Reimagining Literacy in the Age of AI

This volume assesses the critical intersection of artificial intelligence (AI) and literacy education. Drawing on the concept of "living literacies," it explores the transformative potential of AI in literacy practices, offering a comprehensive narrative that bridges theoretical frameworks with practical applications.

The book goes beyond the conventional understanding of AI literacy as mere technological proficiency. Instead, it positions AI as a catalyst for expansive, inclusive, and multifaceted literacy practices in the digital age. Scholars from different parts of the world examine how AI is not just changing what we read and write but how we think, create, and express ourselves in a post-human context.

KEY FEATURES

- Explores AI literacy that encompasses critical thinking, ethical reasoning, and creative expression
- Offers insights into the role of educators and researchers in cultivating AI literacy among learners
- Discusses how creativity and identity intertwine with AI literacy
- Suggests practical approaches to integrating AI into classroom instruction across different age groups

This timely work serves as an essential guide for educators, researchers, and learners by navigating the evolving terrain of literacy in a world increasingly augmented by AI.

CRC Press Reference Books in Computer Science

CRC Press Reference Books in Computer Science series offers advanced and authoritative resources for students, researchers, and professionals across the field of computer science. Books in this series serve as indispensable references which present rigorously researched and innovative approaches to current and complex issues.

Reimagining Literacy in the Age of AI: Theory and Practice
Edited by Jason D. DeHart, Suriati Abas, Raúl Alberto Mora, and Damiana Gibbons Pyles

Generative AI in Higher Education: Guiding Principles for Teaching and Learning: Volume 1
Emmanuel K Nartey

Governing the Future: Digitalization, Artificial Intelligence, Dataism
Henning Glaser and Pindar Wong

Reimagining Literacy in the Age of AI

Theory and Practice

Edited by
Jason D. DeHart, Suriati Abas,
Raúl Alberto Mora, and Damiana Gibbons Pyles

CRC Press
Taylor & Francis Group
Boca Raton London New York

CRC Press is an imprint of the
Taylor & Francis Group, an **informa** business
A CHAPMAN & HALL BOOK

Designed cover image: Shutterstock

First edition published 2025
by CRC Press
2385 NW Executive Center Drive, Suite 320, Boca Raton FL 33431

and by CRC Press
4 Park Square, Milton Park, Abingdon, Oxon, OX14 4RN

CRC Press is an imprint of Taylor & Francis Group, LLC

ISBN: 978-1-032-83976-9 (hbk)
ISBN: 978-1-032-83981-3 (pbk)
ISBN: 978-1-003-51063-5 (ebk)

DOI: 10.1201/9781003510635

Typeset in Minion
by Newgen Publishing UK

Contents

Foreword

As I read the chapters in *Reimagining Literacy in the Age of AI*, I found myself thinking about T.S. Eliot's "The Love Song of J. Alfred Prufrock." The part of the poem that came to mind is near the end when Eliot reflects, "*If one, settling a pillow by her head, Should say: 'That is not what I meant at all; That is not it, at all*'" (Eliot, 1917). The stanza came to me because chapters in this book explore the abundant ways today that people research and represent an idea and people's insatiable appetite for information. However, this part of Eliot's poem has quite a different meaning from the ideas and concepts featured in this book; in the poem, Eliot reflects on his deep feelings of lost youth. But, thinking about the poem while reading the collection moved me into Open AI to ask about the poem's message, and it generated the QR code in Figure F.1.

This information was not enough for me, I wanted more of a multimodal sense about "*If one, settling a pillow by her head, Should say: 'That is not what I meant at all; That is not it, at all'*" (Eliot, 1917), so I then asked for a picture and Open AI then generated this:

> ***Picture Prompt:*** *A scene with two people engaged in a conversation. The first person, in the foreground, has a frustrated and confused expression, raising their hands slightly as if trying to explain themselves. The second person, in the background, looks puzzled or apologetic, showing that they misunderstood what the first person meant. The setting is a cozy, softly lit cafe with warm colors. The focus is on their facial expressions and body language, capturing the tension and miscommunication between them.*

… And then the QR code in Figure F.2 appeared.

Do I think that this picture depicts Eliot's fears, insecurities, and his inability to express desire? Not really, no, but, I found the searching

FIGURE F.1 QR-Code for Screenshot of an OpenAI prompt about Eliot's poem.

FIGURE F.2 QR-Code for AI-generated picture inspired by "The Love Song of J. Alfred Prufrock".

interesting/fun/compelling and it sent me down a rabbit hole for a different visual via the QR code in Figure F.3:

This half-an-hour of meandering and prompting artificial intelligence (AI) software felt incredibly fitting as I thought about writing this foreword.

This is a book about negotiating with machines. Yes, it is about how AI functions and AI's seeming omnipotent character. Yes, it uncovers complex layers of platforms, algorithms, and anticipatory software. Nonetheless, ultimately, each chapter helps readers to think multimodally, critically, even disruptively about AI and algorithmic life. What felt reassuring is that chapter authors gave their content and research a lived, human overlay and many applied work that I have done with Kate Pahl on living literacies (Pahl & Rowsell, 2020). I really admire the ways that authors uncover

FIGURE F.3 QR-Code for Visual representation inspired by "The Love Song of J. Alfred Prufrock".

human mediations with AI. Through these varied lived engagements, machine learning and AI become less scary, omnipotent, even nefarious, and more like a tool to be tamed ethically and meaningfully. I love the way that DeHart articulates it below:

> *When it comes to creation, the boundaries between AI technology and AI literacies inevitably point not to the existence of these technologies, as this is now a given, but to the ways in which users take them up and critically apply them in compositional forms.*
>
> *DeHart, this volume*

Indeed, scholars like DeHart and Gibbons-Pyles in their work have consistently uncovered the critical, the creative, the fearlessly curious ways that children, young, people, and adults recognize the affordances of technologies, platforms, and software, and how they also are able to build boundaries to protect themselves. Surely part of our job as digital literacy researchers is to help teachers teach young viewers and consumers of platforms, algorithmic patterns, and AI searches to be critical and vigilant and also have fun.

Jennifer Rowsell
August 2024

REFERENCES

Eliot, T. S. *Prufrock and Other Observations* (London: The Egoist, 1917), 9–16.

Pahl, K., & Rowsell, J. (2020). *Living literacies: Literacy for social change*. MIT Press.

Editors

Jason D. DeHart earned a PhD in 2019 at the University of Tennessee, Knoxville. His research interests include digital literacy, graphic novels and comics, and adolescent literacy. DeHart is the author of *Building Critical Literacy and Empathy with Graphic Novels* (NCTE).

Suriati Abas is an Assistant Professor in the Department of Elementary Education and Reading at the State University of New York (SUNY) Oneonta. Her research interests center on critical, multimodal, and spatial literacies within school and in out-of-school contexts. Her most recent publications titled "Critical Multimodal Literacy Practices in Student-Created Comics" and "Fostering Artificial Intelligence (AI) Literacy in Higher Education" were published in *Literacy* and *Teaching Media*, respectively. Suriati was awarded the Divergent Award for Excellence in the Implementation of Literacy in a Digital Age in 2022 for the university–community partnership (i.e., involving pre-service teachers, teachers, authors, librarians, and children in K–12 schools) in promoting diverse social justice–themed picture books through in-person book-reading events and digital platforms. She teaches literacy, diversity, and children's literature to pre-service and in-service teachers.

Raúl Alberto Mora is an Associate Professor at the School of Education and Pedagogy at Universidad Pontificia Bolivariana in Medellín, Colombia (while teaching remotely from Norway), where he also chairs the award-winning Literacies in Second Languages Project research lab. He is also a visiting professor at the Doctorate in Education (ELT Emphasis) at Universidad del Valle and has served as visiting faculty at universities in Colombia, Mexico, and Poland. His research has explored literacy theories' conceptual and practical applications to understand second-language practices in city, virtual, and school spaces. Raúl was awarded the Divergent

Award for Excellence in Literacy in a Digital Age Research in 2019 for his contributions to the field of literacy studies and the Clare de Silva Award by the Colombian Association of English Teachers (ASOCOPI) in 2024 for his impact on the English-language teaching community in Colombia.

Damiana Gibbons Pyles is a Professor in the Department of Learning, Teaching, and Curriculum at Appalachian State University. Her research interests focus on media production, identity, and media literacy practices in order to understand the intersections of the visual, the spoken, the written, and the performed in digital and print literacies. Recent publications include her book *Literacy and Identity through Streaming Media: Kids, Teens, and Representation on Netflix* (2023) and several publications, such as scholarship about turning Red and Asian American representation and teaching using different media, i.e., *The Last Kids on Earth*. She currently teaches courses for pre-service and practicing teachers to learn how to integrate media and technology for teaching and learning. Her most recent projects focus on how censorship legislation is impacting how teachers perceive how they can and should teach in their classrooms.

Contributors

Suriati Abas
Department of Elementary Education and Reading
State University of New York (SUNY) Oneonta
Oneonta, New York, USA

Yolanda Álvarez Amigo
Department of Teaching of Language, Literature and Social Science
Autonomous University of Barcelona
Barcelona, Spain

Arild Michel Bakken
Norwegian Reading Centre
University of Stavanger (UiS)
Stavanger, Norway

Patrick Burke
School of Language, Literacy and Early Childhood Education
Dublin City University
Dublin, Ireland

Basil Cahusac de Caux
Liberal Arts Department
American University of the Middle East
Egaila, Kuwait

Ismail Celik
Department of Education and Psychology
University of Oulu
Oulu, Finland

Jason D. DeHart
Wilkesboro County Schools
Wilkesboro, North Carolina, USA

Selcuk Dogan
Faculty of Education
Georgia Southern University
Statesboro, Georgia, USA

Maryam Amir Haeri
Section of Cognition, Data and Education (CoDE)
Department of Learning, Data Analytics and Technology (LDT)
University of Twente
Enschede, Netherlands

Sandra Jamieson
Professor of English and Director of Writing across the Curriculum
Drew University
Madison, New Jersey, USA

Jens Lloyd
English Department
Drew University
Madison, New Jersey, USA

Raúl Alberto Mora
Literacies in Second Languages Project/School of Education and Pedagogy
Universidad Pontificia Bolivariana (UPB)
Medellín, Colombia and Trondheim, Norway

Clarice M. Moran
Department of English
Appalachian State University
Boone, North Carolina, USA

Lynette Pretorius
School of Curriculum, Teaching and Inclusive Education
Faculty of Education
Monash University
Melbourne, Australia

Christopher Proctor
Graduate School of Education
University at Buffalo (SUNY)
Buffalo, New York, USA

Damiana Gibbons Pyles
Department of Learning, Teaching, and Curriculum
Appalachian State University
Boone, North Carolina, USA

Ryan M. Rish
Graduate School of Education
University at Buffalo (SUNY)
Buffalo, New York, USA

Erik Roelofs
Section of Cognition, Data and Education (CoDE)
Department of Learning, Data Analytics and Technology (LDT)
University of Twente
Enschede, Netherlands

Alex Rudniy
Mathematics and Computer Science Department
Drew University
Madison, New Jersey, USA

Johannes Steinrücke
Section of Cognition, Data and Education (CoDE)
Department of Learning, Data Analytics and Technology (LDT)
University of Twente
Enschede, Netherlands

Madalena Teixeira
Department of Education and Psychology/CIDTFF
University of Aveiro
Aveiro, Portugal

Kristen Hawley Turner
Division of Curriculum and Teaching
Fordham University
New York, New York, USA

Bente R. Walgermo
Norwegian Reading Centre
University of Stavanger (UiS)
Stavanger, Norway

Manuela Yepes-Mora
Universidade Portucalense
Porto, Portugal

Introduction

Luke (2005) asserts that "literacy is a malleable repertoire of practices, not an unchanging or universal set of skills" (qtd. in Pahl & Rowsell, 2020); scholars have focused their work at the end of the last century and the beginning of this one trying to understand how the literacy landscape has shifted over the years. Mills (2016) explores how literacy has taken a digital turn, which she defines as "the rapid digitalisation of literacy practices generated by human action, across a growing number of spheres of practice…" (p. 1). In her book, Mills walks the reader through different ways of seeing literacy from socio-cultural, critical, and multimodal to socio-spatial, socio-material, and sensory literacies. Her work highlights how much literacies have broadened as its "spheres of practice" grow through time, space, and place. As such, we are finding that the convergence of artificial intelligence (AI) and literacy education marks an unprecedented juncture in the evolution of pedagogy.

We are now in another huge shift in how literacy can be understood with the emerging AI technologies that have become a part of the literacy landscape. Using Bloom's Taxonomy as a framework, Ng et al. (2021) explored how scholars are discussing AI in their research. They found that many researchers used

> *different types of "literacies", which had recently been applied to define skill sets in other disciplines. Most researchers advocated that instead of merely knowing how to use AI applications, learners should learn about the underlying AI concepts for their future careers and understand the ethical concerns in order to use AI responsibly.*
>
> *p. 9*

In this sense, the idea of AI literacy as a concept necessarily needs to move beyond a skill-based definition toward broader, deeper understandings. What these understandings would entail is a driver for this book.

DOI: 10.1201/9781003510635-1

As literacy scholars, we acknowledge that AI is here to stay and will continue to evolve with time (Mora & Semingson, 2023). Thus, grounding the contributions in this book within the context of an ever-changing landscape of literacy education, we draw on the concepts of "living literacies" to reframe our understanding of what it means to be literate in a digital era. A living literacies approach focuses on "the ways in which meaning is made as people conduct everyday activities" (Pahl & Rowsell, 2020). It pays particular attention to routine activities such as scrolling through websites, viewing TikTok reels, creating artistic work digitally, and even keeping abreast with current news through mobile apps. The merging of the digital with other means of interaction and creation has been a regular feature of society for decades now, and the increasing reality is that technological advancements have become increasingly sophisticated with fascinating implications for researchers to consider.

Moreover, it might be argued that daily reality is not only shaped by, but is in some degree dependent on, advanced technology. To be a literate person and to be conscious of the vicissitudes of modern life in society is to be at least somewhat post-human. Viewing through the lens of living literacies, the traditional concept of literacy expands beyond discrete skills of reading and writing in our daily engagements within school and in out-of-school contexts. It encompasses a kaleidoscope of skills, competencies, and dispositions required to navigate, comprehend, and effectively communicate in an interconnected, multimodal world. It underscores the significance of multimodal literacies wherein the fusion of text, images, sounds, and digital technologies forms the bedrock of communication and expression. We wake up to interact with a smorgasbord of living literacies that is invincible and has indeed become a part of our daily literacy landscape.

This consideration of living literacies aligns with our collective view of the work of readers, writers, viewers, communicators, and composers, which we have taken up in a range of ways in our work. We recognize that the increased development of AI is unprecedented, while also noting that our view of literacy exists within the context of a long range of researched conversation about literacy as agentical and student-driven (Street, 2003), liberatory (Freire, 1970; Parker, 2022), and complex, social, and situated (Gee, 2017). The development of AI in the context of a literacy lens, with attention to the ways literacy practices occur in daily life, leads to many questions. Not the least of these questions is the role of the author/creator/initial voice, as well as the ways that AI reflects and misinterprets lived realities. If texts are a means of expressing and reflecting life, what does the work of an AI reveal and/or obfuscate about humanity?

In this context, AI emerges as a catalyst, offering an intriguing dimension to literacy practice and instruction. At its essence, AI literacy encapsulates the ability to engage critically and proficiently with AI-driven technologies in the realms of reading, writing, and communication. Some of the popular examples of AI tools include MagicSchool.ai, CurryPod, ChatGPT, Twee, and DALL.E. To utilize any AI tools requires going beyond technological fluency and shifting the emphasis to a nuanced understanding and adept use of AI tools to enhance traditional literacy practices. As AI permeates literacy education, literacy scholars and educators will have to undergo a significant transformation within a post-human context. This notion of the post-human marks a period in which readers, writers, and creators have the opportunity to advance conceptualizations of what communication means, and where critical thinking takes on new notions of critique and capacity for innovative use of meaning-making systems. The move from using simple to complex systems might be considered in the context of the movement past redundancy and replication in communication, to the essence of what the human offers in a post-human landscape. We have to shoulder the responsibility of unraveling the complex ethical, societal and pedagogical implications of integrating AI into educational settings. AI presents layers of complexities which impact human cognition, societal structures, and educational equity urging for critical reflections on the intersection of AI and literacy. Hence, as literacy scholars and educators, we stand as pivotal agents in cultivating AI literacy among learners – work that necessarily involves theoretical advancement rather than resistance.

Our role must transcend technical instruction, encompassing the cultivation of critical thinking, ethical reasoning, and creative expression within an educational landscape that is augmented by AI's transformative influence on literacy. Within Al literacy, we believe creativity and identity are intertwined and it offers learners opportunities to craft, remix, and co-create digital narratives that blend human creativity with AI-driven functionalities. While trends in AI might be treated as a subject of fear or further speculation, we embrace a speculative stance in literacy education which stems not only from the acknowledge of advanced digital tools, including AI, but which revolves around a thoughtful and intentional, ongoing conversation about what such tools entail for the individual (and society) engaged in living a literacy-rich life.

ABOUT THE BOOK

Given the fluidity and exploratory nature of AI, we invite readers to join us in our attempts to unpack our understandings of the following: *What is AI Literacy? What place does AI have in literacy practice and instruction? What role do researchers and teachers have in a post-human context? Where do creativity and identity fit in AI literacy?* The chapters in this book argue that AI literacy does not primarily involve interacting with AI systems but leveraging them as instruments for amplifying literacy skills and communicative capacities. In this way, the human is an active participant and is involved with critical engagement, exploring new designs, methods, and experiences for using technological tools.

This book takes on a living literacies (Pahl & Rowsell, 2020) approach to AI in literacy education. While existing literature often compartmentalizes AI's role or focuses solely on technological aspects, this book endeavors to weave a comprehensive narrative that melds theoretical frameworks with practical applications. Building upon the insights of Jennifer Rowsell, Kate Pahl, et al.'s work, this book delves into the intricate interplay between living literacies and AI, shedding light on the transformative potential of AI in shaping literacy practices. The innovative aspect of this book lies in its emphasis on fostering critical AI literacy, intertwining ethical considerations, identity construction, and creative expression within pedagogical frameworks. Rather than viewing AI as an isolated entity within literacy education, this book positions it as a catalyst for expansive, inclusive, and multifaceted literacy practices in the digital age. This book embarks on a pioneering expedition, illuminating the synergistic convergence of AI and literacy education while critically examining its implications on creativity, identity, and the ever-evolving nature of human-machine interactions. It serves as an invitation to educators, researchers, and learners alike to navigate the transformative landscape of AI literacy and redefine the contours of literacy in the digital era.

Leander and Burriss (2020) have noted the need to expand our theoretical formulations of what these new developments in technology, including AI, bots, and algorithms, suggest about what it means to be critically literate. We seek to expand on this conversation within the context of increasingly accessible AI applications to explore how post-humanity is an increasingly resonant reality, and how these developments in technological tools lead us back to questions of daily, lived literacy practices. Chapters in this book take up both the theoretical and conceptual, as well as the practical, as educators and researchers seek to make sense of post-human literacy pedagogies in terms of ethics, conceptualizations among researchers, emerging definitions and delineations, and explorations of AI-reflective approaches across student age groups.

ORGANIZATION OF THE BOOK

This edited volume will draw on a broad variety of expert voices who have been exploring the use of AI in classrooms, with a specific focus on literacy. We invite voices from the educational field to comment on research and practices surrounding the use of AI in relation to literacy concepts. The book will be broken into sections with work related to AI in particular educational contexts. If we, as educators, believe that literacy learning is socially constructed, is there a place for AI? What does AI offer in terms of critical and authentic literacies?

In each of the chapters, contributors begin with a definitional framework related to their work in literacy/literacies. Each contributor tackles the question of the ways/spaces in which they situate themselves in relation to literacy/literacies? These questions are examined in primary/elementary, secondary, and post-secondary contexts, and we have divided the book into four sections, with a final conclusion acting as a coda based on our work with one another and with additional contributors.

Section I: Ethical Considerations

The two chapters in this section (Pretorius & Cahusac de Caux; DeHart) will explore the technology-centered questions of AI tools and applications, focusing on literacy instruction. Though these chapters are not specifically practical, their foundational structure leans toward both the conceptual and in-situ educational approaches.

Section II: Practical Applications in Educational Contexts

The four chapters in this section (Moran & Gibbons Pyles; Abas; Celik & Dogan; Bakken et al.) put practicality to the forefront with implications that speak directly to classroom practice, with a firm grounding in the research literature. The authors in this section offer specific ideas and strategies for working with students across age groups.

Section III: Theoretical Grounding and Future Applications

The final three chapters comprising this section (Proctor & Rish; Lloyd et al.; Mora & Yepes-Mora) take on a speculative (Bozkurt et al., 2023; Garcia & Mirra, 2023) look at the possibilities of AI literacies in education. Grounded in the authors' research and lived experiences with digital literacies and AI, each chapter discusses the potential of AI while staying mindful of the pitfalls and challenges we will need to face as AI becomes more ubiquitous in our educational systems.

CONCLUSION

As we introduce this volume, we recognize both an uncertainty about the ways in which AI will continue to shape conceptualizations of literacy and the ways that AI will impact the daily practices of educators and students. Yet, we also note a responsibility as researchers and educators in the literacy field to take up these questions and explore them and acknowledge the work of our contributors in helping us lead this line of inquiry.

REFERENCES

Bozkurt, A., Junhong, X., Lambert, S., Pazurek, A., Crompton, H., Koseoglu, S., ... & Romero-Hall, E. (2023). Speculative futures on ChatGPT and generative artificial intelligence (AI): A collective reflection from the educational landscape. *Asian Journal of Distance Education, 18*(1), 53–130.

Freire, P. (1970). The adult literacy process as cultural action for freedom. *Harvard Educational Review, 40*(2), 205–225.

Garcia, A., & Mirra, N. (2023). Other suns: Designing for racial equity through speculative education. *Journal of the Learning Sciences, 32*(1), 1–20. https://doi.org/10.1080/10508406.2023.2166764

Gee, J. P. (2017). Identity and diversity in today's world. *Multicultural Education Review, 9*(2), 83–92.

Leander, K. M., & Burriss, S. K. (2020). Critical literacy for a posthuman world: When people read, and become, with machines. *British Journal of Educational Technology, 51*(4), 1262–1276.

Luke, C. (2005). New literacies-new media: Mediascapes and infoscapes. *Pacific Archive of Digital Data for Education and Learning*, 1-19.

Mills, K. A. (2016). *Literacy theories for the digital age: Social, critical, multimodal, spatial, material, and sensory lenses.* Multilingual Matters.

Mora, R. A., & Semingson, P. (2023). AI and literacy education: Consider the challenges, embrace the possibilities, make your classroom even more human. *Literacy Today (July/August/September)*, 54–58. https://publuu.com/flip-book/24429/445819/page/56

Ng, T. K., Leung, J. K. L., Chu, S. K. W., & Qiao, M. S. (2021). Conceptualizing AI literacy: An exploratory review. *Computers and Education: Artificial Intelligence, 2*, 1–11. Doi: 1016/j.caeai.2021.100041

Pahl, K., & Rowsell, J. (2020). *Living literacies: Literacy for social change*. MIT Press.

Parker, K. N. (2022). *Literacy is liberation: Working toward justice through culturally relevant teaching*. ASCD.

Street, B. (2003). The limits of the local: 'Autonomous' or 'disembedding'. *International Journal of Learning, 10*(1), 2825–2830.

I

Ethical Considerations

CHAPTER 1

The AI Literacy Framework for Higher Education

A Grounded Theory Exploration of the Foundational, Social, Conceptual, Ethical, and Affective Domains of AI Literacy

Lynette Pretorius and Basil Cahusac de Caux

INTRODUCTION

Artificial intelligence (AI, tools that are capable of performing complex tasks that used to require human intelligence, see Pretorius, 2023) has become ubiquitous in modern society. Since 2023, however, significant advancements in AI technologies have resulted in the development of various generative AIs capable of performing tasks which, in the past, would have required human creativity (e.g., art). Lim et al. (2023) define generative AI as "a technology that (i) leverages deep learning models to (ii) generate human-like content (e.g., images, words) in response to (iii) complex and varied prompts (e.g., languages, instructions, questions)" (p. 2). Generative AI is considered a *game-changer* for society (Lim et al., 2023) and has significant implications for educational reform.

DOI: 10.1201/9781003510635-3

The development of generative AI led to a certain amount of consternation among educators, with some condemning generative AI because it would erode traditional skills and could encourage students to cheat (see, e.g., Cotton et al., 2023; Currie, 2023; Farrokhnia et al., 2023; Ho, 2024). Many others, however, have acknowledged the need to leverage generative AI to support student learning (see, e.g., Guo et al., 2024; Law, 2024; Lim et al., 2023; Pretorius, 2023; Pretorius et al., 2024). In this study, AI literacy is defined as understanding "how to communicate effectively and collaboratively with generative AI technologies, as well as evaluate the trustworthiness of the results obtained" (Pretorius, 2023, p. T3). We believe that generative AI should be considered as an aide that can help students in their learning and academic development (Pretorius, 2023; Pretorius et al., 2024). However, this requires a cultural shift in higher education to encourage educators to use generative AI in a more educative manner to foster AI literacy.

While institutions have begun incorporating AI tools, such as generative AI, into teaching and learning processes, there remains a notable gap in understanding how to effectively foster AI literacy among educators and students. This gap presents a critical challenge: without a comprehensive AI literacy framework, educators may struggle to prepare students for an increasingly AI-driven world, risking a divide between those who can leverage AI effectively and those who cannot. Recognising this challenge, we sought to address this gap by reflecting on our own experiences with generative AI.

In this chapter, we explore our experiences as two higher education lecturers who navigated the emergence of generative AI over the past two years. We start by explaining how we initially engaged with generative AI in limited ways, discovered the power of generative AI in our teaching practices, and became advocates for AI literacy in both our teaching and research practices. We use a grounded theory approach combined with collaborative autoethnography as a data generation method to analyse our experiences and construct an AI literacy framework for higher education. Our framework highlights the foundational, social, conceptual, ethical, and affective domains of AI literacy.

METHODOLOGY

Research Paradigm

This study is situated within the constructivism paradigm. As researchers, we believe that our realities are multiple and context-dependent, socially (re)constructed through our experiences (Lincoln & Guba, 2016; Pretorius, 2024a). In this chapter, therefore, we explore how we co-constructed our understanding of AI literacy through our experiences as well as during our discussions with each other and our various generative AIs. In this context, it is important to note that we consider our generative AIs to be important interlocutors within our experiences, helping us develop our understanding of generative AI within the higher education sector.

Research Philosophy

We utilised a grounded theory approach with collaborative autoethnography as our data generation method. Initially developed by Glaser and Strauss (1967/1999), grounded theory is an approach that allows researchers to construct a theory systematically by analysing experiences. As an inductive research approach, grounded theory involves the collection and coding of data to identify patterns, constant comparison throughout the data coding phase, and theoretical sampling (Glaser & Strauss, 1967/1999). In other words, grounded theory allows researchers to describe, understand, and analyse actions and changes so as to generalise these experiences through abstraction and theory construction (Morse et al., 2021). Applying a grounded theory approach allowed us to utilise our narratives and the interactions we had with each other and our generative AIs to gain deeper insights into the collaborative co-construction of knowledge.

Collaborative Autoethnography

Since we utilised our own stories in this study, we needed to use a data generation method that accepts and values the researcher's insider knowledge. Autoethnography allows researchers to purposely explore their own experiences in order to highlight cultural phenomena (Adams & Herrmann, 2023; Adams et al., 2022; Ellis et al., 2011). We have previously utilised autoethnography to explore the experiences of doctoral researchers and academics (see Cahusac de Caux et al., 2022; Pretorius et al., 2019). In these studies, we showed that the higher education system can be considered a unique culture that creates a complex dynamic of experiences for those within the space (see, e.g., Pretorius & Cutri, 2019; Pretorius, 2022). Consequently, we argued that higher education can only be truly understood through insider exploration (Pretorius & Cutri, 2019). Additionally, we consider the recent developments related to how generative AI should be used within higher education as representing a cultural phenomenon, if not a societal transformation. Autoethnography allowed us to explore this cultural phenomenon through our own experiences to share common insights for others to apply in their teaching and research practices.

In this study, we combine and analyse both of our experiences to construct a shared understanding. As such, this chapter can be considered a collaborative autoethnography of teaching experience (see Chang et al., 2013, for information about collaborative autoethnography). To employ collaborative autoethnography in our study, we started by meeting together via Zoom to discuss our intentions for this chapter. This discussion resulted in a draft outline of what we wanted to discuss, as well as a plan to explore the analytical lens we wanted to utilise. Both authors reflected on their experiences of using generative AI during the preceding year. To prompt our reflections, we utilised a minimalistic reflective prompt strategy (Pretorius & Cutri, 2019; Pretorius & Ford, 2016). These prompts allowed us to explore what prompted us to engage with generative AI for our practices, examine how our use of generative AI affected our practices, reflect on our thoughts and feelings at the time and now, as well as understand what we could learn from the experience.

At this point, it is important to discuss the generative AIs used in this chapter. ChatGPT (Open AI, https://chat.openai.com/) allows for the customisation of the GPT 4 platform. Lynette developed a customised generative AI that was able to browse the internet, create artwork using DALL-E, conduct qualitative data analysis and technical reporting, and write conversational English posts about academic articles and datasets. This generative AI was trained to respond in Lynette's tone and writing style. She initially developed this generative AI for personal use to explore the capabilities of generative AI technology. Based on her success with this customised generative AI in pilot studies, Lynette has been awarded two grants in part to assess the viability of this model for research data generation and analysis.

Basil developed his customised generative AI to generate additional insights on his undergraduate students' formative assessments (reports, etc.). He did this initially because he wanted to provide richer and more meaningful feedback that students could use to constructively improve their academic work. Since then, he has found that his customised generative AI can be used, with proper prompting, to assess how effectively students' work aligns with the rubric(s) contained in a formative assessment. He plans to use his customised generative AI in the future to refine his own grading rubrics further in ways that engage students and promote learning.

To write about our experiences, we each wrote our sections individually and submitted them to each other for critical feedback and discussion, a method we have previously employed (see Pretorius, 2022). This strategy allowed us to collaboratively construct the themes we used to develop our AI literacy framework. We also consulted relevant artefacts during our writing process. Lynette consulted a previous AI literacy paper she had written (Pretorius, 2023) to better understand her motivations for utilising generative AI in her teaching. She also consulted her blog, lesson plans, workshop slides, assignment instructions, and previous conversations with her generative AI. Basil consulted his lesson plans, workshop slides, assignment instructions, and conversations he had previously had with his generative AI.

The process of writing and rewriting our stories allowed us to engage more deeply with our motivations and experiences, creating vivid and thick descriptions of our experiences. We also took deep care throughout the research process to ensure that no other person was identified in our stories, a key ethical consideration of autoethnography (Edwards, 2021). We applied reflexive thematic analysis (Braun & Clarke, 2006, 2019, 2022) throughout our iterative collaborative writing process, as we acknowledge that knowledge co-construction is not a linear but rather a circular process. As we reflected on comments from each other, we were prompted to go back and explore our experiences in more detail, thereby generating new data for analysis. A key aspect during this process was our researcher reflexivity, which helped us to construct themes relevant to our contextual understandings as higher education educators. These themes were then used to construct the components of our AI literacy framework.

Lynette's Narratives from Australia

When generative AI was first introduced, I was excited to explore its potential. I played with it primarily for my own interest and discovered that it was a good tool that could be utilised in my teaching and research. At that time, there was considerable discussion in higher education about the dangers of generative AI, particularly with regard to its impact on academic integrity. As I explored its uses, I became convinced that it should not be seen as a danger but rather as a tool. As I noted in a paper at that time (see Pretorius, 2023), we should embrace the technology, teaching students how to use it effectively as AI literacy would become an essential transferable skill in the future.

Using Generative AI as an Academic Language and Literacy Tutor

One of my core teaching and research philosophies is to privilege the inclusion of diverse perspectives. English is not my first language, and I recognise that knowledge and culture are embedded within the languages we use. As such, I try, wherever possible, to promote student's critical thinking using their diverse perspectives and understandings of the world. The reality in the classroom, however, is that we assess learning through English expression. Meaning is hindered through poor academic language (i.e., sentence structure, punctuation, grammatical elements, spelling, and vocabulary; see Podorova, 2016, 2017) and inadequate academic literacy (i.e., the organisation and development of ideas, the academic style and voice within the writing, and the appropriate use of referencing; see Podorova, 2016, 2017).

Since generative AI has become more freely available, I have started encouraging my students to use it as an academic language and literacy tutor. For example, I teach an entry-level Master's unit where the student population is overwhelmingly from non-English-speaking backgrounds. I actively encourage these students to utilise ChatGPT as an academic language and literacy tutor, explicitly showing them how to write prompts and use ChatGPT (see, e.g., Pretorius, 2024b). I also spend a significant amount of time explaining the importance of asking ChatGPT to explain why it made the changes so that my students can see the generative AI not just as a useful tool but as an active interlocutor in their learning journey. I also highlight that the free version of ChatGPT is able to do this in order to help ensure equity of access to this technology.

I have been gratified to see a gradual improvement in students' written work sent to me for feedback or assessment. I do not think that this is a reflection of a changing student population; my university still has a substantial international student cohort. Instead, I interpret this as a greater understanding of the importance of clear communication of ideas where generative AI has helped to augment and improve students' learning. I firmly believe that encouraging students to effectively use these technologies will allow them to focus more on their higher-order thinking skills, emphasising deeper learning and engagement.

Using Generative AI to Promote Creativity in Data Generation

This year, I was fortunate to be given the privilege of teaching a final-semester unit in one of our Faculty's Master's programmes. This unit was designed to teach students the benefits of subjective research through autoethnography or self-study. The major assignment for this unit required the students to conduct a small-scale autoethnography or self-study of approximately 5,000 words. I had recently been reading some more creative autoethnographies, which utilised poems (Rangarajan & Daneshfar, 2022), photos (Patel, 2022), and artwork (Kalenjuk et al., 2022), and was trying to explore ways in which I could be more creative in my research. However, while I appreciated these creative forms of expression, I always considered myself as *not artistic enough* to be able to create what I considered beauty through art. At the same time, I had previously created an artwork as part of a book project using a generative AI, and this greatly impressed me (see Pretorius, 2023). I realised that generative AI could be a way for my students to create artwork to use in their assignments, particularly if they felt like I did, that they were not really artistic enough.

As part of my assignment instructions, I ran a workshop outlining what was expected for the autoethnography or self-study project. This workshop was important because students had not previously had the chance to write an assignment that was even close to what they were expected to do now. I really wanted to encourage students to be more creative, so my research plan example included the following: "For Assignment Two, I plan to do an autoethnography. [...] I will write reflective diaries, conduct a reflective interview with myself using Zoom, and create an artwork representing my experiences using DALL-E." I also wanted to show them how useful such a strategy could be, so I decided to create an example artwork myself for an imaginary project where I was exploring my own academic identity. In the workshop, I showcased to the students the various iterations of the artwork created by DALL-E, exploring what I had typed as a prompt, why I had typed it in that way, how I used my feelings in response to a generated image to help me think about how I wanted it refined, and finally, what the artwork was that I decided was representative of my academic identity as an educator and researcher. The final images I generated can be seen in the preprint version of this chapter (see Pretorius & Cahusac de Caux, 2024).

Students were very engaged in this discussion, asking questions and providing further insights into why they thought I may have made particular changes. At one point during my image generation discussion, DALL-E created a picture of me that would have been better suited to the cover of a modelling magazine, which elicited strong reactions from me. I explained to students why I did not like the photo, highlighting my emotional reactions as well as my personal need to challenge societal attitudes towards how women are embodied. I did this to showcase to them how I thought I would be able to discuss this if I had decided to write an autoethnography using this method of data generation.

When I recently marked students' final assignments, I was glad to see that some students had taken up the challenge to include more creative expressions in their assignments, including photos and poems. While none had included artwork generated by generative AI in their final assignment, several noted that they had used conversations with generative AI to improve their understandings and reflections. The discussions I had with students also highlighted that they were interested in further exploring the use of generative AI.

Using Generative AI to Encourage Deeper Data Analysis and Reflection

Recently, I have started exploring the potential of using my customised generative AI to conduct qualitative data analysis. For example, one of my research projects is designed to explore the experiences of doctoral students in academia. This project consists of an extensive qualitative dataset, including 40 qualitative surveys and 21 interviews. Given the size of this dataset, I decided to explore the possibility of utilising my customised generative AI as a way to conduct an initial analysis of individual interview transcripts, providing me with a starting point for further analysis. To do this, I developed a series of question prompts for the generative AI based on the theories and concepts I was interested in exploring in my project. With consent from my participants, I then uploaded participant transcripts (using pseudonyms only) to my customised generative AI and interrogated the document using my developed prompts.

I have been particularly impressed by my customised generative AI's capacity to detect implicit meaning within texts. While I expected that it would be able to detect explicit mentions of concepts, I was not expecting it to make connections between ideas which were not explicitly articulated. The conversation in Table 1.1 illustrates one example of this. Based on my pilot analysis for one of my research projects, I have obtained ethics approval to further explore my model's potential for data analysis. I am also working to integrate examples of this data analysis process into my teaching to showcase a new and innovative approach to my students.

In my project, I have sought explicit consent from participants to utilise my customised generative AI. I have also offered participants

TABLE 1.1 Data Analysis Using a Customised ChatGPT

Author	Response
Lynette	In this study, imposter syndrome (also termed imposter phenomenon) is considered to be feelings of being a fraud despite objective evidence to the contrary. Highlight any examples of imposter syndrome in the transcript.
Customised Generative AI	In the transcript, [...] there are nuanced indications that could be interpreted as reflections of imposter syndrome, albeit not explicitly stated as such. [Participant pseudonym]'s narrative is primarily characterised by a strong sense of purpose, ambition, and critical engagement with his educational journey. However, certain moments and expressions hint at underlying doubts or internal conflicts that resonate with the characteristics of imposter syndrome: [...] While [the participant] confidently navigates the academic and bureaucratic structures of his educational context, there's an implicit sense of being an outsider trying to find his place within these structures. His reflections on understanding and managing academic expectations and procedures might hint at moments of self-doubt or the internal questioning of his belonging in these academic spaces. [several additional examples provided]

Note: The data used in this example are part of a project that was approved by Monash University's Human Research Ethics Committee (project number 37132).

the opportunity to access the data it generated for their own interest. All participants consented to their data being used for analysis by the customised generative AI and just over 80% of the participants (17/21) took up the opportunity to receive their results. Given that my participants in this project are doctoral students and early career researchers, this reflects a genuine interest from the academic community in exploring the potential of this tool as a collaborator for data analysis. So far, participants have been very enthusiastic about the responses, with one participant simply replying that he was "genuinely stunned".

Ethical Considerations and Challenges

There are, of course, some ethical considerations of using generative AI that should be taken into account. First, users need to be aware of the importance of not submitting sensitive personal information to generative AI platforms, as these data could be used to train the generative AI. I have been successful in obtaining grant funding to upgrade my ChatGPT to an enterprise-level system, which means that no data I share can be used for data mining and training of the Open AI systems. As ethical researchers, it is also important to ensure that research participants are fully informed about the project and how their data will be used. Second, there is an ethical concern that generative AIs were trained with artwork without express consent from artists (see, e.g., Appel et al., 2023). Third, there are debates as to whether generative AI should be considered an artist because it generates original content or whether it is only reproducing elements of other artists' work because of the way the model was trained. I believe that it can be considered an artist because it combines components of art in new and unique ways that were not done before. Importantly, I consider the interaction between the generative AI and me as the prompter integral in the art-creation process. We are working together, generating work that would not have been possible separately. Fourth, it is important to note that there is a risk that the generative AI may reflect biases present in the training data (Lund & Wang, 2023), thereby perpetuating stereotypes or discrimination. An example of this bias was evident in the pictures it generated for me, which reflected problematic attitudes towards the female form in one of the images it created. Finally, it has recently been highlighted that the use of generative AI does contribute significantly to the user's carbon footprint, with one image generation estimated to necessitate the equivalent amount of energy needed to fully charge a smartphone (Luccioni et al., 2024). As such, the utilisation of such tools should be weighed against the energy costs and emissions it would generate.

BASIL'S NARRATIVES FROM KUWAIT

Universities in Kuwait, as in many other parts of the world, are aware of the myriad challenges and opportunities surrounding the use of generative AI in educational contexts. ChatGPT and other large language models (LLMs) are used by faculty and students to perform numerous tasks: brainstorming, drafting papers, reviewing external sources, and summarising large tracts of text/numerical data. Since the adoption of LLMs by faculty and students, my university has attempted to address the use and abuse of generative AI in learning contexts. Importantly, though, the university has yet to establish clear guidelines for generative AI. Many of the proposed guidelines resemble a Band-Aid approach to the widespread use of generative AI. For instance, in mid-2023, the university introduced a blanket ban on the use of text generated through generative AI for submission-based assignments. In effect, this meant that students were penalised for submitting any work that contained content generated by LLMs – even if generative AI input was minimal.

Despite such reactive measures, many faculty (including myself) were excited by the seemingly limitless potential of generative AI. During lectures, faculty began introducing students to tools such as ChatGPT and DALL-E in an attempt to guide students on the ethical and effective use of such tools. One of my lectures on digital literacy in early 2023 explored several generative AI tools with the intention of familiarising students with the academic potential of such tools. At the time of the lecture, many students were aware of the existence of ChatGPT. However, only some had heard of DALL-E. This text-to-image generator has gained a significant following since the time of my lecture. It is also important to note that, with the merger of AI tools such as ChatGPT and DALL-E, multimodal tools are now reaching wider audiences and are set to become a mainstay of academic work at almost all levels.

Exposing Students to Generative AI-Based Tools

In early January 2023, I was responsible for giving a lecture on digital literacy, with a focus on how technology has aided our ability to organise, process, and produce information. What was missing from the lecture, however, was a meaningful discussion of the role that generative AI was beginning to play in completing everyday tasks. I immediately filled this glaring omission with material on generative AI tools. In the lecture material, I incorporated a brief introduction to the use of generative AI tools and then presented a detailed discussion and case study revolving around DALL-E.

On the day of the lecture, I asked my students how many of them had heard of generative AI and AI-based tools. The majority raised their hands. I then asked how many had used them. Approximately half had. Then, I asked them if they had heard of DALL-E. At that point, not a single hand remained raised. I demonstrated the use of DALL-E to a group of approximately 40 students. Many were struck by the sophisticated images generated by the tool; some were impressed by its adaptability and robustness. Shortly after the lecture ended, a group of students visited my office to learn more about DALL-E. They claimed that they wanted to use DALL-E to generate images for a graduation project they were currently working on as a group, indicating that students were interested in using generative AI for academic purposes. It was also a sign that such tools could be included in assessments.

Incorporating Generative AI in Assignments

Due to my students' interest and curiosity in generative AI tools, I decided to design an assignment that would give them an opportunity to use generative AI to boost their creativity. The assignment itself had already been created; my main task was to incorporate generative AI into the overall design. The assignment was relatively straightforward: students would work in groups to create a publication awareness campaign related to one or two of the United Nations' Sustainable Development Goals (see United Nations, n.d.). This task required students to carefully craft a campaign based on clear messaging, sound research, and informative visuals. Students were then asked to create an infographic poster, which may be displayed on campus and social media accounts to further raise awareness.

I aimed to incorporate the use of DALL-E in the assignment. I did this for two reasons: (1) to familiarise students with the use of a generative AI-based tool that converts text to image, and (2) to boost students' creativity through precise prompts. In order to successfully incorporate DALL-E into the assignment, I needed to thoroughly introduce students to the workings of this generative AI-based tool during a lecture. This was done when explaining the requirements of the assignment. I made sure to demonstrate the use of DALL-E to all students, to provide detailed explanations on how to write prompts, select and manipulate images, and download the images that are generated. I also included detailed instructions on the use of DALL-E on the course learning management system.

Ethical Considerations and Challenges

While demonstrating and explaining the use of DALL-E, I strived to highlight the importance of transparency in academic work. From the outset, students were informed of the ethical conventions concerning the use of generative AI. For instance, students were told that they needed to clearly acknowledge that they had used DALL-E (or a similar platform/tool) to generate images used in their assignments – even if such tools were only partially used. Acknowledging the use of generative AI would be done in two ways: (1) through a statement to that effect in the introduction to the assignment and (2) in the form of a label tagged to every image created through the use of generative AI.

Some students were concerned that using tools such as DALL-E would amount to cheating or academic misconduct. I reassured the students that in the case of the assignment in question, using DALL-E and other similar tools to create images would not constitute a breach of academic integrity or be viewed as an instance of cheating. It would also not affect their grades. I gave the students the option to find images online, generate images through the use of generative AI, or create their own images (e.g., digitally or manually). By giving the students these options, they were less likely to worry about being penalised for using generative AI.

Several groups of students used DALL-E to create eye-catching visuals on the theme of sustainable ecotourism. The images, which I unfortunately do not have permission to share, were aesthetically pleasing and designed in a way that evoked calm and a sense of duty to nature/the environment. They were typically centred on the importance of minimising our carbon footprint. Some of the images also emphasised the importance of local (versus global) tourism. Given the timeframe of the assignment (approximately three weeks), I often wonder whether students would have been able to create such powerful images without the help of generative AI.

Faculty Development and Generative AI

A year later, in January 2024, I participated in my department's very first faculty development day. The main aim of the event was to provide faculty members in my department with the opportunity to share and transfer practical knowledge and skills related to research and teaching. For my presentation, I decided to introduce my colleagues to generative AI through six practical tips, which could help faculty streamline their day-to-day duties by using ChatGPT or Bard/Gemini.

The tips I shared with faculty can be divided into three themes: generative AI for time management and organisation, generative AI for content creation, and generative AI for feedback and insights. With generative AI for time management and organisation, I demonstrated how tools such as ChatGPT can be used to assign students to groups and schedule assignments such as presentations. Many faculty members said this would save them time, as they are usually doing these tasks manually by printing lists of students prior to assigning them to groups.

With generative AI for content creation, I demonstrated two useful capabilities: (1) creating exam revision sheets using a prompt and lecture slides, and (2) drafting presentation/lecture slides using a prompt and link to an external source such as an open-access research paper. Students often ask for revision sheets in preparation for midterms and final exams. Using generative AI to create exam revision sheets, which could then be made available to students online, would greatly benefit students. During my demonstration, I stressed the importance of post-editing and proofreading; I had previously found that the output occasionally contained minor stylistic errors or slight problems with the content itself (e.g., a key piece of information may be missing).

As for feedback and insights, I demonstrated how ChatGPT can review uploaded assignments and – when properly prompted – provide feedback according to the grading rubric(s) attached to the assignment. This was a revelation for some faculty, who said they would use it to gain additional insights into the work that their students submit. Some faculty jokingly asked whether this feature could be used to assign grades to students' work. Naturally, I pointed out the importance of subject experts such as ourselves in terms of assigning a final grade for assignments. One faculty member – who also happened to be presenting on the use of generative AI at the event – also touched on the fact that different generative AI platforms and tools would assign different grades to the same assignment. This demonstrates that there is an issue with reliability and consistency when using such tools. In any case, I made it clear that the feedback feature should only be used to gain additional insights or to provide more detailed feedback to students submitting formative assessments. It should not be used to blindly grade the work of students without recourse to faculty members' knowledge and expertise.

DISCUSSION

To better understand our experiences, we inductively coded them to see where they overlapped. These codes were collapsed into five themes: foundational, conceptual, social, ethical, and emotional. We also utilised Lynette's customised generative AI to validate the themes we generated. We have illustrated these themes in Table 1.2.

We noticed that we had spoken about elements reflective of the theory of literacies. The traditional definition of *literacy* focuses on the abilities of reading and writing, where literacy is considered a skill that can be

TABLE 1.2 Data Analysis Using a Customised ChatGPT

Theme	Codes
Foundational	Deploying Specific Functionalities of the Generative AI Platforms Familiarising Our Students with the Capabilities of the Platform Familiarising Ourselves with the Capabilities of the Platform Selecting Appropriate Generative AI Platforms Understanding the Collaborative Role of Generative AI
Conceptual	Locating Information Organising Information Evaluating Information Using Information Repurposing Information
Social	Dialogues with Customised Generative AI for Research Insights Generative AI as a Co-creator of Artistic Creations Generative AI as a Partner in the Learning Process Using Generative AI as an Interlocutor
Ethical	Acknowledging AI Contributions Addressing Artistic Integrity and Environmental Impact Ensuring Data Privacy and Informed Consent Transparency and Limitations of Generative AI
Emotional	Emotional Aspects of Evaluating Generative AI Output Emotional Reactions to Generative AI Data Analysis Emotional Reactions to Generative AI Feedback Reflection on Biases and Stereotypes

cognitively taught and assessed (Bloome & Green, 2015; Chakraborty et al., 2021). In contemporary educational settings, however, literacy is much more often considered a social practice. In this view, literacy is fluid and multimodal rather than fixed and discrete, constructed through everyday interactions, and laden with power and privilege (Barton & Hamilton, 2012; Gee, 1989; Lea, 2004; Lea & Street, 1998, 2006; Rowsell & Pahl, 2015; Street, 1984, 1994). Given the multiplicity that literacy entails, the term *literacies* is used instead. In this study, therefore, literacies are understood to be the socially and contextually constructed multimodal use of language.

In more recent years, literacies as a concept has been further developed to incorporate the digital turn, which Mills (2010) describes as "new literacy practices in digital environments across a variety of social contexts" (p. 246). Through the use of technology, the ways in which people connect have broadened in scope, influencing the ways people make meaning within digital spaces, leading to the term digital literacies (Bawden, 2008; Summey, 2013; Tour, 2017). Importantly, digital literacies are "collaborative, participatory, interactive, distributive, non-linear, highly multimodal and creative" (Tour, 2017, p. 414). With the advent of generative AI technologies, where people socially interact *with technology*, digital literacies have become even more important.

In our reflections, we found key foundational skills enabled our effective use of generative AI, including familiarising ourselves and our students with the capabilities of the platform, selecting appropriate generative AI platforms, deploying specific functionalities of the generative AI platforms, and understanding the collaborative role of generative AI in our practices. This led us to develop stronger conceptual understandings, including how to locate, organise, evaluate, use, and repurpose information from our interactions with generative AIs. We also discovered the social dimension of generative AI when we started to use generative AI as an interlocutor, co-creator, and partner, encouraging our students to do the same.

Importantly, our reflections underscored our commitment to acting ethically in the digital realm. By emphasising transparency, informed consent, and the consideration of broader ethical implications, we showcased how educators can model digital citizenship, guiding students to engage with generative AI technologies thoughtfully and responsibly. Finally, our reflections also highlighted the significant role of the affective domain in our experiences and approaches to using generative AI. Researchers have noted that digital literacies by themselves do not account for the positionality of the user with regard to information, proposing that emotional self-awareness is a key factor in successfully navigating the digital world (see, e.g., Lincenberg, 2021). Emotional factors not only influenced how and why we integrated and interacted with generative AI in our teaching and research but also shaped the ethical considerations and creative processes with which we engaged. The affective domain, therefore, can be considered a critical aspect of engaging with generative AI, driving both the practical application of these technologies and the reflective evaluation of their implications.

CONCLUSION

In conclusion, we have constructed a framework that showcases how educators and researchers can foster a culture of AI literacy in higher education (see Figure 1.1). In the framework, we highlight the following key features:

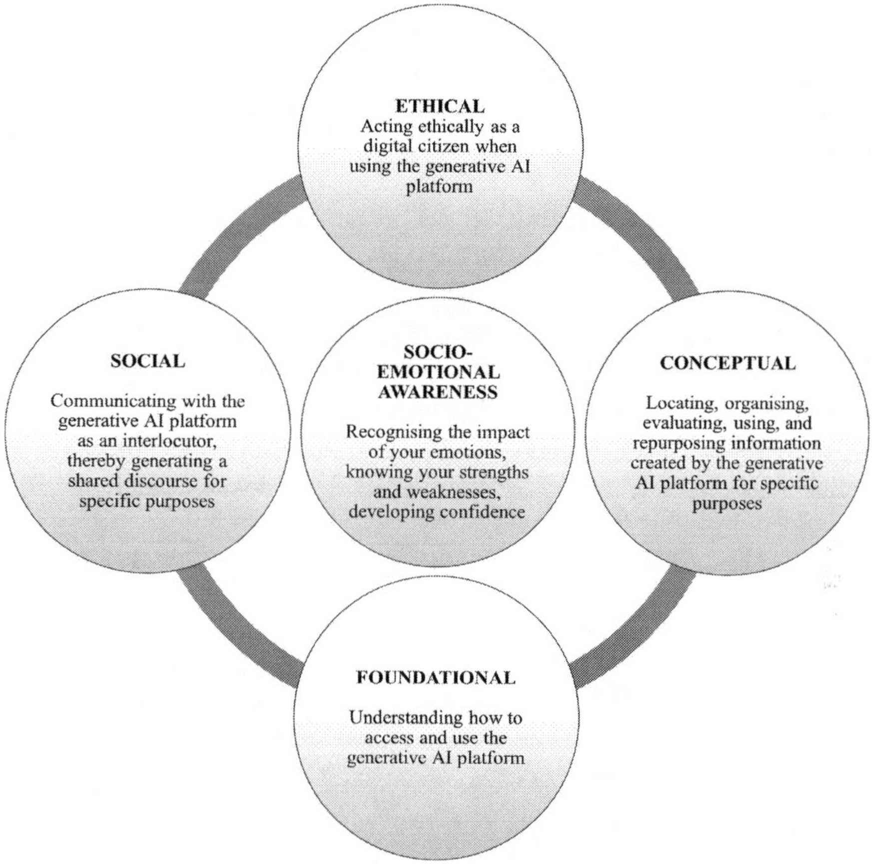

FIGURE 1.1 AI Literacy Framework for Higher Education.

1. Effective generative AI use necessitates a foundational understanding of how to access and use the platform.
2. Effective generative AI use involves locating, organising, evaluating, using, and repurposing information for specific purposes.
3. Effective generative AI use involves communication with the platform as an interlocutor to generate a shared discourse for specific purposes.
4. Effective generative AI use should be underscored by ethical actions as a digital citizen.
5. Effective generative AI use is underpinned by socio-emotional awareness.

STATEMENTS, DECLARATIONS, AND DATA AVAILABILITY

Both Dr Lynette Pretorius and Dr Basil Cahusac de Caux contributed to the conceptualisation, investigation, methodology, data curation, formal analysis, validation, project administration, and writing (both draft and final version) of this study.

This chapter was made available via pre-print on 6 June 2024. The pre-print can be accessed here: https://doi.org/10.26180/25965178 We chose to make our research available via pre-print for two key reasons. First, we had already received a significant amount of interest in the development of our framework, so we decided to share our findings promptly to allow other scholars to build on our work without delay. Second, we are committed to democratising knowledge creation and dissemination in academia, so we sought to make our full research as widely accessible as possible to foster inclusivity and collaboration across the scholarly community.

The authors did not receive any specific grants from funding agencies in the public, commercial, or not-for-profit sectors for the preparation or publication of this manuscript. Once the pre-print was published, Dr Lynette Pretorius received a consultancy fee to help further develop the AI literacy framework described in this chapter into an AI literacy curriculum.

ACKNOWLEDGEMENTS

We would like to thank Rev Chris Pretorius for his technical assistance in helping Dr Lynette Pretorius develop her customised AI ChatGPT 4 model described in this manuscript. We would also like to acknowledge the members of our writing groups for helpful discussions while preparing this manuscript. In particular, we would like to thank Jing Zhang for valuable suggestions to further refine our AI literacy framework.

REFERENCES

Adams, T. E., & Herrmann, A. F. (2023). Good autoethnography. *Journal of Autoethnography, 4*(1), 1–9. https://doi.org/10.1525/joae.2023.4.1.1

Adams, T. E., Holman Jones, S., & Ellis, C. (2022). *Handbook of autoethnography* (2nd ed.). Routledge.

Appel, G., Neelbauer, J., & Schweidel, D. A. (2023, April 7). Generative AI has an intellectual property problem. *Harvard Business Review*. https://hbr.org/2023/04/generative-ai-has-an-intellectual-property-problem

Barton, D., & Hamilton, M. (2012). *Local literacies: Reading and writing in one community*. Routledge.

Bawden, D. (2008). Origins and concepts of digital literacy. In C. Lankshear & M. Knobel (Eds.), *Digital literacies: Concepts, policies and practices* (pp. 17–32). Peter Lang.

Bloome, D., & Green, J. (2015). The social and linguistic turns in studying language and literacy. In J. Rowsell & K. Pahl (Eds.), *The Routledge handbook of literacy studies* (pp. 19–34). Routledge.

Braun, V., & Clarke, V. (2006). Using thematic analysis in psychology. *Qualitative Research in Psychology, 3*(2), 77–101. https://doi.org/10.1191/1478088706qp063oa

Braun, V., & Clarke, V. (2019). Reflecting on reflexive thematic analysis. *Qualitative Research in Sport, Exercise and Health, 11*(4), 589–597. https://doi.org/10.1080/2159676X.2019.1628806

Braun, V., & Clarke, V. (2022). *Thematic analysis: A practical guide*. SAGE.

Cahusac de Caux, B., Pretorius, L., & Macaulay, L. (2022). *Research and teaching in a pandemic world: The challenges of establishing academic identities during times of crisis*. Springer. https://doi.org/10.1007/978-981-19-7757-2

Chakraborty, D., Soyoof, A., Moharami, M., Utami, A. D., Zeng, S., Cong-Lem, N., Hradsky, D., Maestre, J., Foomani, E. M., & Pretorius, L. (2021). Feedback as a space for academic social practice in doctoral writing groups. *The Educational and Developmental Psychologist, 38*(2), 238–248. https://doi.org/10.1080/20590776.2021.1972764

Chang, H., Ngunjiri, F. W., & Hernandez, K. C. (2013). *Collaborative autoethnography*. Left Coast Press.

Cotton, D. R. E., Cotton, P. A., & Shipway, J. R. (2023). Chatting and cheating: Ensuring academic integrity in the era of ChatGPT. *Innovations in Education and Teaching International, 61*(2), 228–239. https://doi.org/10.1080/14703297.2023.2190148

Currie, G. M. (2023). Academic integrity and artificial intelligence: Is ChatGPT hype, hero or heresy? *Seminars in Nuclear Medicine, 53*(5), 719–730. https://doi.org/10.1053/j.semnuclmed.2023.04.008

Edwards, J. (2021). Ethical autoethnography: Is it possible? *International Journal of Qualitative Methods, 20*, 1–6. https://doi.org/10.1177/1609406921995306

Ellis, C., Adams, T. E., & Bochner, A. P. (2011). Autoethnography: An overview. *Historical Social Research/Historische Sozialforschung, 36*(4), 273–290. www.jstor.org/stable/23032294

Farrokhnia, M., Banihashem, S. K., Noroozi, O., & Wals, A. (2023). A SWOT analysis of ChatGPT: Implications for educational practice and research. *Innovations in Education and Teaching International, 61*(3), 460–474. https://doi.org/10.1080/14703297.2023.2195846

Gee, J. P. (1989). Literacy, discourse, and linguistics: Introduction. *Journal of Education, 171*(1), 5–17. www.jstor.org/stable/42743865

Glaser, B. G., & Strauss, A. L. (1967/1999). *The discovery of grounded theory: Strategies for qualitative research*. Transaction Publishers.

Guo, K., Pan, M., Li, Y., & Lai, C. (2024). Effects of an AI-supported approach to peer feedback on university EFL students' feedback quality and writing ability. *The Internet and Higher Education, 63*, Article 100962. https://doi.org/10.1016/j.iheduc.2024.100962

Ho, P. X. P. (2024). Using ChatGPT in English language learning: A study on IT students' attitudes, habits, and perceptions. *International Journal of TESOL & Education, 4*(1), 55–68. https://doi.org/10.54855/ijte.24414

Kalenjuk, E., Subban, P., Laletas, S., & Wilson, S. (2022). Using art therapy to explore researcher identity as a prelude to dysgraphia study: An autoethnography. *JoCAT: Journal of Creative Arts Therapies, 17*(2), 1–17. www.jocat-online.org/a-22-kalenjuk

Law, L. (2024). Application of generative artificial intelligence (GenAI) in language teaching and learning: A scoping literature review. *Computers and Education Open, 6*, Article 100174. https://doi.org/10.1016/j.caeo.2024.100174

Lea, M. R. (2004). Academic literacies: A pedagogy for course design. *Studies in Higher Education, 25*(6), 739–756. https://doi.org/10.1080/0307507042000287230

Lea, M. R., & Street, B. V. (1998). Student writing in higher education: An academic literacies approach. *Studies in Higher Education, 23*(2), 157–172. https://doi.org/10.1080/03075079812331380364

Lea, M. R., & Street, B. V. (2006). The "Academic Literacies" model: Theory and applications. *Theory into Practice, 45*(4), 368–377. https://doi.org/10.1207/s15430421tip4504_11

Lim, W. M., Gunasekara, A., Pallant, J. L., Pallant, J. I., & Pechenkina, E. (2023). Generative AI and the future of education: Ragnarök or reformation? A paradoxical perspective from management educators. *The International Journal of Management Education, 21*(2), Article 100790. https://doi.org/10.1016/j.ijme.2023.100790

Lincenberg, J. (2021). Emotional self-awareness as a digital literacy. In J. Cowls & J. Morley (Eds.), *The 2020 yearbook of the digital ethics lab* (pp. 22–34). Springer. https://doi.org/10.1007/978-3-030-80083-3_3

Lincoln, Y. S., & Guba, E. G. (2016). *The constructivist credo*. Routledge. https://doi.org/10.4324/9781315418810

Luccioni, S., Jernite, Y., & Strubell, E. (2024). *Power hungry processing: Watts driving the cost of AI deployment?* Proceedings of the 2024 ACM Conference on Fairness, Accountability, and Transparency, Rio de Janeiro, Brazil, June 3–6.

Lund, B. D., & Wang, T. (2023). Chatting about ChatGPT: How may AI and GPT impact academia and libraries? *Library Hi Tech News, 40*(3), 26–29. https://doi.org/10.1108/LHTN-01-2023-0009

Mills, K. A. (2010). A review of the "digital turn" in the new literacy studies. *Review of Educational Research, 80*(2), 246–271. https://doi.org/10.3102/0034654310364401

Morse, J. M., Bowers, B. J., Charmaz, K., Clarke, A. E., Corbin, J., Porr, C. J., & Stern, P. N. (2021). *Developing grounded theory: The second generation revisited* (2nd ed.). Routledge. https://doi.org/10.4324/9781315169170

Patel, S. V. (2022). Balancing growth and grief: Narratives of an immigrant doctoral student navigating academia during the COVID-19 pandemic In B. Cahusac de Caux, L. Pretorius, & L. Macaulay (Eds.), *Research and teaching in a pandemic world: The challenges of establishing academic identities during times of crisis* (pp. 59–75). Springer. https://doi.org/10.1007/978-981-19-7757-2_5

Podorova, A. (2016). Academic language feedback toolkit: Making progress with post-entry language skills development. *Journal of Academic Language and Learning, 10,* A141–A154. https://journal.aall.org.au/index.php/jall/article/view/401

Podorova, A. (2017). *Academic language feedback guide.* https://alf-tool.monash.edu/

Pretorius, L. (2022). A harmony of voices: The value of collaborative autoethnography as collective witnessing during a pandemic. In B. Cahusac de Caux, L. Pretorius, & L. Macaulay (Eds.), *Research and teaching in a pandemic world: The challenges of establishing academic identities during times of crisis* (pp. 25–33). Springer. https://doi.org/10.1007/978-981-19-7757-2_3

Pretorius, L. (2023). Fostering AI literacy: A teaching practice reflection. *Journal of Academic Language & Learning, 17*(1), T1–T8. https://journal.aall.org.au/index.php/jall/article/view/891/435435567

Pretorius, L. (2024a). Demystifying research paradigms: Navigating ontology, epistemology, and axiology in research. *The Qualitative Report, 29*(10), 2698-2715. https://doi.org/10.46743/2160-3715/2024.7632

Pretorius, L. (2024b). *Developing AI literacy in your writing and research.* The Scholar's Way. www.lynettepretorius.com/the_scholars_way_blog/developing-ai-literacy-in-your-writing-and-research/

Pretorius, L., & Cahusac de Caux, B. (2024). *The AI literacy framework for higher education: A grounded theory exploration of the foundational, social, conceptual, ethical, and affective domains of AI literacy.* [Pre-print]. Monash University Research Repository. https://doi.org/10.26180/25965178

Pretorius, L., & Cutri, J. (2019). Autoethnography: Researching personal experiences. In L. Pretorius, L. Macaulay, & B. Cahusac de Caux (Eds.), *Wellbeing in doctoral education: Insights and guidance from the student experience* (pp. 27–34). Springer. https://doi.org/10.1007/978-981-13-9302-0_4

Pretorius, L., & Ford, A. (2016). Reflection for learning: Teaching reflective practice at the beginning of university study. *International Journal of Teaching and Learning in Higher Education, 28*(2), 241–253. www.isetl.org/ijtlhe/pdf/IJTLHE2142.pdf

Pretorius, L., Huynh, H.-H., Pudyanti, A. A. A. R., Li, Z., Noori, A. Q., & Zhou, Z. (2024). *Empowering international PhD students: Generative AI, Ubuntu, and the decolonisation of academic communication.* [Pre-print]. Monash University Research Repository. https://doi.org/10.26180/26923231

Pretorius, L., Macaulay, L., & Cahusac de Caux, B. (2019). *Wellbeing in doctoral education: Insights and guidance from the student experience.* Springer. https://doi.org/10.1007/978-981-13-9302-0

Rangarajan, R., & Daneshfar, S. (2022). Processing uncertainty during COVID-19: A collaborative autoethnography of two stranded international PhD students. In B. Cahusac de Caux, L. Pretorius, & L. Macaulay (Eds.), *Research and teaching in a pandemic world: The challenges of establishing academic identities during times of crisis* (pp. 37–57). Springer. https://doi.org/10.1007/978-981-19-7757-2_4

Rowsell, J., & Pahl, K. (2015). *The Routledge handbook of literacy studies.* Routledge.

Street, B. V. (1984). *Literacy in theory and practice.* Cambridge University Press.

Street, B. V. (1994). What is meant by local literacies? *Language and Education, 8*(1–2), 9–17. https://doi.org/10.1080/09500789409541372

Summey, D. C. (2013). *Developing digital literacies: A framework for professional learning.* Corwin Press.

Tour, E. (2017). Understanding digital literacy practices: What can be learnt with visual methods? *Changing English, 24*(4), 413–425. https://doi.org/10.1080/1358684X.2017.1304815

United Nations. (n.d.). *The 17 goals.* https://sdgs.un.org/goals

CHAPTER 2

Exploring the Speculative

AI Literacies and Creativity

Jason D. DeHart

Suppose you connected strongly with a book or piece of art. Then suppose you met the creator of this art piece and they told you that they had generated the response with AI. Would that change your sense of connection?

CONTEXT AND FRAMING

The development of artificial intelligence (AI) in educational settings might be seen as having evolved with relative speed, seemingly since the COVID-19 pandemic – a time of isolation in which the prominence of screens, as well as the divide between those who have access to technology and those who do not, was made evident. However, conversations about and prognostications of AI have been part of both speculative and educational conversation for decades, including the work of literacy scholars. Olson (1996) has historically written about the possibilities of writing and creating with technological assistance, noting that the use of the term "cyborg" denotes the foregrounding of some types of machine or supportive communication method. The question that leads this chapter is one of authorship

DOI: 10.1201/9781003510635-4

and connection, and one that the author has posed in his classroom for his students to consider. The role of creativity and the human consciousness in light of the development of AI raises new questions of design, authorship, and ethics.

Whether the additional component consists of speech-to-text or digitalized commentary for choosing the proper driving route, the use of technology alongside human beings for creative and efficient purposes has roots in the Industrial Revolution, and throughout time. In literacy scholarship, this focus on technology can be traced back through a variety of paradigms, including multiliteracies, New Literacies, digital literacy, and media literacy. In the context of this work, I particularly focus on New Literacies and will define this term and framing as a means of discussing the possibilities of AI and what the future might hold for theoretical developments within literacy.

The use of advanced technology to solve and sometimes complicate social problems has been richly explored in fictional texts, but now researchers and educators have the reality of this technology to wrestle with and explore. At the same time, this author notes a movement toward more complicated questions revolving around the detection of the use of AI, issuing in a kind of surveillance mentality surrounding the phenomenon. While this chapter includes the drawbacks and complications of AI, there are several possible benefits and fascinating possibilities as well. It is with a hopeful view of the nature and possibilities of informed and critical literacy practices across modes, or meaning-making spaces, as well as theorized and actualized spaces for the production of communication that the author endeavors to consider the phenomenon of AI and its implications for creativity from a literacy/literacies perspective.

This perspective, hewn from the wider corpus of literacy/literacies studies, links with New Literacies (Cervetti et al., 2006), a description of communication and creation practices that are located in and made possible by new technological platforms, linking to multimodal synthesis of human voices and experiences. The textual ontology of this mode of creating and exploring is multimodal both in terms of the artistry involved and in terms of the technological design (Van Leeuwen, 2005). Under this view, literacy is not simply a set of practices related to generating or decoding printed words but is instead a tapestry of social and cultural engagements and interactions, encompassing a range of meaning-making and communication practices.

From a literacy/literacies perspective, the author engages with these questions of benefits and dilemmas from the vantage of theorizing what is made possible through the use of AI. As with many developing technologies and advances, AI creates a complex network of considerations, including ethical implications and legalities. This chapter is by no means intended to assuage all concerns, explore all issues, or speak to all social and industrial purposes and possibilities with AI – rather, within the educational context and with attention on literacies, the author intends to probe questions of what is made possible and what problems might occur in a speculative framing of AI literacies, including the materials that student/teacher creators can take up and make use of as further developments occur.

Chiefly, this chapter considers questions of AI from a framework that links multimodality (New London Group, 1996) and multicreativity (Kaufman et al., 2010).

THE DEVELOPMENT OF MULTIMODAL TECHNOLOGIES

As early as 1996, the New London Group began to speculate about what literacy/literacies might look like, given the rise of Internet technologies. These scholars noted the already present and increasingly developing thoroughfare of information that would come to be part of reading, writing, and creating for future generations. Kist (2000) explored notions of what crafting and expression would look like in classrooms that featured new technologies and ways of creating, or "New Literacies." The terminology of "New Literacies," however, predates both of these sources as Buckingham (1993) applied this concept to emerging ways of creating and making meaning through media and technology. Within these speculative and realized visions from scholarship, there is a thread of creativity, a focus on communication, and interwoven questions of ethics and power, including the redistribution of power and literacy structures within classroom spaces as ludic, interactive engagements with a range of materials. Rowsell (2014) has noted this ludic aspect of game-based literacy interactions as an endemic aspect of creating/crafting and thinking across modes of textual distribution.

Bezemer and Kress (2015) pointed out that multimodality could be a social and communicative conceptualization as simple as a gesture or as well known as the images in a classic text – adding modes of meaning-making and communication systems to run parallel with the extant text. To this end, multimodal formulations have been around, arguably, since the origin of language itself. Human beings draw upon a range of communication systems to share information and commemorate events. What is always evolving and deictic, to borrow Leu et al.'s (2013) term, is the emerging role of technology of formal educational systems, as well as in social systems, and the degree to which communicators have access to a range of tools that make complex interactions more seamless and accessible in a broadened conceptualization.

It is this sense of the social system of communication which links multimodality with multicreativity, particularly in what has been termed consideration of the polymath – the communicator who is able to develop artistic and innovative responses across forms. Kaufman et al. (2010) pointed the rarity of the creative polymath and developed this potentiality through questions of what it ultimately means to be creative. This polymathic expression links with the research/writer/composer who has multiple perspectives on ways to engage with content and the necessary components of design elements. Perhaps it is the case that more open accessibility to AI affords more potential for polymathic creative expression. In order to think about this question, it might be helpful to first consider a balance of conversation about AI, including the potential drawbacks.

In addition to the positive and possible, there has been tentative and concerned conversation around these swiftly developing technologies.

OWNERSHIP AND COMPENSATION

This democratizing of complex creation has led to a number of questions for both legal and creative entities. *Billboard* reported in 2024 that legislation was being passed in Europe that would safeguard copyrighted songs and musical arrangements from creative applications with AI. This resource noted that legislation was aimed at establishing a set of "controls," including "the use of copyrighted music" (Smirke, 2024, n.p.), and this was a development from active participation from both musical and technology companies with interest in the matter. In early 2024, Reuters reported that such legislation could be harmful to the development of the AI industry. On the other hand, creatives have expressed concerns over the fair and ethical use of AI, a major cause of the Screen Actors Guild strikes of Summer 2023 (Selk & Chery, 2023). While science fiction authors have dreamed about possibilities for developments in technology, they have also coupled these dreams with warnings; in our present age, this linking of advancement and uncertainty has been demonstrated in the public and corporate reception and interaction with AI technologies.

Ethics and ownership have been endemic aspects of considering multimodal texts and elements of design for some time. There are, indeed, elements of power and particular foci of discourse within multimodal texts presented in media, with some texts proving beneficial and others causing more complication and sense of harm (Fairclough, 2013; Hobbs, 2020). In the next section, affordances of AI in literacy/AI literacies will be explored, as will some of the further ethical and economic complications that this technology brings along with it.

There are various layers of ethical concerns when it comes to the use of technologies, and AI is certainly no exception.

ETHICAL IDENTITY PRACTICES

Concerns across digital spaces include anonymity, the ways in which messages are communicated and conveyed, and the enacting of identity in thoughtful ways in largely anonymous spaces (Buchholz et al., 2020). The affordances of online spaces, digital interaction, and technological tools are considerable; AI opens up even more questions and possibilities. Along with these affordances could particular notes of concern. Hagendorff (2020) pointed to the persisting call for ethics in AI-supported engagements and creating, with particular attention on questions of accountability, as well as concerns about privacy and fairness. These concerns focus on the ethical use of data and the ways that individuals or groups are held accountable for the uses of existing data. Lauer (2021) spoke to this concern as a question of responsibility, particularly of social media spaces and their role in providing space for interaction. Additional long-standing ethical considerations within the framework of digital literacy include critical consumption, the use of media tools for positive social ends (Banaji & Buckingham, 2009), as well as the use of creative methods and approaches to research-based problems (Buckingham, 2009). Ultimately, Hagendorff's (2020) conclusion is that the benefits of AI outweigh the potential for problematic behaviors and situations.

CORPORATIONS AND SETTING APPROPRIATE LEGAL BOUNDARIES

Kazim and Koshiyama (2021) further defined the specific ethical considerations for AI, including the "blockchain," a trail of digital interactions that can be generated; the concept of "big data analytics," or the ways that concentrations of collected information are processed and considered; and algorithmic concerns (p. 2). Additionally, Flick and Worrall (2022) noted concerns related to copyright laws. These concerns are seated in the context of digital literacy, and all are linked with the concept of humanity as a chief center of concern. The ethical in this sense is balanced with the energizing possibilities for a creativity.

An AI-centered pedagogy of creativity and composition must, in its fullest form, hold in focus the concerns of the ethical, and this lens can help students share their thinking about both affordances and appropriate boundaries. Lauer (2021) called for a sustained ethical sensibility at the crux of work with AI, noting both the ubiquity of this technology, and pointed to the process of forming standards and protocol for negotiating AI.

In effect, a theory of AI literacies and creativity points to, in tandem, the range of compositional interactions and designs that AI affords while also noting underlying questions of authorship and the type of bricolage that can be involved in weaving working together from an online pool of data. This sense of play and work brings to mind remixing and metacreative literacy practices, as explored by Navas (2022). In this way of approaching the creative possibilities of AI, one might frame what is made possible by growing technology as the next natural step in postproduction and remixing. Under this view, the integrity of the original remains intact, while the new product, brought together or transformed in some material and essential way, points to an altogether different message or set of questions brought about by the new remixed product/text.

Navas (2022) used the term metacreativity from the world of the *Dungeons and Dragons* stories to consider how paradigms shift and change, and how paradigms are formed interstitially between existing paradigmatic structures. When it comes to literacy education, Rowsell and Harwood (2015) spoke of a reconfigured sense of who the child is as composer/creator, including roles that speak to consumption and invention. The economic sensibilities applied to creativity can lead to this notion of the consumer, while the role of remixing and making use of tools to innovate and explore link to invention.

LINKS WITH LITERACY PRACTICES/CREATING

From a linguistically developmental perspective, the emergence and advancement of technology, however practiced and actualized, stems from the human and from human encounters, planning, and programming. From this vantage, the use of AI is not a replacement of but a parallel structure to the development of human storytelling and creation. The invention of the printing press did not, in effect, replace authorship or act in opposition to the notion of what it means to be an author. Notions of authorship lead to questions of ownership, including the ways that rights are distributed and negotiated when creating for a wide audience and when thinking about work that is created or shared as part of instruction purpose.

Of course, the printing press and advanced AI technologies are two matters and work very differently; however, from an ethical stance and a definitional approach, the use of typography to replace human handwritten configurations, the use of digital design tools to replace images crafted from ruled lines, and the use of autocorrection technology to ensure accurate and clear communication all work in parallelism with, not in opposition to, human creation. Yet, the vicissitude of ownership, authorship, and copyright in terms of AI literacies are yet to be determined at the time of this writing. In a recent social media post, a comics creator and cartoonist shared an image of an AI-generated forest scene with the words "AI Trash" scrawled in red print across the page. Other creators have pledged to ban users who incorporate AI into their work from social media spaces, creating a separation from their work and the products that are generated through AI technologies.

Of particular interest, in this case, is the ways that the voice and compositional possibilities of AI might give rise to further types of communication. No technology is an end to itself; otherwise, the social and cultural practice of the technology swiftly becomes an anachronism. The use of speech-to-text technologies provides possibilities for communication to occur, and it is this notion of communication by means of technological support and engagement that is perhaps at this stage most fascinating as a development. The ways in which AI might act as a set of practices by which further access to creation and languaging might be democratized in a fascinating consideration in terms of both literacy practices and ethically distributing tools for open lines of interaction and understanding to occur. Visualization, for example, is one of many aspects of the complicated process of reading and processing information (Serafini, 2014); yet, the existence of AI might help to generate pathways and allow for production in visual and multimodal compositions for readers/viewers/thinkers who are exploring ways of making sense of textual worlds. The possibilities of such visualizing and

AI languaging systems lead then to questions of what is possible in terms of intercultural communication practices.

From a speculative perspective, authors and creators like Gene Roddenberry envisioned times when universal translators might be possible, opening up interactions and communications across galactic spaces. Yet, interactions are stymied in daily life: what possibilities exist for the use of AI languaging systems? When it comes to creation, the boundaries between AI technology and AI literacies inevitably point not to the existence of these technologies, as this is now a given, but to the ways in which users take them up and critically apply them in compositional forms.

A polymathic expression of creativity with AI might best be described through a holistic understanding of the tools themselves, ways to navigate these tools and developing tools that do not exist for public use yet, and an understanding of the ethical application of multiple questions regarding what creativity means in social and even legal terms.

TOWARD A THEORETICAL FRAMING OF AI ARTS AND CREATIVITY

In Foucault's framing of the panopticon and synopticon, the image of a central tower or all-seeing eye is prominent and is a means by which order is kept in some social systems. Within this context of punitive and limiting use of technology, there is a striking presence of possibility but absence of interaction. One never knows if the all-seeing eye is turn on, or simply blinking and present in an effort to ensure complicity. This human versus technology framing is far from what is ideal when it comes to developments and innovations in communication systems. The practice of utilizing technology, in this view, is a central component of what it means to be literate and is not removed from instructional or creative contexts but rather critically considered in alignment with already-existing tools and means of language and image production.

Technology might be seen as panopticonal when physical devices are used, but the digitized and wireless reality of AI lends itself toward a synopticonal framing in which technology is invisible, endemic, and assumed to be present. Indeed, even in moments when the presence of technology is not ascertained, the signals of human communication might well be possible and enacted. In a recent podcast discussion, two creative writers/artists pointed out the underlying belief that more is available in terms of AI than is being currently released to the public. The notion of a pervasive system of AI, already present and yet unseen in much of daily life, is a conceptualization made all the more possible by the integrated technological framework with which people now navigate their daily lives. This leads to the conceptualization of a framing of technology and literacy which assumes production and capability that is not yet democratized but being further developed for maximum economic gain.

In the same conversation, the speakers noted that not only was AI detection an existing reality in technology, but that an AI detection detector was also a realized product. Given this swift movement to surveillance, it might be ascertained that there will likely be a continuation of development in terms of technologies related not just to the generation of AI products but in order to determine the authenticity of communications that might have been composed using AI. Systems that set up boundaries and alert users to the presence of AI-generated texts will likely continue to be as profligate as the mechanisms that can generate AI responses themselves. To date, the reliability of such detection, particularly through individual and singular methods, has not been clearly established (Anderson et al., 2023).

Returning to the initial question of authorship and connection that leads this chapter, the sense of connection might dissolve, but the appreciation of a piece of work that offers that connection might persist. This is an anomalous reality in which it is the work itself a human being connects with – absent of the presence of the person or individual's voice. The end product is achieved in terms of a physical text that connects with a reader, but the strength and quality of that connection are questionable as the voice of author is a mingled transfusion of other voices received by the reader and then interpreted in their own manner. In this example, reading and consuming text is no longer viewed as a transferal of idea and experience from one author or set of authors, with the assistance of an editorial, to a readership; rather, it is the culling of multiple points of human experience, spun together in a mechanical centrifuge, and then generated with an interlinking of themes and aspects of lived experience that essentially stem from a range of experiences. It is a manufactured experience, drawn from the ether.

Yet, the experience of an author is always a manifestation of a range of experiences, including the role of faulty memory, as well as the choice to intentionally lace truth with fiction. The art of this decision-making process, including the ways the narrative is conveyed, might be seen as craft. Yet, there is something of the human voice which remains consistent in original creation that is absent from a manufactured product. One might value an original drawing more so than a careful tracing. While the tracing is enjoyable and achieves an expect of production, an aesthetic experience with the work might be mitigated by its origins as a traced/replicated work.

Still yet, a tracing of ideas is more helpful and connective than an absence. If, for example, a creator lacks access to the tools or means by which to produce a response, the AI-generated method of assisting and sharing content, derived from a wellspring of thought patterns and experiences, might point to the possibility of a shared experience that would otherwise be impossible. The linking of human voice to human voice, as supported by an AI system, does not negate the possibility for creativity, connection, or criticality. These essential elements are the concluding implications of this chapter and its theoretical terminus.

In terms of creativity, the design and diffusion of technologies includes its own sense of craftsmanship, as does the potential for thinking about the utilization of these technologies for communication purposes; in terms of connection, the linking of a visual or typographical composition, or a melding of the two, serves as a means by which one idea can be transferred, linked together, or made visually manifest by an AI technology, issuing into a defined literacy practice of both composition/utterance and reception. The defining and limiting of text within socially acceptable hierarchies has been a tenet of my research trajectory for some time; AI might be useful as a means to reconsider what constitutes text as the products which are instantly manifest with these technologies can be shaped and reshaped based on the use of design elements.

The receptive component of a communicative exchange is not a *sine qua non* in order for literacy/literacies to have occurred or to have been drawn upon – a novel in a drawer hidden from readership is still a novel – but the element of composition and utterance might be seen a more essential feature of language production in order to be taken up as an autonomous literacy practice. This consideration of isolation and community with online creating links with the concepts of audience which have been a notable aspect of online spaces for some time in the literature (Hoechsmann, 2008; Wee, 2017).

Finally, the notion of criticality stems from further thinking about what AI means in terms of authorship as well as the discussions that can surround AI creations.

From this chapter's consideration of AI and creativity, there are a number of salient points which might be helpful in positioning and exploring the next phase of what AI literacies look, sound, (feel?), and read like. Namely, these commitments of a speculative AI literacies pedagogy, with particular attention to the visual and verbal aspects of creation and interaction, might include:

1. A paradigmatic approach to AI literacies which is both solid and temporal; a framework that can speak to the now as well as the next simultaneously and be adapted to further questions as they arise. The ongoing evolution of technology means that the tools we imagine for tomorrow's world might, indeed, be part of tomorrow's world. This is a rich space for the imagination and a place for innovative conversations about the ways human beings can continue to explore, grow, support, and be supported through the use of communicative AI technologies.
2. A central sense of ethos that permeates all aspects of literacy, both online and offline, monolingual and multilingual, monomodal and multimodal, and which holds the human as the essential element of continued ethical inquiries and developments. This aspect of pedagogy is social and cultural, and illustrates the central importance of the human story and human voice. These are essential aspects of literacy as human beings share narratives, and this ethos means that voices and practices are included, rather than excluded.
3. A reconsideration and playful reinterpretation of the role of creator and author, as when auteur theory was applied to film, with a focus on the integrity of original works, invention in remixing with existing works, and the economic implications of producing and consuming creative works. While the role of an author or artist is honorable, and should be, the democratizing of content creation is a continually evolving possibility within the span of available technologies. A pedagogy focused on the possibilities of AI literacies should (and will likely) include a focus on the architectural space of these technologies – the interconnected dimension of online space. Within this space, power shifts and voices can be magnified that might otherwise be silenced.
4. A commitment to fearless criticality, the questioning and requestioning, as well as the freedom to posit new questions as

ways of composing come to be and challenge human ontology. As mentioned earlier, the worry that AI will replace human creativity has been palpable among the creative community; the possibilities of AI are fascinating, while critical questions of authenticity and critical descriptions of creation processes continue to be important for literacy/literacies.

With these elements in mind and in practice, literacy as a field might be further enriched and challenged by AI. A number of possible questions continue to emerge, including the thinking processes of readers and writers that can be supported through AI, the ways in which a visualizing and verbalizing component to AI might support a manifesting of existing content with more immediate access for information literacy, and the continued role of the individual citizen/consumer in forming what is popular and possible with these quickly developing tools. As a literacy researcher and educator with an affinity for the digital and all that technological tools afford, I am optimistically curious to see how institutions and individuals will continue to shape and explore discourse around these tools. A thoughtful system of pedagogy and research will always reflect trends, transitions, and developments.

REFERENCES

Anderson, N., Belavy, D. L., Perle, S. M., Hendricks, S., Hespanhol, L., Verhagen, E., & Memon, A. R. (2023). AI did not write this manuscript, or did it? Can we trick the AI text detector into generated texts? The potential future of ChatGPT and AI in Sports & Exercise Medicine manuscript generation. *BMJ Open Sport & Exercise Medicine*, *9*(1), e001568.

Banaji, S., & Buckingham, D. (2009). The civic sell: Young people, the internet, and ethical consumption. *Information, Communication & Society*, *12*(8), 1197–1223.

Bezemer, J., & Kress, G. (2015). *Multimodality, learning and communication: A social semiotic frame*. Routledge.

Buchholz, B. A., DeHart, J., & Moorman, G. (2020). Digital citizenship during a global pandemic: Moving beyond digital literacy. *Journal of Adolescent Adult Literacy*, *64*(1), 11–17.

Buckingham, D. (1993). *The development of television literacy: Talk, text and context* [Doctoral dissertation, Institute of Education, University of London].

Buckingham, D. (2009). Creative visual methods in media research: Possibilities, problems and proposals. *Media, Culture & Society*, *31*(4), 633–652.

Cervetti, G., Damico, J., & Pearson, P. D. (2006). Multiple literacies, new literacies, and teacher education. *Theory into Practice*, *45*(4), 378–386.

Fairclough, N. (2013). *Language and power*. Routledge.

Flick, C., & Worrall, K. (2022). The ethics of creative AI. In C. Vear & F. Poltronieri (Eds.), *The Language of Creative AI: Practices, Aesthetics and Structures* (pp. 73–91). Springer International Publishing.

Hagendorff, T. (2020). The ethics of AI ethics: An evaluation of guidelines. *Minds and Machines, 30*(1), 99–120.

Hobbs, R. (2020). *Mind over media: Propaganda education for a digital age*. WW Norton & Company.

Hoechsmann, M. (2008). Audience incorporated (Inc.): Youth cultural production and the new media. *Journal of Curriculum Theorizing, 24*(1), 60–70.

Kaufman, J. C., Beghetto, R. A., & Baer, J. (2010). Finding young Paul Robeson: Exploring the question of creative polymathy. In R. J. Sternberg, & D. D. Preiss (Eds.), *Innovations in educational psychology* (pp. 141–162). Springer Publishing Company.

Kazim, E., & Koshiyama, A. S. (2021). A high-level overview of AI ethics. *Patterns, 2*(9), 1–12.

Kist, W. (2000). Beginning to create the new literacy classroom: What does the new literacy look like? *Journal of Adolescent & Adult Literacy*, *43*(8), 710–718.

Lauer, D. (2021). You cannot have AI ethics without ethics. *AI and Ethics, 1*(1), 21–25.

Leu, D. J., Forzani, E., & Kennedy, C. (2013). Providing classroom leadership in new literacies: Preparing students for their future. In S.B. Wepner et al. (Eds.), *The Administration and Supervision of Reading Programs*, 200–213.

Navas, E. (2022). *The rise of metacreativity: AI aesthetics after remix*. Routledge.

New London Group. (1996). A pedagogy of multiliteracies: Designing social futures. *Harvard Educational Review*, *66*(1), 60–92.

Olson, G. A. (1996). Writing, literacy and technology: Toward a cyborg writing. *JAC*, *16*(1), 1–26.

Rowsell, J. (2014). Toward a phenomenology of contemporary reading. *The Australian Journal of Language and Literacy*, *37*(2), 117–127.

Rowsell, J., & Harwood, D. (2015). "Let it go": Exploring the image of the child as a producer, consumer, and inventor. *Theory into Practice, 54*(2), 136–146.

Selk, A., & Chery, S. (2023). What to know about the looming SAG-AFTRA strike, its impact on Hollywood. *The Washington Post.* https://go.gale.com/ps/i.do?id=GALE%7CA756862747&sid=googleScholar&v=2.1&it=r&linkaccess=abs&issn=01908286&p=AONE&sw=w

Serafini, F. (2014). *Reading the visual: An introduction to teaching multimodal literacy*. Teachers College Press.

Smirke, R. (2024). European Union passes 'world first' AI legislation that would safeguard copyrighted music. *Billboard.* www.billboard.com/business/business-news/european-union-ai-legislation-laws-copyrighted-music-passes-1235631846

Van Leeuwen, T. (2005). Multimodality, genre and design. In R.H. Jones & S. Norris (Eds)., *Discourse in Action: Introducing Mediated Discourse Analysis* (pp. 73–93). Routledge.

Wee, V. (2017). Youth audiences and the media in the digital era: The intensification of multimedia engagement and interaction. *Cinema Journal*, *57*(1), 133–139.

II

Practical Applications in Educational Contexts

CHAPTER 3

Teachers First

Building AI Literacy to Address Mundane Tasks and Enhance Creative Applications in Secondary English Classrooms

Clarice M. Moran and Damiana Gibbons Pyles

As artificial intelligence (AI) finds its way into the classroom, teachers are left wondering if they should welcome it in or keep it out. Some hope to use AI to reduce mundane tasks, jazz up lesson planning, and augment learning goals. Others fear it will take over the role of the teacher and lead students to rely on machine-generated work instead of creative output. It is a push-pull that confounds even the most enthusiastic techies. What do we do with AI? Are we supposed to use it, avoid it, maintain our suspicion of it?

In this chapter, we will address the growing importance of AI in secondary education and the need to equip teachers (both inservice and preservice) with the skills and knowledge necessary to effectively integrate AI in their daily, lived practice. This new AI literacy will, we argue, become increasingly integral to operating in the world. Teachers will require a new set of tools for this type of "living literacy" (Rowsell & Pahl, 2020), tools that equip them to address both new and old problems in education. In this sense, teachers will need to develop transliteracies that take into account multiple ways of knowing (Stornaiuolo et al, 2017). They must be able to move from analog to digital worlds seamlessly, integrating AI while maintaining a "literacies before technologies" stance (NCTE, 2018). This

DOI: 10.1201/9781003510635-6

Herculean task is among the most confounding of modern times. It appears that AI is not going anywhere soon, so grappling with its implications, ethical considerations, and abilities is essential for teachers who are often considered among the most important adopters of technologies (Celik et al, 2022; Seufert et al, 2021).

The chapter will begin by examining the current landscape of AI in education, particularly how it is affecting teaching and learning in secondary schools, then discuss how AI can assist in both mundane and creative tasks in the secondary English classroom. The chapter will provide a framework for understanding what it means to be AI literate and offer suggestions for integrating AI into daily teacher life, as well as guidelines for teacher preparation programs.

THE STORY SO FAR: AI IN SECONDARY EDUCATION

Though some worries exist for teachers how they can use digital platforms for their students' learning, AI can help teachers with some of their mundane, everyday tasks. One concern is that teachers might tailor their teaching to the design of the app rather than their own pedagogical goals (LeBlanc et al, 2023). This could potentially be even more of a concern if teachers are using AI to design the lesson itself, especially if teachers are not using their own knowledge and autonomy to double-check the lesson. Moreover, there are inherent biases within algorithms themselves (Noble, 2018), and given that AI platforms are built on algorithms, this could be a concern. If these concerns are addressed, however, AI can be useful for teachers. Not only can AI platforms help teachers to create lesson plans in multiple subjects, including English language arts (ELA), but they can also revise those lesson plans when prompted by the teachers to improve them (Hashem et al, 2023).

Although research on AI is still emerging, many scholars have found that AI has a variety of benefits for teachers and students, including reducing teacher burnout (Hashem et al, 2023), improving students' understanding of language (Chao et al, 2023), developing preservice teachers' pedagogical knowledge (Su et al, 2022), and acting as a comprehensive educational resource (Chen, 2023). Concerns about AI include apprehension over the veracity of the outputs (Lathrop & Johnson, 2023; Sison et al, 2023), fear that the machine will take over jobs (Reed, 2022), and anger over how it was programmed (Reed, 2023). In short, controversy has dogged AI since it was introduced. However, by developing AI literacy, teachers can leverage the benefits of the technology and, potentially, enhance their pedagogy and reduce their workload.

THEORETICAL FRAMEWORK AND CONSIDERATIONS

One of the tenets of our chapter is that the everyday, lived experiences of teachers matter. In particular, we would like to focus on the "small stories" of teachers' lives (Watson, 2007), in which the way that teachers discuss their own experiences creates the way that they construct their own identities, even when discussing everyday experiences. Similar to Gee's (2001) "identity kits," teachers express their identities through the stories they tell about their everyday experiences in the classroom.

The environment in which teachers construct their own small stories is often a stressful one, especially when it comes to the increasing demands of the teaching profession – from the push for high student test scores to increased responsibilities due to teacher shortages. One of the many stressors teachers have, in particular, is the mundane administrative and planning tasks that they have to do every day, which only add to their workload (Ardvisson et al, 2019). After all, most teachers got into the profession to make a difference with young people, but there is so much more to the job of teaching that has nothing to do with students.

Researchers have found that using AI to assist with these mundane tasks can counter burnout, leading to new ways of teachers' understanding of their own roles. Hashem et al (2023) found that teachers could use ChatGPT to plan lessons that were effective as long as the teachers used their human knowledge to revise the lessons along with the machine to create a lesson that would teach the content while meeting their students' needs. This interaction did lessen the teachers' feelings of burnout. In a sense, these teachers' "small stories" are adding new characters in the form of AI partners, which can help them to see themselves in a new, less-stressed perspective.

What AI brings to the interaction with teachers, though, is not completely straightforward. To understand this dynamic, the posthuman theoretical framework can lend its insights. Posthumanist theory decentralizes the role of human beings in the world, suggesting that other organisms, including machines, have an equal part to play in interactions with humans (Wolfe, 2010). In this sense, rather than being a passive tool, AI would be an "active participant" (Barad, 2007, p. 13) when teachers are using it, so that the way AI interacts with the teachers, including what AI produces and how, is an important factor in its own right and helps us understand the interaction between the AI and the teachers themselves.

In particular, posthumanism offers a lens into how ELA teachers can work with technologies in their classrooms. Opening up the idea of interactions between nonhuman entities and humans in a classroom changes the way that literacy itself is defined. Lenters and McDermott (2020) collaborated with a group of literacy scholars to define literacy as "[c]ommunicative practices for forming and making sense of the world through intentional and sustained encounters with human and more-than-human entities and for opening spaces for new becomings" (p. 4). In this view of literacy, the "new becomings" encompass not only what the teachers produce with AI for learning but also how the teachers see themselves in the process, which is why we pair posthumanism with critical literacy as well.

Critical literacy involves viewing the world with a "critical" eye and taking into account students' "funds of knowledge" or the background that they bring into the classroom (Gonzalez et al, 2006), as well as multimodal and multilingual practices (Lau, 2012; Vasquez et al, 2019). Often posthumanism and critical theories are pitted against one another, but we can see how they can work together (Kuby et al, 2020). Critical literacy, together with posthumanist theory, provides a way to expand the definition of literacy and acknowledge the joint contributions of humans and machines. Posthumanism helps to shed light on how machines are participating in the dynamics while humans are interacting with them and while critical literacy opens up questions of representation, identity, and agency to include AI alongside teachers and students. Drawing on both posthumanism scholarship and critical literacy allows us to address the human and nonhuman systems of power that contribute to knowledge.

AI LITERACY

Although it seems as if AI burst into public consciousness in November 2022, the idea of AI actually was first proposed back in 1955 in a paper titled, "A Proposal for the Dartmouth Summer Research Project on Artificial Intelligence" (McCarthy et al, 2006). In that paper, McCarthy et al (2006) proposed that machines could be "programmed to use language" (p. 12) and recommended using a computer to "carry out activities which may best be described as self-improvement" (p. 14). Then, as now, the authors were interested in employing technology to make life easier.

Much of the current furor over AI has surrounded the chatbot ChatGPT, a large language model (LLM) released by OpenAI that uses an algorithm to predict which English word naturally comes next in a string of English words to produce human-like conversation. Trained on the Common Crawl dataset of billions of publicly available web pages, ChatGPT analyzes language and looks for common patterns to answer queries. Controversy has dogged ChatGPT since its debut with some publications calling it a "global phenomenon" (Reed, 2022) and others worrying about its "ethical and social dangers" (Mehrishi, 2023). Eager to cash in on the Capitalist advantages that ChatGPT might offer, Microsoft introduced its own LLM, "BingChat," in February 2023 (since renamed Copilot), and Google launched its version, called "Bard," in March 2023 (since renamed "Gemini").

In the ensuing months, teachers have grappled with the technology and wondered how much they should allow in their classrooms. This struggle has led to a need for renewed *AI literacy*, a term that we believe should join the growing list of multiliteracies necessary for teacher competency (Cazden et al, 1996; Cope & Kalantzis, 2009). In addition to literacy in reading, writing, and multimodalities (which include social media, digital tools, visual and aural awareness), teachers now must develop an understanding of how to manipulate and critically evaluate AI. It is no longer enough to understand how to use basic digital tools, such as Google Docs, or to be able to teach in an online space. Teachers now need to develop an understanding of how to talk to students about AI, integrate AI in their own pedagogy, and guide students through their use of AI. This expanded view of literacy goes beyond traditional literacy practices and includes embedding social practices (Bailey, 2009) as well as the use of technology (Swenson et al, 2006). Teachers now must integrate the traditional with the new in a way that leverages the affordances of both (Boche, 2014).

Before 2022, a review of literature that attempted to define AI literacy found that the definitions centered around learning how to use AI as well as flagging concerns around its use for teachers and students (Ng et al, 2021). Ng et al (2021) described AI literacy as demonstrating abilities in programming and searching in digital spaces, emphasizing teachers' "computational techniques" (p. 507). Likewise, Celik et al (2022) found in a systematic review that early AI was helpful in classifying students and scoring exams. However, these analyses of AI stopped short of the capabilities demonstrated by the new LLMs introduced at the end of 2022.

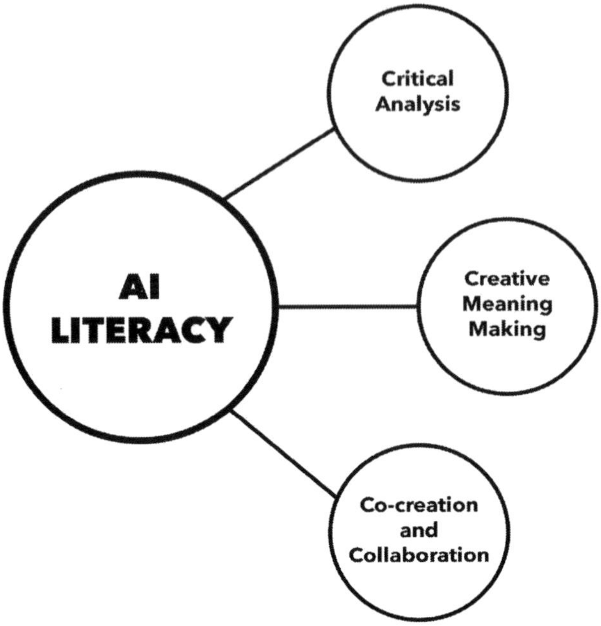

FIGURE 3.1 Components of AI Literacy. (Graph created by authors.)
Note: The graph details the specific competencies needed for teachers to develop AI literacy.

The previous definitions of AI literacy did not take into consideration the natural language abilities of programs like ChatGPT. Therefore, we propose a new definition of AI literacy that includes a broader context and takes into consideration the affordances of the new technology. An AI literate teacher would have these three competencies: critical analysis, creative meaning making, and co-creating. Figure 3.1 describes this multilayered competency.

- *Critical analysis* – Teachers must develop the ability to critically evaluate images and text to determine if they were created by a machine. They must be able to discuss this critical analysis with their students and help them develop skepticism toward any text, image, soundbyte, video, or other multimodal creation. Teachers can draw on critical media literacy frameworks, such as the one developed by the Center for Media Literacy, to encourage students to unpack spurious images and texts before accepting their legitimacy (Crovitz & Moran, 2020).

- *Creative meaning making* – Teachers should understand some of the creative capabilities of AI and be able to leverage it in their classrooms. From brainstorming and drafting to editing and publishing, AI can serve as a creative source for teaching and learning (Maloy et al, 2024). Teachers must learn to manipulate AI and use it as a source to augment their creativity.
- *Co-creation and collaboration* – AI-generated written work is clunky at best and completely false at worst (Lathrop & Johnson, 2023; Moran, 2024). Teachers should guide students (and themselves) in rewriting and editing any AI-generated text so that the language sounds more like their own voice. Using an LLM, such as ChatGPT or Copilot, as a co-creator requires careful attention to ethical issues (Burriss, 2024), but students and teachers can rewrite and reimagine the initial brainstorming efforts of the machine, co-creating and collaborating with the computer so that the work becomes more original and more human-like. AI literacy also includes careful attention to the prompt given to the LLM, since this can be the key to success or failure in generating the desired output (Dang et al, 2022; Oppenlaender et al, 2023; Woo et al, 2023).

Understanding the process behind prompting is one of the keys to co-creating and collaborating with AI. Carefully crafting a specific prompt is known as *prompt engineering* (PE) and is the process of writing a command that causes the machine to produce work that successfully meets the needs of the writer. For example, asking ChatGPT to simply "write a lesson plan on the setting *Of Mice and Men*" will not produce the same result as the more surgical request to "write a lesson plan for a 10th grade English class that asks students to investigate the setting *Of Mice and Men* and its connection to the Great Depression." The more specific and targeted the prompt, the better the resulting output (Pando & Marlatt, 2024). There are myriad prompts that teachers can tailor to their own students, classroom, curricula, and needs. Working to craft an appropriate prompt so that the LLM creates an acceptable product is one of the hallmarks of AI literacy.

However, simply typing a prompt into an LLM does not go far enough. We recommend a specific, six-step process when employing AI. This process will leverage the power of the machine as well as the critical, creative, and collaborative competencies of teachers who are AI literate, as described above.

A Process for Teachers Using AI

Using AI in the classroom will require careful attention by teachers to the output and then tweaking it to suit the needs of the students and curriculum. While some state departments of instruction have suggested general ways of using AI in the classroom (North Carolina Department of Instruction, 2023), we want to provide a more detailed process for both inservice and preservice teachers when using GenAI:

Step 1 - Decide what you want to teach or create using GenAI.

Step 2 - Prompt the machine, taking care to wordsmith the prompt so that you are very specific about the output you want. (Remember, it is only a machine and does not know how to provide lesson objectives, for example, unless you tell it.)

Step 3 - Receive the results and then critically analyze them. Is the output accurate? Does it meet your needs? Check and double-check for factual errors or "hallucinations."

Step 4 - Reprompt, fine-tuning the words so that you receive the output you seek.

Step 5 - Edit the result so that it fits your needs.

Step 6 - Teach.

Figure 3.2 describes this process.

Teachers will need to apply the six-step process repeatedly for each new task they attempt with GenAI. It is an iterative process that teachers can use multiple times as they create with AI. We recommend using the process in both mundane and creative tasks to ensure that the outcome is suitable for each teacher's specific needs.

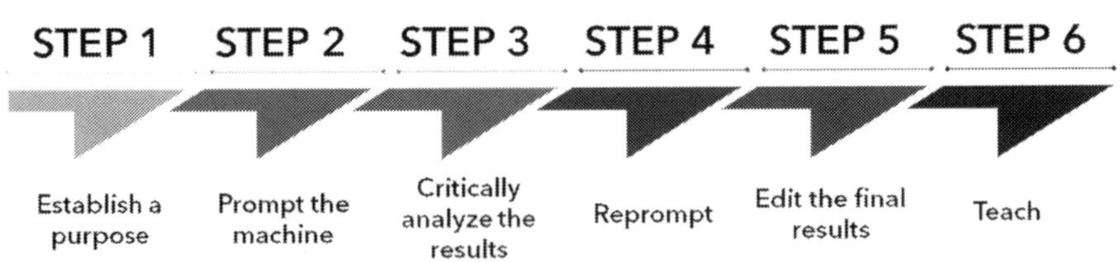

FIGURE 3.2 A Process for Using GenAI.

Note. The graph describes a step-by-step process for generating content from an artificial intelligence program and then using it to teach.

In the following section, we provide some ideas for using GenAI in teaching and daily work. Applying the six-step process when implementing each of these ideas will generate a more viable end product.

IDEAS FOR USING AI

Using AI for lesson planning, assessment, and creative tasks has become a strongly suggested or mandated activity in some school districts near us in North Carolina (Gibbons, 2023; Walkenhorst, 2024). We worry that this is, in essence, putting the cart before the horse, since many teachers are unsure of AI and lack professional development for implementing it. This reminds us of the flipped classroom craze in the early 2000s when teachers were being asked (even required in some districts) to employ the flipped method without any guidance or professional development (Moran & Young, 2014; Young & Bush, 2004).[1]

We offer here some ideas for inservice teachers who are either interested in or required to use some aspect of AI. This is, by no means, an exhaustive list. However, we hope that we might provide a creative spark for capitalizing on the affordances of AI in ELA and support teachers.

AI and Mundane Tasks

One of the most interesting applications of GenAI is its use as a tireless workhorse for mundane teaching chores that many teachers dislike, such as creating rubrics, scoring assessments, or (for some) creating lesson plans.

Allowing AI to take over the more tedious parts of teaching allows humans to focus on the relational aspects of the job, according to Sal Khan, the founder of the online school Khan Academy and Hadi Partovi, the founder of code.org recorded a video titled, "A Fireside Chat with Sal Khan and Hadi Partovi," as part of the *AI 101* video series aimed at familiarizing teachers with AI (Code.org & Khan Academy, 2023). Partovi says in the video:

> *And what I believe AI is going to do is enable more personalized learning, less busy work on the job of the teacher, more coaching and facilitating and working with that kid who has something that is blocking them or they're struggling with something or they need a motivation boost or whatnot.*

Using AI for mundane tasks can help teachers who want to offer additional support to Multi-Language Learners (MLLs). ChatGPT, for example, is available in more than 20 languages, which makes it possible for teachers to translate worksheets, guided notes, literature summaries, and other handouts into a variety of languages for MLLs – something previously impossible without a multilingual teacher aide. In addition, AI can rewrite the levels of reading passages and design activities to help teachers with differentiation. In one recent survey, teachers said their favorite use of AI was for designing short quizzes or writing prompts (Blose, 2023).

Below are some ideas for using AI to complete some of the more mundane tasks of teaching.

Lesson Plans. There are many free and paid platforms that use GenAI to create lesson plans. Not only does ChatGPT write lesson plans tied to specific standards (including state standards), but other platforms have popped up, hoping to capitalize on the monetary aspects of lesson plan writing. Some of the sites we are aware of include Magic School AI (www.magicschool.ai), Eduaid.ai (www.eduaide.ai/), and Copilot (https://educationcopilot.com/).

PE (see *Co-creation and collaboration* in AI Literacy, above) is key to producing a lesson plan that meets the needs of each student. The AI can differentiate, include standards, write objectives based on Bloom's Taxonomy, and offer activities – but the user needs to tell it to include these things. In addition, using *critical analysis* to assess the accuracy of the lesson plan is important, since some AI-generated plans are very basic or even inaccurate (St. George & Svrluga, 2023) (see the six-step process above). We suggest prompting the machine to "act as if." This specific instruction is based on *New York Times* reporter Brian Chen's (2023) experimentation with ChatGPT and discovery that the "golden prompt" "*Act as if*" is a collection of "magic words" that "will instruct the bot to emulate an expert."

A sample prompt might be:

> *Act as if you are a ______ -grade ______ teacher. Write a _____-minute long lesson on ______ that includes ________ standards. Include students using technology and a formative assessment at the end that ties into the lesson objectives.*

Be aware that LLMs have no real understanding of students or teaching and may generate a lesson that is impossible to complete in just one class period. We put the following sample prompt into ChatGPT 4:

> *Act as if you are a 10th grade English teacher. Write a 90-minute long lesson on characterization in The Great Gatsby by F. Scott Fitzgerald*

that includes standards from the North Carolina standard course of study. Include students using technology and a formative assessment at the end that ties into the lesson objectives.

We got back a fairly basic lesson plan that advised us to *discuss characterization*, then have students *use their computers or tablets to create a presentation* (ChatGPT 4 response). There was no specific program or digital tool suggested, and there was no guidance on HOW to direct students to use their computers. The lesson plan included the final assessment of *ask each student to write a brief paragraph on an index card, answering the following question: "How does Fitzgerald's characterization of [choose one character] contribute to the overall theme of the novel?"* (ChatGPT 4 response).

This is, in our opinion, the most basic of lesson plans and something that teachers will need to tweak (see our suggested AI process in Figure 3.2). However, it is a good starting point for beleaguered and overworked teachers.

Rubrics. Designing a rubric can be a tedious task, especially if the teacher is interested in creating an analytic rubric on a grid. However, in one metastudy, Jonsson and Svingby (2007) found that rubrics can increase the consistency of scoring, reduce value judgments, and promote learning. And, as many teachers know, rubrics offer extra "CYA"[2] insurance against grumpy students or parents. There are a few rubric-generating websites that cater to teachers, such as Quick Rubric (www.quickrubric.com) and Rubric Maker (https://rubric-maker.com). However, we have found that GenAI programs do a decent job of creating rubrics, although they will not create a grid. It is as simple as prompting the machine to **"create a rubric on____"** and describing the assessment. Teachers can copy and paste the suggested rubric categories and point values into their own table or grid, tweaking as they go to fit the needs of their students and assignments.

Assessments. Although we advocate for authentic assessment that focuses on project-based learning, student understanding, and course goals (Darling-Hammond & Snyder, 2000), we do recognize that sometimes a quick quiz or multiple-choice assessment is required. GenAI can help design these short assessments. Teachers should prompt the machine very surgically to get what they want. For example, they can ask it to "**Design a multiple choice quiz with five questions on ______.**" The LLM will provide the questions and the correct answers.

GenAI can help think of other more interesting assessments as well, such as essay topics or projects. We prompted ChatGPT4 with **"What are some**

final project ideas for a 10th grade English class studying The Great Gatsby?" We received a list of ideas that included a multimodal presentation, a 1920's newspaper project, a creative writing assignment, a character trial, a digital storybook, a 1920's party, an art project, and a podcast. All of these ideas would need to be fleshed out in more detail but could offer a great starting point for a project-based assessment.

Translations. ChatGPT can effectively translate text into more than 20 languages, including Spanish, French, German, Chinese (Mandarin), Japanese, Korean, Arabic, Portuguese, Italian, Russian, Dutch, and others. This can be a fantastic support for teachers with MLLs in their classroom. Copy and paste the English text from a short story, speech, essay, worksheet, or assignment, and ask the machine to "translate the above text into ______." While MLLs should be encouraged to speak and write in English, translations can help them strategically analyze text and increase their comprehension in English (Goodwin & Jiménez, 2016). Teachers also can provide a word bank to accompany the text with a few, specific words translated and defined.

Leveled Reading Passages. As literacy scholars, we support student choice in both reading and writing, and we believe that students should not be forced to read at a specific Lexile level (or other level determined by a standardized test). Literature of all kinds can offer students the opportunity to experience other lives and new worlds, and we want them to choose the books that reflect their passions and interests – not a specific word count. In fact, research demonstrates that requiring students to read leveled texts, such as Reading Recovery books, does not increase fluency or encourage students to read at increasingly higher levels (Cunningham et al, 2005). However, sometimes teachers may find it necessary to level a reading passage as a form of differentiation. GenAI offers a way for teachers and media specialists to level the same passage within a classroom. If, for example, the teacher has a student who is reading far below grade level, and a particular essay is required reading, AI can level the essay and make it more digestible for the student.

In our experience, GenAI sometimes becomes stuck when asked to level a passage. When we asked ChatGPT4 to level Martin Luther King Jr.'s 1963 "Letter from Birmingham Jail" to a fourth-grade reading level, it could not answer and eventually gave us an error message. The key is to copy and paste short snippets of text to be leveled so as not to overwhelm the machine. A suggested prompt is **"Put the following passage into a ______ reading level"** and then paste the passage.

The biggest issue with leveling is that the original music and rhythm of the writing is lost. For example, in response to King's (1963) beautiful words "Moreover, I am cognizant of the interrelatedness of all communities and states. I cannot sit idly by in Atlanta and not be concerned about what happens in Birmingham. Injustice anywhere is a threat to justice everywhere." ChatGPT4 leveled the passage to a fourth-grade reading level and wrote: *Dr. Martin Luther King Jr. said that all places and people are connected. He believed that if something unfair was happening in one city, like Birmingham, he should care about it even though he lived in Atlanta. He thought that if there is unfairness anywhere, it could hurt fairness everywhere* (ChatGPT 4 response)..

Writing Prompts. Although there are a myriad of writing books available with writing prompts for generating provocative or authentic writing, sometimes teachers need a writing prompt specifically tied to what they are reading or studying in class. GenAI can produce writing prompts for students at every grade level (see Appendix). It is important to differentiate for the machine what kind of writing you want students to produce. If, for example, you want them to freewrite, you will need to ask the LLM to generate a "freewrite prompt." If you want students to write a longer essay, narrative, or just a paragraph, you will need to specify this in your prompt. Be detailed on the content of the writing you want as well. We suggest asking the LLM: **"Generate a writing prompt that asks ____-grade students to write a ____ on ______."** This should result in a prompt that is interesting and targeted.

Information on Canonical Texts. We have been teaching and reading for more than 20 years, and we still haven't read every canonical text available. Certain novels or plays have eluded our attention, although we are embarrassed to admit that we don't know the characters or plot. Although it does not take the place of reading, GenAI can offer basic summaries, characters, and information about canonical texts. We caution against trusting everything the AI program generates, though, since it often makes mistakes, hallucinates, or "bullshits" answers (Lathrop & Johnson, 2023). An internet search and Wikipedia also can provide background information on canonical texts, but for quick summaries, ChatGPT can't be beat. A prompt that works well is "**Summarize the basic plot of ____.**" Teachers can also ask the program to "**Describe the main characters in ____**", "**Describe the setting of ____**", "**Describe the main theme of ____**", and even **"Provide two key quotes from ____."** These basic textual analysis features can help teachers fact-check their own knowledge and provide them with more self-confidence when teaching.

Letters and Emails. One of the most tedious and mundane tasks of a teacher's work is writing emails and letters. We are required to write emails to parents, informing them of their child's progress in our class, and we are required to write letters of recommendation for colleges and jobs. Although many teachers have developed their own templates for these types of correspondence, LLMs also can produce a letter or email. Prompting is important here, since the program does not know context, so we recommend putting in as many details as possible. One recent prompt we used is:

> *Act as if you are a 10th grade English teacher. Write a short email to a parent whose child has missed too many days of school. Tell the parent that the child will need to make up work and his grade will be affected by his absences.*

ChatGPT generated a thoughtful and professional email that included a game plan for getting the student back on track.

Letters of recommendation (tweaked following the six-step process) and newsletters detailing classroom activities all can be started through an LLM. This can drastically reduce the teacher workload and offer free time for a work-life balance.

AI and Creative Uses

Although a mistrust of new technology may hamper educators' wholehearted embrace of GenAI (Mishra & Heath, 2024), the technology also may inspire creative ideas. Using GenAI in unusual ways makes good use of the capabilities of the technology and can potentially spur new applications and ideas. AI has the potential to be a creative collaborator and envision interesting ways to remix or generate content. Ethan Mollick, a professor at the Wharton School of Business and an innovative educator who uses AI in interesting ways in his own work, believes that creativity is one of the best features of GenAI for teachers. In a 2023 article in the online publication *Tech Trends*, Mollick is quoted as saying, "If educators are not using AI as creative tools, they are in trouble" (Henriksen et al, 2023, p. 5). We agree with this sentiment and believe GenAI has the potential to change instructional practices in positive ways.

Brainstorming and Editing. GenAI is an excellent resource for brainstorming and overcoming creative blocks. Student writers often find themselves with a seed of an idea or a broad concept they'd like to explore but struggle with how to begin. Teachers can have students prompt an LLM to generate a list of thought-provoking questions to narrow down their topic. Additionally, the LLM can provide valuable information to guide students in their research and writing processes. Teachers can encourage students to utilize this tool as a prewriting activity, fostering a more focused and informed approach to their assignments.

For example, teachers who assign research papers can encourage students to prompt an LLM to come up with main points on which to focus in their writing. When we put a general prompt into Microsoft's Copilot, it replied with a list of 20 possible essay topics. Our prompt was **"I need to write a paper on transcendentalism. What are some topics I can write about?"** The AI generated a variety of topics, including this one: *Transcendentalism in Modern America: Investigate how transcendentalist principles continue to resonate in contemporary American culture. Consider examples from literature, art, and popular media that reflect transcendentalist themes* (Chat GPT 4 response).

The programs also make good editors for students who have finished a rough draft. Teachers can ask students to copy and paste their rough drafts into a GenAI program and direct it to **"Edit this rough draft."** This will result in a quick turnaround of an edited document – although the machine does not have a good ear for voice and will change the text into a somewhat robotic piece. Teachers should encourage students to use the six-step process we detailed earlier in an effort to get a better product. Teachers also should ask students to compare the AI-edited document with suggestions from their peers. This triangulation helps students see errors in their writing and cuts down on teachers' grading and correcting of mechanical errors.

Sketching Characters. One of our favorite ways to use GenAI is to encourage our students to use it in writing fiction. Sometimes it is difficult for new writers to imagine a character or flesh one out so that it seems to have a realistic backstory. GenAI can provide some details that student writers may not have considered. Teachers faced with students who say "I don't know what to write about" can direct them to an LLM. Teachers can suggest that students ask the program: **"Help me create a character for a**

story" and then provide as much detail as possible about a potential character. We prompted ChatGPT4 with "**Help me create a character for a story. The character is a transgender boy who is 15 and wants to start a business. What can his name be? What is his backstory?"** The result was a fantastic list of potential character traits (innovative, resilient, empathetic), a backstory about his life, and his challenges and goals. It was enough of a push to get our creative juices flowing and make us feel as if we could write a story about this character.

Teachers can encourage students to prompt the LLM, or they can prompt the LLM themselves and provide the character outline to students. Teachers may want everyone in the class to write a creative narrative about a specific oddball character, and they can use AI to help flesh out some of the details.

Co-creating Poems. Since the GenAI programs have been trained on many canonical texts, including poems, they are pretty good at helping to design poems in a particular form. They can follow the basic template of a haiku, a limerick, and a sonnet. Teachers can give the program a particular form and a topic, and see what it creates. This can offer students inspiration for their writing or act as a mentor text for analysis. Teachers can ask students: "What do you like in this poem? What do you dislike? What features make this poem work? What would you change?" The GenAI poems do not take the place of great poetry by human writers, but they can provide a quick tool for analysis.

Writing Sentence Starters. Another idea is to ask the GenAI to create sentence starters to help get essays going. Sometimes students need this extra scaffolding to help them begin, especially MLLs and those who struggle with writing tasks (Edgerly et al, 2018; Grapin et al, 2021). A sentence starter is exactly what it sounds like: a sentence to get you started. This doesn't necessarily need to be the first sentence of an essay (or even be included at all), but it is enough of a support to help students know how to start writing. For example, teachers who want students to write an argumentative essay can ask the GenAI program to generate sentence starters on both sides of the argument to get students started with their thinking.

If, for example, teachers want students to write an argumentative essay on the importance (or unimportance) of homework, a sample prompt is: **"Write 5 sentence starters for an argumentative essay on the necessity of homework."** And then, again, **"Write 5 sentence starters for an argumentative essay on the unimportance of homework."** A response we received from ChatGPT after these prompts was: "*While many argue that homework is an essential part of learning, I believe that it often detracts from students' well-being and extracurricular engagement, making it more of a burden than a benefit*" (ChatGPT 4 response).

Sometimes coming up with sentence starters is a Herculean task for teachers, so using an LLM to generate a few can reduce the teacher workload.

Modifications for Teacher Educators

Teacher educators hoping to prepare future teachers for the new world of GenAI will need to address issues of ethics and the use of GenAI in the classroom. One suggested way to talk about GenAI is to ask preservice teachers to design lesson plans with and without GenAI, comparing and analyzing each for effectiveness. Although novice teachers often write lesson plans that lack detail, veteran teachers know that comprehensive and detailed lesson plans result in higher student engagement and more effective class time (Allahverdi & Gelzheiser, 2021). In one study, preservice teachers who practiced writing lesson plans and then taught them to students came to see lesson plan-writing as an important component to teaching (Parker et al, 2017). Although the types of lesson plans – and the style in which they are written – vary dramatically, a lesson plan is, in general, a blueprint or "dress rehearsal" that allows teachers to think through things before they occur (Hoover & Hoover, 1967).

Moran and Coward (2024) asked a cohort of nine preservice teachers to use ChatGPT to write lesson plans for a fictional ELA class. After generating disappointing results, the preservice teachers were instructed to critique the output, alter their prompt, and try again. Last, they were instructed to edit the final machine-generated plans to make them better and suit the needs of their fictionalized class. (This process was identical to the six-step process we recommend above.). The preservice teachers were surveyed on their thoughts and ultimately decided that the GenAI lesson plans were a mixed bag. Some enjoyed using GenAI to create lesson plans, and others concluded that the machine made "weird errors" (p. 23) – such as writing a three-day plan instead of the requested one-day plan, writing a plan for 120 minutes instead of the requested 90, and creating "basic" assessments like asking students to write a paragraph instead of something more creative.

It also may be helpful for teacher educators and preservice teachers to read through the *Blueprint for an AI Bill of Rights* (White House, 2022), the most comprehensive ethics guide for using GenAI. Instructors can ask preservice teachers to think about the principles suggested in the document and the ethics questions it raises.

We suggest that teacher educators work intentionally with preservice teachers to guide them through the use of GenAI and discuss resulting errors. This critical analysis will help develop the multiliteracies (Cope & Kalantzis, 2009) essential to operating in the new world of GenAI. In addition, this head-on look at GenAI will provide preservice teachers the opportunity to experiment with and understand LLMs within the safety of the university classroom before trying them out on real students. We recommend that all Methods courses offer some type of AI instruction to develop preservice teachers' AI literacy.

DISCUSSION AND CONCLUSION

Left to their own devices, AI tools can create patterns from any kind of data, which can make them a powerful asset (Celik et al, 2022); however, teachers who become *AI literate* have learned how to forge a partnership with the tools to leverage their potential and manage both mundane tasks and creative activities. We contend, though, that the human teacher still should have the final say in using anything that AI creates.

After all, teachers are the ones who know how humans interact with one another. Teachers are the ones who know if an AI-generated classroom newsletter has the right tone to communicate to parents. Teachers are the ones who know if their students can handle an AI-generated lesson or quiz based on their understanding of the material. Teachers are the ones who know if their students can handle using AI for editing or creative writing assistance. AI literacy is another tool that teachers can add to their toolboxes, but it is not a stand-in for the knowledge and skills about content and students that teachers have and continue to build.

AI tools do not have social or emotional understanding about the world – but teachers do, and teachers are the ones who must pair AI use with ethical considerations, content knowledge, and pedagogical skills. They are the experts not only in human–human interaction but also in their own teaching and their students' learning. Through the six-step process we describe, teachers can not only create effective prompts for the AI but also provide a check on what it produces and how they teach with it. In addition, teachers can use the three-pronged approach to develop and increase their AI literacy. This means evolving their own critical analysis of what AI generates for their students and for them, using AI for creative meaning-making in the classroom and co-creating with AI to complete both mundane administrative tasks and creative activities. We firmly believe that teachers should maintain control over all AI tools used in the classroom, since they are the ones with the skills and knowledge. And while we have only begun to consider how to use AI and the broad implications it may have for the future, starting the conversation with teachers at the forefront is a good place to begin.

NOTES

1 In the flipped classroom method, the teacher makes a video in which they provide direct instruction or a lecture. Students watch the video outside the classroom and then use in-class time to work on activities related to the instruction. The idea is to "flip" the delivery method so that traditional homework is done in class, and traditional instruction is viewed at home.

2 CYA is an acronym that means "cover your ass" and refers to something that protects or safeguards.

REFERENCES

Allahverdi, F. Z., & Gelzheiser, L. (2021). Comparison of a more effective and a typical teachers' lesson plan detail in the psychological engagement of students. *Sakarya University Journal of Education, 11*(1), 83–100. DOI: 10.19126/suje.797461

Arvidsson, I., Leo, U., Larsson, A., Håkansson, C., Persson, R., & Björk, J. (2019). Burnout among school teachers: Quantitative and qualitative results from a follow-up study in southern Sweden. *BMC Public Health, 19*(1), 1–13. DOI: 10.1186/s12889-019-6972-1

Bailey, B. (2009). *Reel literacies: Digital video production as a literacy practice.* University of Rochester.

Barad, K. (2007). *Meeting the universe halfway: Quantum physics and the entanglement of matter and meaning.* Duke University Press.

Blose, A. (2023, April 12). As ChatGPT enters the classroom, teachers weigh pros and cons. *NEAToday*. Retrieved from www.nea.org/nea-today/all-news-articles/chatgpt-enters-classroom-teachers-weigh-pros-and-cons

Boche, B. (2014). Multiliteracies in the classroom: Emerging conceptions of first-year teachers. *Journal of Language and Literacy Education [Online], 10*(1), 114–135.

Burriss, S. (2024). An ethics primer for educators: Learning and practicing AI ethics with students. In C. M. Moran's (Ed.), *Revolutionizing English education: AI in the classroom.* (pp. 179–194). Lexington.

Cazden, C., Cope, B., Fairclough, N., Gee, J., Kalantzis, M., Kress, G., Luke, A., Luke, C., Michaels, S., & Nakata, M. (1996). *A pedagogy of multiliteracies: Designing social futures. Harvard Educational Review, 66*(1), 60–92.

Celik, I., Dindar, M., Muukkonen, H., & Järvelä, S. (2022). The promises and challenges of artificial intelligence for teachers: A systematic review of the research. *TechTrends, 66*, 616–630.

Chao, J., Ellis, R., Jiang, S., Rosé, C., Finzer, W., Tatar, C., Fiacco, J., & Wiedemann, K. (2023, June). Exploring artificial intelligence in English language arts with StoryQ. *Proceedings of the AAAI Conference on Artificial Intelligence, 37*(13), 15999–16003.

Chen, B. X. (2023, May 25). Get the best from ChatGPT with these golden prompts. *The New York Times*. Retrieved from www.nytimes.com/2023/05/25/technology/ai-chatbot-chatgpt-prompts.html?campaign_id=158&emc=edit_ot_20230609&instance_id=94628&nl=on-tech%3A-a.i.&regi_id=78988964&segment_id=135129&te=1&user_id=9932ec07b97634b3033ba77c3dd8eb65.

Code.org & Khan Academy. (2023). Fireside chat with Sal Khan and Hadi Partovi. [Video]. *AI 101 for Teachers*. Retrieved from https://code.org/ai/pl/101

Cope, B., & Kalantzis, M. (2009). "Multiliteracies": New literacies, new learning. *Pedagogies, 4*(3), 164–195. https://doi-org.proxy006.nclive.org/10.1080/15544800903076044

Crovitz, D., & Moran, C. M. (2020). Analyzing disruptive memes in an age of international interference. *English Journal, 109*(4), 62–69.

Cunningham, J. W., Spadorcia, S. A., Erickson, K. A., Koppenhaver, D. A., Sturm, J. M., & Yoder, D. E. (2005). Investigating the instructional supportiveness of leveled texts. *Reading Research Quarterly, 40*(4), 410–427.

Dang, H., Mecke, L., Lehmann, F., Goller, S., & Buschek, D. (2022). *How to prompt? Opportunities and challenges of zero- and few-shot learning for human-AI interaction in creative applications of generative models.* Retrieved from https://doi.org/10.48550/arXiv.2209.01390.

Darling-Hammond, L., & Snyder, J. (2000). Authentic assessment of teaching in context. *Teaching and Teacher Education, 16*(5–6), 523–545.

Edgerly, H., Wilcox, J., & Easter, J. (2018). Creating a positive feedback culture. *Science Scope, 41*(5), 43–49.

Gee, J. P. (2001). Reading as situated language: A sociocognitive perspective. *Journal of Adolescent & Adult Literacy, 44*(8), 714–725. www.jstor.org/stable/40018744

Gibbons, A. (2023, Nov. 18). Robeson county school district gets $4 million grant to develop AI program in art classes. *WBTW*. Retrieved from www.wbtw.com/news/state-regional-news/robeson-county/robeson-county-school-district-gets-4m-grant-to-develop-ai-program-in-art-classes

Gonzalez, N., Moll, L. C., & Amanti, C. (Eds.). (2006). *Funds of knowledge: Theorizing practices in households, communities, and classrooms.* Routledge.

Goodwin, A. P., & Jiménez, R. (2016). TRANSLATE: New strategic approaches for English learners. *The Reading Teacher, 69*(6), 621–625.

Grapin, S. E., Llosa, L., Haas, A., & Lee, O. (2021). Rethinking instructional strategies with English learners in the content areas. *TESOL Journal, 12*(2), e557.

Hashem, R., Ali, N., El Zein, F., Fidalgo, P, & Abu Khurma, O. (2023). AI to the rescue: Exploring the potential of ChatGPT as a teacher ally for workload relief and burnout prevention. *Research and Practice in Technology Enhanced Learning, 19*(23): 1–26. DOI: 10.58459/rptel.2024.19023.

Henriksen, D., Woo, L. J., & Mishra, P. (2023). Creative uses of ChatGPT for education: A conversation with Ethan Mollick. *TechTrends, 67,* 595–600. https://doi.org/10.1007/s11528-023-00862-w

Hoover, K. H., & Hoover, H. M. (1967). Lesson planning: Key to effective teaching. *The Clearing House, 42*(1), 41–44.

Jonsson, A., & Svingby, G. (2007). The use of scoring rubrics: Reliability, validity and educational consequences. *Educational Research Review, 2*(2), 130–144.

King, M. L., Jr. (1963). *Letter from Birmingham jail.* Retrieved from www.csuchico.edu/iege/_assets/documents/susi-letter-from-birmingham-jail.pdf.

Kuby, C. Spector, K., Johnson Thiel, J. (2020). *Posthumanism and literacy education Knowing/becoming/doing literacies.* Routledge.

Lathrop, B. N., & Johnson, T. S. (2023). Researchers beware: ChatGPT is a bullshitter. *English Education, 55*(3), 219–221.

Lau, S. M. C. (2012). Reconceptualizing critical literacy teaching in ESL classrooms. *The Reading Teacher, 65,* 325–329.

LeBlanc, R. J., Aguilera, E., Burriss, S., de Roock, R., Fassbender, W., Monea, B., Nichols, T. P., Zacher Pandya, J.,Robinson, B., Smith, A., & Stornaiuolo, A. (2023). *Digital platforms and the ELA classroom: A policy brief.* James R. Squire Office, National Council of Teachers of English. Retrieved from https://ncte.org/resources/policy-briefs

Lenters, K. & McDermott, M. (2020). Introducing affect, embodiment, and place in critical literacy. In K. Lenters & M. McDermott's (Eds.), *Affect, embodiment, and place in critical literacy: Assembling theory and practice.* (pp. 1–18). Routledge.

Maloy, R., Trust, T., & Edwards, S. (2024). Teaching writing in the era of generative AI: Strategies for making learning meaningful. In C. M. Moran (Ed.), *Revolutionizing English education: AI in the classroom.* (pp. 81–106) .Lexington.

McCarthy, J., Minsky, M. L., & Rochester, N. (2006). A proposal for the Dartmouth summer research project on artificial intelligence. *AI Magazine, 27*(4), 12–14.

Mehrishi, M. (2023, Feb. 7). The dangers of ChatGPT: How it can put you at risk. *OpenGrowth.* Retrieved from www.opengrowth.com/resources/the-dangers-of-chatgpt-how-it-can-put-you-at-risk.

Mishra, P., & Heath, M. K. (2024). The (Neil) Postman always rings twice: 5 questions on AI and education. In M. Searson, E. Langran, & J. Trumble (Eds.), *Exploring new horizons: Generative artificial intelligence and teacher education.* (pp. 14–24). Association for the Advancement of Computing in Education.

Moran, C. M. (2024). Introduction. In C. M. Moran's (Ed.), *Revolutionizing English education: AI in the classroom.* (pp. xii–xiv). Lexington.

Moran, C. M., & Coward, M. (2024). 'The AI did my job well': Using ChatGPT to develop lesson plans. In C. M. Moran (Ed.), *Revolutionizing English education: AI in the classroom.* (pp. 15–29). Lexington.

Moran, C. M., & Young, C. A. (2014). Active learning in the flipped English language arts classroom. In J. Keengwe, G. Onchwari, & J. Oigara (Eds.), *Promoting active learning through the flipped classroom model* (pp. 31–78). IGI Global.

National Council of Teachers of English (NCTE). (2018). *Beliefs for integrating technology into the English language arts classroom.* Retrieved from https://ncte.org/statement/beliefs-technology-preparation-english-teachers

Ng, T. K., Leung, J. K. L., Chu, K. W. S., & Qiao, M. S. (2021). AI literacy: Definition, teaching, evaluation and ethical issues. *Proceedings of the Association for Information Science and Technology, 58*(1), 504–509.

Noble, S. U. (2018). *Algorithms of oppression.* New York University.

North Carolina Department of Instruction. (2023). *NCDPI releases guidance on the use of artificial intelligence in schools.* Retrieved from www.dpi.nc.gov/news/press-releases/2024/01/16/ncdpi-releases-guidance-use-artificial-intelligence-schools

Oppenlaender, J., Linder, R., & Silvennoinen, J. (2023). *Prompting AI art: An investigation into the creative skill of prompt engineering.* DOI: 10.48550/arxiv.2303.13534

Pando, M., & Marlatt, R. (2024). Prompting the chatbot: Presenting a teaching case using generative AI models in secondary education. In C. M. Moran (Ed.), *Revolutionizing English education: AI in the classroom.* (pp. 107–124). Lexington.

Parker, E. C., Bond, V. L., & Powell, S. R. (2017). A grounded theory of preservice music educators' lesson planning processes within field experience methods courses. *Journal of Research in Music Education, 65*(3), 287–308.

Reed, B. (2022, Dec. 5). What is AI chatbot phenomenon ChatGPT and could it replace humans? *The Guardian.* Retrieved from www.theguardian.com/technology/2022/dec/05/what-is-ai-chatbot-phenomenon-chatgpt-and-could-it-replace-humans

Reed, B. (2023, July 5). Authors file a lawsuit against open AI for unlawfully "ingesting" their books. *The Guardian*. Retrieved from www.theguardian.com/books/2023/jul/05/authors-file-a-lawsuit-against-openai-for-unlawfully-ingesting-their-books.

Rowsell, J., & Pahl, K. (2020). What is living literacies? In K. Pahl and J. Rowsell (Eds.), *Living literacies: Literacy for social change* (pp. 1–22). The MIT Press.

Seufert, S., Guggemos, J., & Sailer, M. (2021). Technology-related knowledge, skills, and attitudes of pre-service and in-service teachers: The current situation and emerging trends. *Computers in Human Behavior, 115*. www.sciencedirect.com/science/article/pii/S0747563220303022?via%3Dihub

Sison, A. J. G., Daza, M. T., Gozalo-Brizuela, R., & Garrido-Merchán, E. C. (2023). *ChatGPT: More than a weapon of mass deception, ethical challenges and responses from the human-centered artificial intelligence (HCAI) perspective*. arXiv preprint: arXiv:2304.11215.

St. George, D., & Svrluga, S. (2023, July 13). Artificial intelligence is already changing how teachers teach. *The Washington Post*. Retrieved from www.washingtonpost.com/education/2023/07/13/ai-education-teachers-lesson-plans/

Stornaiuolo, A., Smith, A., & Phillips, N. (2017). Developing a transliteracies framework for a connected world. *Journal of Literacy Research, 49*(1), 68–91.

Su, J., Zhong, Y., & Ng, D. T. K. (2022). A meta-review of literature on educational approaches for teaching AI at the K-12 levels in the Asia-Pacific region. *Computers and Education: Artificial Intelligence, 3*, 100065.

Swenson, J., Rozema, R., Young, C. A., McGrail, E., & Whitin, P. (2006). Extending the conversation: New technologies, new literacies, and English education. *English Education, 38*(4), 351–369.

Vasquez, V. M., Janks, H., & Comber, B. (2019). Critical literacy as a way of being and doing. *Language Arts, 96*(5), 300–311.

Walkenhorst, E. (2024, Jan. 16). AI in NC schools: DPI says teachers and students should use it, provides guidance on how. *WRAL*. Retrieved from www.wral.com/story/ai-in-nc-schools-dpi-says-teachers-and-students-should-use-it-provides-guidance-on-how/21239386

Watson, C. (2007). Small stories, positioning analysis, and the doing of professional identities in learning to teach. *Narrative Inquiry, 17*(2), 371–389.

White House. (2022, Oct.). *Blueprint for an AI bill of rights*. Retrieved from www.whitehouse.gov/ostp/ai-bill-of-rights

Woo, D. J., Guo, K., & Susanto, H. (2023). *Cases of EFL secondary students' prompt engineering pathways to complete a writing task with ChatGPT*. doi: 10.13140/RG.2.2.31464.85762.

Wolfe, C. (2010). *What is posthumanism?* (Vol. 8). University of Minnesota Press.

Young, C. A., & Bush, J. (2004). Teaching the English language arts with technology: A critical approach and pedagogical framework. *Contemporary Issues in Technology and Teacher Education [Online serial], 4*(1). Retrieved from www.citejournal.org/vol4/iss1/languagearts/article1.cfm

Appendix

Tasks and Prompts for GenAI in ELA

Task	GenAI Prompt[a]
Lesson plan	Write a ____-minute long lesson on ______ that includes _______ standards. Include a formative assessment at the end that ties into the lesson objectives.
Rubrics	Create a rubric on____
Assessments	Design a multiple choice quiz with ___ questions on ____. What are some final project ideas for _____ (name of novel, play, type of unit).
Translations	Translate the above text into _____.
Leveled reading passages	Put the following passage into a _____ reading level.
Writing prompts	Generate a writing prompt that asks ____-grade students to write a ____ on ______.
Information on canonical texts	Summarize the basic plot of ____ . Describe the main characters in ___. Describe the setting of ____. Describe the main theme of ___. Provide two key quotes from ____.
Letters and emails	Write a short email to a parent whose child has _ ___. Tell the parent that the child ____.
Brainstorming and editing	I need to write a paper on ____. What are some topics I can write about? Edit this rough draft.
Sketching characters	Help me create a character for a story about __ __.
Co-creating poems	Write a ____ (sonnet/haiku/poem) about ___.
Writing sentence starters	Write ___ sentence starters for ____.

[a] *The first eight prompts should be preceded with "Act as if you are a ___th grade English teacher."*

CHAPTER 4

When AI Literacy Meets Computational Creativity

Vignettes of a Preservice Teacher's Journey with Generative AI

Suriati Abas

INTRODUCTION

Creating comics involves a unique blend of the visual and verbal language to craft narratives that seamlessly interweave text and images (McCloud, 1994). In this context, creativity is taken as novel or original ideas and effective or impactful products (Kaufman & Sternberg, 2010; Sternberg, 2016). While creativity is a fundamental feature of human intelligence (Cross, 2011; Boden, 2004), the emergence of generative artificial intelligence (AI) has ushered in a new era of computational creativity, reimagining the process of creating comics. Colton and Wiggins (2012) refer to computational creativity as the ability of computer systems to generate novel and meaningful content, often in collaboration with human creators. As an interdisciplinary field, computational creativity offers valuable insights into the nature of human creativity using computational methods (Boden, 2009; Colton et al., 2009; Wingström et al., 2022), where software acts as a creative collaborator to push the boundaries of creative expression (Pérez y Pérez, 2015). With AI able to assist in generating visual elements, narrating

DOI: 10.1201/9781003510635-7

ideas, automating creative processes, and fostering AI literacy, the ability to understand, evaluate, and utilize AI systems (Long & Magerko, 2020) becomes essential for harnessing these technologies effectively.

Building upon this foundation, it is important to note that while numerous studies have investigated comic creation across educational levels from elementary to higher education, there remains a significant gap in research examining the use of generative AI for comic creation, particularly in teacher education courses (Sperling, et al., 2024). Previous studies have demonstrated the potential of preservice teachers' comic creation, with findings demonstrating their critical multimodal literacy practices (e.g., Abas, 2023), suggesting enhanced bilingual and multimodal literacy skills (e.g., González Ybarra & Marroquin, 2024), the connection between life stories and school experiences (McGarr et al., 2020), and the learning of scientific concepts (Romagnoli et al., 2018). However, the application of generative AI in this domain remains largely unexplored, presenting a critical area for investigation given the rapid advancements in AI technology and its potential to revolutionize creative processes.

This chapter aims to address this research gap by examining how a preservice teacher engages with and experiences generative AI for creative expression and multimodal composition. By employing the notions of multiliteracies (New London Group, 1996) and living literacies (Pahl & Rowsell, 2020), I seek to understand the implications of AI-assisted comic creation on literacy education and teacher preparation. This exploration is particularly timely as it intersects with the growing need for AI literacy in educational settings, offering insights into how future educators navigate the complexities of computational creativity in their pedagogical practices.

THEORETICAL FRAMEWORK

In this chapter, I join scholars who work from a multiliteracies perspective to capitalize on expanding definitions of literacy which include visual and multimodal texts. The New London Group's (1996) seminal work on multiliteracies has paved the way for reconceptualizing literacy in the digital age, recognizing the importance of equipping students with the skills to navigate and create meaning across diverse modes and media (Kalantzis & Cope, 2024). This framework becomes particularly relevant in the context of AI literacy, as generative AI technologies like text-to-image models open up new possibilities for multimodal composition and creative expression. The concept of "living literacies" (Pahl & Rowsell, 2020) further expands the multiliteracies framework by emphasizing the everyday experiences of individuals as they engage with AI within and beyond official schooled activities (e.g., asking Alexa, a virtual assistant, for the latest news updates, reading social media posts or creating a website). Living literacies acknowledge that literacy practices are deeply embedded in our daily lives, shaped by their social, cultural, and technological contexts (Barton & Hamilton, 1998; Street, 2003). In the era of generative AI, living literacies encompass the ways in which individuals interact with, create, and make meaning through AI-powered tools and platforms.

Connecting living literacies to AI thus calls for the importance of understanding how AI technologies are experienced and utilized in everyday contexts, rather than solely focusing on their technical aspects or creative potential. By examining AI literacy through the lens of living literacies, we can gain insights into how preservice teachers navigate, critically evaluate, and creatively employ generative AI tools in their personal and professional lives. Studies of computational creativity, often in collaboration with human creators (Colton & Wiggins, 2012), have the potential to unlock greater understanding of human creativity (Boden, 2004). However, the field still grapples with the frequently asked question: Can computers be creative?

From the standpoint of living literacies, this question becomes less central, as the focus shifts to how AI technologies are actively shaping and transforming literacy practices in real-world contexts. To gain an in-depth understanding on the AI literacy of preservice teachers, I employed narrative inquiry (Clandinin & Connelly, 2000), focusing on the experience of an undergraduate student who does not have any experience with using AI in any other courses at the university where she studies.

NARRATIVE INQUIRY AS A METHOD

Narrative inquiry, a qualitative research method that focuses on the study of human experience through the lens of stories (Clandinin & Connelly, 2000), is well-suited for investigating how preservice teachers engage with AI technologies for creative purposes, such as crafting comics given the storying/narrative nature of the medium. By employing narrative inquiry, valuable insights on how preservice teachers make sense of these technologies, navigate the creative process, and construct their identities as educators and creators in the digital age can be obtained (Clandinin,

2013; Webster & Mertova, 2007). To add on, this method allows for a rich, contextualized understanding of the challenges, opportunities, and transformative potential that generative AI presents for preservice teachers, as they grapple with questions of agency, authenticity, and creativity in their collaborations with AI technologies

Taken from a larger study conducted on preservice teachers over the course of a 15-week semester, this chapter focuses on the experience of one student named Linda (preferred pseudonym). While it may not accurately represent the AI literacy of all preservice teachers, this student's experience opens up discussions for thinking about moving forward with integrating AI in teacher education courses and considerations for incorporating generative AI. The data for the study comprised (a) three informal face-to-face conversation sessions to share about the project, raise concerns, and ask questions about the content and AI; (b) a social justice creative project that involves the use of generative AI to create a comic that communicate a social justice issue of concern; (c) a student reflection paper that articulates the successes, challenges, and potential applications in K-12 classrooms; and (d) an AI documentation that details the processes of constructing prompts (or otherwise known as prompt engineering) and the semiotic choices for including a particular AI-generated visual among others. Analysis of these data involves identifying themes, patterns, and meanings that emerge from the preservice teacher's narrative. In addition to employing a thematic analysis (Riessman, 2008), I invited Linda to do "member checking" (Creswell & Miller, 2000). This ensures that the interpretations and themes accurately represent her experiences. By seeking the insights of the participant as findings are developed, I am additionally adding credibility to the findings. Through this collaboration which took place mostly after the semester was over and the grades were released, I offer vignettes of the narratives that captured critical moments of her experiences with generative AI.

A PRESERVICE TEACHER'S JOURNEY WITH GENERATIVE AI

Brief Background

Linda is a preservice teacher majoring in childhood education. She identifies herself as an able-bodied, bisexual, cisgendered Caucasian woman. She belongs to a lower middle-class family; her husband is the sole breadwinner while she and her three children go to school every day. She claims that she is not adept at drawing. Prior to working on this project,

FIGURE 4.1 QR Code to Access Linda's AI-Generated Comic.

Linda does not have any opportunity to experiment with AI as all of her professors refrained students from using it (Check-in session #1, March 2024). However, for one of my course sessions, she was tasked to unpack the concept of "intersectionality", a term coined by Kimberley Crenshaw, to describe the double bind of simultaneous racial and gender prejudice, by creating a superhero of color (see Zulkarnain & Abas, 2024). Working in trios, Linda and her peers used MagicAI, a generative AI tool embedded in Padlet, a platform typically used for uploading, organizing, and sharing content virtually. Excerpts of Linda's narratives were chosen to discuss AI literacy as she was one of the participants who expressed strong interest in having open conversations about examining her work closely. Besides, she had used a similar theme of superheroes building on prior in-class experiences of using generative AI. Despite claiming to have limited drawing skills, Linda harnessed the power of generative AI to create her first memoir, titled *Can ANY BODY Help Me?* (Refer to Figure 4.1). In the memoir, Linda used combinations of generative AI tools: several free comic design templates from Canva, a web-based graphic design tool, and the *I can't draw* generative AI feature embedded in Padlet. This memoir chronicles Linda's experiences with body shaming as a white woman growing up and residing in rural Upstate New York. In the memoir, Linda is the protagonist and the female superhero:

> *I chose a brunette superhero to mirror myself as I am a brunette woman. Growing up, brunette hair was always something I was ashamed of because in my time, petite blonde women were favored, something I found myself the polar opposite of. I also think that when*

> *we speak about diversity, having a brunette character holds significant power in representing women who are not the mascot of white supremacy. Many women with origins from non-European countries have brunette or black hair such as myself, and our beauty and our features deserve to be represented in a context that empowers women and allows us to feel beautiful and strong. This is especially important when thinking about creating characters that will reach the eyes of young children who should have the opportunity to see their features represented- as many characters such as princesses are blonde haired and blue eyed.*
>
> *Narrative Text #1*

Besides, having given much thought about the character, Linda creatively injected a pun to the title by spelling the word anybody as "any body" to refer to her body as the primary subject of the AI-generated comic. Through her narrative, we gain insight into how generative AI can empower students who may not consider themselves traditionally artistic to engage in creative expression and visual storytelling, thereby broadening the scope of literacy practices and pedagogical possibilities in the 21st-century classroom.

INITIAL ENCOUNTERS AND THE PROCESSES OF USING GENERATIVE AI

As a mother of three children, comic books were never in Linda's family's reading list; growing up, she was not exposed to comic books or graphic novels. Her first encounter was through a graphics, *Dangerous Conversations: Persistent Tensions in Teacher Education* by Stephanie Jones and James F. Woglom (2014), which was part of our course reading. Linda took the initiative to refer to popular superhero comics that serve as models for developing her own comic:

> *I do not have any prior experience with comic books or graphic novels of any sort. However, with the assignment I wanted to make sure that I was presenting a quality assignment so I browsed through several popular comics by Marvel and DC brands who I know have had very successful comics such as Superman, Thor, and Batman. I also rented some popular children's graphic novels from the Huntington Library such as Bug Scouts. AI was also a new concept for me, as I graduated with my first degree before AI was created, so this process forced me*

in the best possible way to challenge my familiarity with new modern technologies.

Narrative Text #2

From Narrative Text #2, it was also evident that Linda had minimal knowledge of recent advancements in generative AI tools, despite AI as a field existing since the early 1950s. For Linda and the other students, the process of creating the comic began by selecting a topic from a range of social justice issues that were in the course content. She chose the topic, "gender identity", and focused on her personal story of body shaming. She met me during student hours to discuss the story ideas and proceeded to create a character sketch, character profiles and a six-panel storyboard that outlines the exposition, rising action, climax, falling action, and resolution.

> *When I first started brainstorming, my project was going in a different direction. Initially I had an idea to have a project centered around the idea of metamorphosis and the life cycle of a woman and the body shaming she may endure at each stage, but I realized I could only go so far as I am only 28 and it was based on my personal experience. Some searches I had [used] were "postpartum body with stretch marks realistic style watercolor paint image" and the images just weren't being generated the way I needed them to be mostly due to censorship. That is when I decided to become more creative and revise. From here, I decided that I wanted to ditch the idea of a watercolor realistic painting and proceed in a version of the story that was true to the comic book culture. I decided to have a play on the superhero tale where the superhero has this "critical flaw" that is her body and being a woman in a field where she may receive such criticisms. I started typing "female superhero comic book style" but realized that the AI generator favored thin, blonde women which is not me.*
>
> *The revisions from this point were manipulating my character to be as similar as I could make it while evolving through different periods of my life where I was "heavy-set," "thin," pregnant, and to points where I have gained acceptance of my body and what my future aged self would want to say about the topic. I found I had to refine my searches for an older superhero as some were hyper-realistic. My search was "older superhero comic book" and I refined it to "female superhero old comic book style image". My final products were generated off the initial prompts. The most difficult revision that*

> *I finished with were the child superheroes. I had to change the hair color of the child superhero so that she wouldn't be confused with my character, so my prompt went from "brunette child female superhero being yelled at by angry citizens comic book style" to "child female superhero being yelled at by angry citizens comic book style."*
>
> *Narrative Text #3*

Creating effective prompts was challenging to Linda as it requires refining the descriptions, which can be arduous. In the next section, she articulates the frustrations and contentment in developing her AI literacy skills through iterative prompts.

DEVELOPING AI LITERACY SKILLS THROUGH ITERATIVE PROMPTS

> *Learning a new skill was frustrating, especially when the skill is embedded in a task that I wasn't strong in to begin with- technology. I believe that it is vital to go outside of my comfort zones, especially if it is a task that will be present in my career and students may take advantage of AI to create assignments. I want to make sure they are using the tool in a responsible and informed way. I did have to change my overall concept [prompts] and that was ok because I was able to create something better than I initially envisioned and I am very proud of my overall result. I believe the template on Padlet was very helpful. Padlet was also a new tool for me this semester and will be a tool I bring into my classroom. The instructions for this assignment were concise and easy to follow.*
>
> *Narrative Text #4*

In the initial phase of this project, Linda had relied on her existing literacy skills, specifically, her knowledge of using search engines – Google or Yahoo, to navigate a generative AI tool. She attempted to use exact keywords such as "body shaming", "fat body", and "postpartum body" to instruct AI to produce the desired images for her comic. However, these prompts did not yield the intended results. This experience highlights the importance of developing new literacy skills, particularly in the context of generative AI. As students engage in the social practice of crafting prompts or prompt engineering, they gain valuable awareness about the unique characteristics of generative AI tools. Unlike Google and Yahoo, which retrieve existing content, generative AI tools can create original text, images, and other forms of media. When provided with explicit examples and strategies for crafting prompts effectively, Linda began experimenting with various techniques independently.

> *I made sure to be as specific as I could to have a sense of uniformity in my superheroes, but because my character fluctuated in size, and age, it did not have to be a perfect fit. The prompts I would tailor to the image I desired were along the lines of "Brunette female superhero comic book style image" but I would add specific indicators such as "with a mask" or "elderly" if I needed something more to the superhero.*
>
> *Reflection, May 1, 2024*

The process of working through trial-and-error, as evidenced in Table 4.1, demonstrates that the development of AI literacy skills involves learning to craft prompts that guide the AI toward producing the desired output (Kandlhofer et al., 2016; Long & Magerko, 2020). The iterative nature of crafting prompts aligns with the principles of multiliteracies, which emphasize the importance of designing and redesigning meaning across various modes and media (Cope & Kalantzis, 2000; New London Group,

TABLE 4.1 A Summary of Prompts Used to Create the Memoir, *Can ANY BODY Help Me?*

Prompt Number	Prompt	Linda's Comments
1	Body shaming	AI produced inappropriate images
2	Postpartum body with stretch marks realistic style watercolor paint image	
3	Female superhero, comic book style	AI generated images of thin, blonde woman which [who] does not represent the comic creator
4	Older superhero, comic book style	AI generated images of male superheroes instead of women
5	Female superhero, old, comic book style	AI generated a female superhero with speech bubbles that are unreadable
6	Brunette child female superhero being yelled at by angry citizens, comic book style	AI generated identical child and mother superheroine characters
7	Child female superhero being yelled at by angry citizens, comic book style	

1996). As Linda refined her prompts based on the AI-generated images, she actively participated in a process of meaning-making that required her to critically evaluate and adapt her communication strategies (Bali, 2024). This experience underscores the significance of fostering literacy skills that enable students to effectively collaborate with AI technologies in the creation of multimodal texts. Unlike search engines, AI tools create opportunities for engaging in dialogues to fine-tune the output until it meets the needs of the users (Oppenlaender, et al.,2023; Markauskaite, et al., 2022). However, to achieve the intended output with AI, Linda described that "a person needs to be colorful linguistically to be able to manipulate the prompts and to better craft an image" (Reflection, May 1, 2024). Linda's experience with crafting prompts highlights the complex interplay between language, creativity, and technology in the context of generative AI. By cultivating AI literacy skills, preservice teachers like Linda can critically engage with generative AI tools, harnessing their potential to create innovative, multimodal texts that reflect their unique perspectives and experiences.

In the next section, I offer guidelines for crafting prompts based on my teaching experience and the data obtained from this study.

GUIDELINES FOR CRAFTING PROMPTS WITH GENERATIVE AI (TEXT-TO-IMAGE)

- **Define the Purpose**: Clearly state the goal for the AI-generated images.
- **Choose the AI Tool**: Select the most suitable text-to-image AI tool based on your needs (e.g., Midjournay, DALL.E, any AI-embedded tools in Canva or Padlet).
- **Provide Detailed Prompts**:
  - Describe the subject, physical characteristics, pose/action, background, and artistic style.
  - Use specific details for accurate results.
- **Iterate and Refine Prompts**: Engage in a creative dialogue by modifying prompts based on the generated output.
- **Specify Artistic Style**: Include instructions for the desired artistic or photographic style.

- **Use Modifiers**: Enhance images by incorporating modifiers like "with a mask", "elderly", or setting details.
- **Document and Track**: Record prompts, AI tool/version, and creation date for transparency.
- **Consider Ethical Implications**: Remain mindful of potential biases or harmful representations in the AI output.

Crafting effective prompts requires practice, experimentation, and a creative mindset to leverage generative AI tools. As Linda became more adept at the craft of developing prompts that produce her desired visuals, she also noticed several biases in the generative AI tool.

NOTICING BIASES IN GENERATIVE AI IMAGES

One of the biases that caught Linda's attention greatly was that which involves gender and identity. When she typed "superhero", AI automatically created an iconic white, male figure that most people identified as Superman; he was clad in a full-body compression garment with a cape, outer boxer, boots, and a large "S" on the chest patch: "AI automatically created Superman for me" (Check-in session #1, April 2024). Then when she added the word "female superhero", the AI-generated images produced several white women with predominantly blonde or brown hair (except one) and a pencil-slim figure to depict a typical heroine. As Linda noted:

> *My comic doesn't take into account that people who are being shamed don't have brown hair and blue eyes and may not fit into "typical" beauty standards. I personally have brown hair, brown eyes, and while I have overcome the bouts of shame that I have endured, I still do not feel as secure as my character or meet her beauty standards, and I can see how others may feel the same.*
>
> *Reflection, April 24, 2024*

Such a strikingly biased representation of a female superhero is tied in part to the machine-generated prompt created from the human-provided "female superhero comic book style" prompt. This observation aligns with the growing body of research that highlights the prevalence of biases in AI systems, particularly in relation to gender, race, and body image (e.g. Shaw et al., 2024; Marinucci et al., 2023; Sperling et al., 2024). The biases present in generative AI outputs are often a reflection of the biases inherent in the training data and the societal norms and stereotypes that shape the development of these technologies (Benjamin, 2020; Crawford & Paglen, 2019; Kim et al., 2022). As literacy scholars engage with generative AI in educational contexts, it is crucial to critically examine and address these biases to promote more inclusive and equitable representations in AI-generated content. Maha Bali's (2024) work on critical AI literacy offers valuable insights into how educators can foster a critical understanding of AI systems among learners. Bali argues that critical AI literacy should encompass not only technical knowledge but also an understanding of the social, ethical, and political implications of AI technologies. By developing critical AI literacy skills, students can learn to recognize and challenge the biases and limitations of generative AI, and actively work toward creating more inclusive and equitable AI-generated content. When prompted how she critically evaluate the AI-generated images to ensure that they were free from biases, stereotypes, or insensitivities, Linda wrote,

> *The nature of my comic was to put the biases and stereotypes on display to show the harms of body shaming, and how my character would be impacted and eventually overcome the insensitivities toward different bodies. My comic's purpose is to empower women to see beyond the labels and stereotypes others place on our bodies and how it "should" look to them.*
>
> *Reflection, April 24, 2024*

Additionally, while crafting prompts, Linda could have included more detailed and concise descriptions to challenge AI's default assumptions and biases. Incorporating a wider range of physical characteristics, ethnicities, and body types in the prompts would generate more diverse and inclusive representations of her character self. However, despite AI's potential to develop characters that are aesthetically pleasing, Linda tried to minimize reliance on the tool. While recognizing these biases was crucial, Linda also grappled with finding the right balance between leveraging AI's capabilities and maintaining her own creative input.

BALANCING HUMAN CREATIVITY AND COMPUTATIONAL CREATIVITY

Although AI can be a valuable tool, Linda was cautious about using it intensely. While recognizing AI's value for ideation and overcoming creative obstacles, she emphasized the primacy of personal inspiration and nurturing inherent creative abilities, stating,

While AI is very helpful with brainstorming and assisting in creating images, the drawback is that people who rely on these tools may lack originality and creativity from their own minds. The tool should be used with cases such as writer's block, or times where creativity may be lacking, but the first point of trial should be to brainstorm and create with personal inspirations. I kept my AI use to a minimum and only really used it in areas where I lacked such as drawing.

Reflection, May 1, 2024

On the contrary, Linda viewed the generative AI tool as an "assistant", helping her to create images for her comics, which she could have otherwise done traditionally using pen and paper. Linda's approach to generative AI exemplifies the notion of living literacies (Pahl & Rowsell, 2020), which acknowledges literacy practices as deeply embedded in individuals' daily lives, shaped by their social, cultural, and technological contexts. Her experience highlights how students could potentially interact with and make meaning through AI-powered tools within their everyday experiences, beyond official schooled activities. To add on, Linda's view that "people also need their own levels of creativity to be able to help AI match their needs" (Reflection, May 1, 2024) resonates with the active engagement aspect of living literacies. Effective use of generative AI necessitates developing skills and knowledge to creatively guide and shape AI's output through well-crafted prompts and clear visions, rather than passively consuming AI-generated content. Thus, there is a need to foster a balanced, critically engaged relationship with AI while maintaining agency, creativity, and the ability to adapt in an ever-evolving technological landscape. This balance, however, is just one of many ethical and pedagogical considerations that arise when integrating AI into educational practices.

ETHICAL CONSIDERATIONS AND PEDAGOGICAL IMPLICATIONS OF AI IN EDUCATION

As AI evolves, it blurs the line between human and AI-assisted creations, particularly in higher education. This raises critical questions about the custodianship of intellectual property and the very nature of creativity (Eshraghian, 2020).

Linda's experience with generative AI illustrates several of these concerns:

I had an overall sense of guilt for using a tool to create images when I probably could have used some creativity and tried my hand at

> *making a comic strip by hand. However, I decided to go outside of my comfort zone and try something I have never experienced before in hopes that it could change my mind. I think it was a good decision because I was allowed to become more familiar with a tool my students may be using.*
>
> *Reflection, May 1, 2024*

Similar to Linda, educators and students would also be faced with ethical dilemmas when integrating AI into creative processes. Some of the key concerns that emerged from Linda's experience include:

- **Authenticity and Creativity**: The potential impact of AI on creativity and originality in student work.
- **Bias and Representation**: The perpetuation of biases and stereotypes in AI-generated content, as evidenced by the narrow, Westernized standard of beauty initially reflected in Linda's superheroine images.
- **Assessment and Attribution**: The need to re-evaluate assessment practices and concepts of authenticity in academic work, including guidelines for crediting AI involvement in student projects.
- **Equity and Access**: Addressing potential inequities in access to AI comic creation tools among students.
- **Pedagogical Implications**: The impact of AI-generated comics on traditional literacy skills and storytelling abilities.

To address these concerns, I developed a set of guiding questions for preservice teachers:

- How can we balance AI assistance with independent creation to foster students' creativity and artistic skills?
- What strategies can we employ to teach students about the capabilities and limitations of AI in content creation?
- How can we ensure that AI-generated content is age-appropriate and aligns with educational objectives?
- What ethical considerations should guide the use of AI-generated representations, particularly regarding diversity and potential biases?
- How might the use of AI in content creation affect students' understanding of narrative structure, character development, and visual storytelling?

These questions aim to encourage critical thinking about the integration of generative AI in educational contexts, addressing key areas such as creativity, intellectual property, content appropriateness, critical thinking, and representation. The integration of generative AI, however, has implications on teacher education programs.

IMPLICATIONS FOR TEACHER EDUCATION PROGRAMS

The insights gained from Linda's experience with generative AI raise several critical areas for consideration in teacher education programs. As generative AI becomes increasingly prevalent in educational settings, it is crucial that preservice teachers are equipped with the necessary skills to navigate these technologies effectively and ethically. Based on Linda's experience, the affordances or merit of using AI includes the potential for fostering interdisciplinary connections and critical thinking about social issues:

> *I found that AI is another mode to work with. I have never created a comic before, but after this project, I decided to use it for another project in another class to voice concerns about 'identity' and 'nationalism' and how such topics play a role in the oppression of racialized black people in America.*
>
> *Reflection, May 1, 2024*

This experience shows how engaging with AI for one project can lead to its application in other academic contexts, broadening students' perspectives and critical thinking skills.

To prepare future educators, teacher education programs should consider incorporating AI literacy modules that cover both technical aspects and ethical considerations. These programs should also provide hands-on experiences with AI tools to develop skills in prompt engineering and creative problem-solving. Furthermore, it is essential to foster critical discussions about AI biases, limitations, and potential impacts on education. Last, developing guidelines for ethical AI use in educational contexts will be crucial for ensuring responsible implementation of these technologies in future classrooms.

LIMITATIONS AND FUTURE RESEARCH

While this study provides valuable insights into one preservice teacher's experience with generative AI, it is important to acknowledge its limitations. As a single case study, the findings may not be generalizable to all preservice teachers or contexts. Future research could expand on this work by examining a larger and more diverse sample of preservice teachers, exploring how factors such as prior technological experience, subject area specialization, or cultural background might influence engagement with generative AI. Additionally, longitudinal studies could investigate how preservice teachers' AI literacy skills develop over time and how these skills translate into classroom practice once they enter the teaching profession.

RECOMMENDATIONS FOR EDUCATORS

Based on the findings of this study, I offer the following recommendations for educators looking to incorporate generative AI into their teaching practices:

- Start with low-stakes, exploratory activities to allow students to familiarize themselves with AI tools.
- Explicitly teach prompt engineering skills, encouraging students to document and reflect on their prompt iterations.
- Incorporate critical discussions about AI biases and limitations into lessons involving AI-generated content.
- Use AI as a complement to, not a replacement for, traditional creative processes.
- Develop clear guidelines for crediting AI contributions in student work.
- Regularly update your own knowledge about AI developments and their educational implications.

CONCLUSION

As generative AI technologies continue to shape literacy education, educators and scholars must adopt a nuanced, critically engaged approach. By cultivating AI literacy skills alongside living literacies and multiliteracies frameworks, we can empower students to become active, critically conscious co-creators with AI systems. The integration of generative AI in education has the potential to reshape literacy practices and pedagogy, leading to new genres of multimodal texts and hybrid forms of authorship. As educators, our role will increasingly focus on guiding students in critical AI literacy, ethical use of AI tools, and leveraging AI to enhance human creativity. However, it is crucial to acknowledge the limitations of these tools and maintain a balance between AI assistance and human creativity. Ultimately, the goal is to use these technologies as catalysts for reimagining creative expression and fostering innovative, socially conscious thinkers and creators. Future research should explore the long-term impacts of AI integration in education, focusing on how it affects student creativity, critical thinking, and multimodal literacy skills. Additionally, ongoing investigations into ethical considerations and best practices for AI use in educational settings will be essential as these technologies continue to evolve.

REFERENCES

Abas, S. (2023). Critical multimodal literacy practices in student-created comics. *Literacy, 57*(2), 161–170. https://doi.org/10.1111/lit.12324

Bali, M. (2024). Where are the crescents in AI? *LSE HE blog.* https://blogs.lse.ac.uk/highereducation/2024/02/26/where-are-the-crescents-in-ai

Barton, D., & Hamilton, M. (1998). *Local literacies: Reading and writing in one community.* Routledge.

Benjamin, R. (2020). *Race after technology: Abolitionist tools for the new Jim code.* Polity.

Boden, M. A. (2004). *The creative mind: Myths and mechanisms.* Routledge.

Boden, M. A. (2009). Computer models of creativity. *AI Magazine, 30*(3), 23–23.

Clandinin, D. J. (2013). *Engaging in narrative inquiry.* Routledge.

Clandinin, D. J. & Connelly, F. M. (2000). *Narrative inquiry: Experience and story in qualitative research.* Jossey-Bass.

Colton, S., Lopez de Mantaras, R., & Stock, O. (2009). Computational creativity: Coming of age. *AI Magazine, 30*(3), 11. https://doi.org/10.1609/aimag.v30i3.2257

Colton, S., & Wiggins, G. A. (2012). Computational creativity: The final frontier? In L. De Raedt, C. Bessiere, D. Dubois, P. Doherty, P. Frasconi, F. Heintz, & P. Lucas (Eds.), *Proceedings of the 20th European conference on artificial intelligence (ECAI)* (pp. 21–26). IOS Press. doi:10.3233/978-1-61499-098-7-21

Cope, B., & Kalantzis, M. (2000). *Multiliteracies: Literacy learning and the design of social futures.* Routledge.

Crawford, K., & Paglen, T. (2019). *Excavating AI.* https://excavating.ai

Creswell, J. W., & Miller, D. L. (2000). Determining validity in qualitative inquiry. *Theory into Practice, 39*(3), 124–130. http://www.jstor.org/stable/1477543

Cross, N. (2011). *Design thinking: Understanding how designers think and work.* Berg Publishers.

Eshraghian, J. K. (2020). Human ownership of artificial creativity. *Nature Machine Intelligence, 2*(3), 157–160. https://doi.org/10.1038/s42256-020-0161-x

Jones, S., & Woglom, J. F. (2014). Dangerous conversations: Persistent tensions in teacher education. *Phi Delta Kappan, 95*(6), 47–56. https://doi.org/10.1177/003172171409500611

Kalantzis, M., & Cope, B. (2004). Designs for learning. *E-Learning and Digital Media, 1*(1), 38–93.

Kandlhofer, M., Steinbauer, G., Hirschmugl-Gaisch, S., Huber, P. (2016). *Artificial intelligence and computer science in education: From kindergarten to university*. In 2016 IEEE Frontiers in Education Conference (FIE); October 12–15, 2016.

Kaufman, J. C., & Sternberg, R. J. (Eds.). (2010). *The Cambridge handbook of creativity*. Cambridge University Press.

Kim, T., Rushmeier, H., Dorsey, J., Nowrouzezahrai, D., Syed, R., Jarosz, W., & Darke, A. M. (2022). Countering racial bias in computer graphics research. In *Special Interest Group on computer graphics and interactive techniques conference talks (SIGGRAPH '22 Talks)*. Association for Computing Machinery. https://doi.org/10.1145/3532836.3536263

Long, D., & Magerko, B. (2020, April). What is AI literacy? Competencies and design considerations. In *Proceedings of the 2020 CHI conference on human factors in computing systems* (pp. 1–16). Association for Computing Machinery (ACM) Digital Library. https://dl.acm.org/doi/10.1145/3313831.3376727

Marinucci, L., Mazzuca, C. & Gangemi, A (2023). Exposing implicit biases and stereotypes in human and artificial intelligence: state of the art and challenges with a focus on gender. *AI & Society, 38*, 747–761. https://doi.org/10.1007/s00146-022-01474-3

Markauskaite, L., Marrone, R., Poquet, O., Knight, S., Martinez-Maldonado, R., Howard, S., Tondeur, J., De Laat, M., Buckingham Shum, S., Gašević, D., & Siemens, G. (2022). Rethinking the entwinement between artificial intelligence and human learning: What capabilities do learners need for a world with AI? *Computers and Education: Artificial Intelligence, 3*. https://doi.org/10.1016/j.caeai.2022.100056

McGarr, O., Gavaldon, G., & Saez de Adana, F. (2020). Using autobiographical comics to explore life stories and school experiences of pre-service early childhood educators. *British Educational Research Journal, 46*(5), 1152–1170.

McCloud (1994). Understanding comics: the invisible art. HarperPerennial.

New London Group (1996). A pedagogy of multiliteracies: Designing social futures. *Harvard Educational Review, 66*, 60–92.

Oppenlaender, J., Linder, R., & Silvennoinen, J. (2023). *Prompting AI art: An investigation into the creative skill of prompt engineering*. https://arxiv.org/pdf/2303.13534.

Pahl, K., and J. Rowsell. 2020. *Living Literacies: Literacy for Social Change*. The MIT Press.

Pérez y Pérez, R. (2015). A computer-based model for collaborative narrative generation. *Cognitive Systems Research, 36–37*, 30–48.

Riessman, C. K. (2008). *Narrative methods for the human sciences.* Sage Publications.

Romagnoli, A., Bazler, J., & Van Sickle, M. (2018). Science education and the graphic novel connection: Pre-service teachers and the creation of graphic novelettes. *Science Educator, 26*(2), 73–80.

Shaw, M. S., Toliver, S. R., & Tanksley, T. (2024). The internet doesn't exist in the sky: Literacy, AI, and the digital middle passage. *Reading Research Quarterly, 59*(4), 690–705. https://doi.org/10.1002/rrq.537

Sperling, K., Stenberg, C.-J., McGrath, C., Åkerfeldt, A., Heintz, F., & Stenliden, L. (2024). In search of artificial intelligence (AI) literacy in teacher education: A scoping review. *Computers and Education Open, 6*. https://doi.org/10.1016/j.caeo.2024.100169

Sternberg, R. J. (2016). Creativity, intelligence, and culture. In V. P. Glăveanu (Ed.), *The Palgrave handbook of creativity and culture research* (pp. 77–99). Palgrave Macmillan/Springer Nature. https://doi.org/10.1057/978-1-137-46344-9_5

Street, B. (2003). What's "new" in the new literacy studies? Critical approaches to literacy in theory and practice. *Current Issues in Comparative Education, 5*(2), 77–91.

Webster, L. L., & Mertova, P. (2007). *Using narrative inquiry as a research method: An introduction to using critical event narrative analysis in research on learning and teaching.* (1st ed.) Routledge.

Wingström, R., Hautala, J., & Lundman, R. (2022). Redefining creativity in the era of AI? Perspectives of computer scientists and new media artists. *Creativity Research Journal, 36*(2), 177–193. https://doi.org/10.1080/10400419.2022.2107850

Ybarra, M.G. & Marroquin, E. (2024). Rethinking and redrawing teaching and learning: Latinx preservice teachers documenting their pedagogies of the home through comic strips. *Journal of Adolescent and Adult Literacy, 67*(6), 389–402. https://doi.org/10.1002/jaal.1348

Zulkarnain, I., & Abas, S. (2024). Fostering artificial intelligence (AI) literacy in higher education: Integrating generative AI and social annotation tools for critical engagement. *Journal of Cinema and Media Studies, 9*(2). Teaching Dossier. https://quod.lib.umich.edu/j/jcms/teachingmedia/

CHAPTER 5

Intelligent-TPACK for AI-Assisted Literacy Instruction

A Novel Technological and Pedagogical Approach to Prepare Teachers for Future Classrooms

Ismail Celik and Selcuk Dogan

INTEGRATION OF AI TECHNOLOGIES INTO EDUCATION

With the rapid advancement of artificial intelligence (AI), educators have an unprecedented opportunity to transform teaching and learning experiences in the classroom. AI-based technologies offer a set of benefits for both teachers and students. Through the affordances of AI, for example, students have the opportunity to have personalized learning experiences specific to their needs (Celik et al., 2022; Salas-Pilco et al., 2022). Such a personalized approach occurs due to the analysis of vast amounts of multimodal data from students. The data, including learners' backgrounds, interests, and motivation are proceeded with AI to deliver personalized learning activities (Cukurova et al., 2020). By timely offering personalized materials, AI-powered systems can promote student engagement (Celik, 2023; Luckin et al., 2022). More specifically, real-time interventions are possible due to opportunities from AI-powered technologies. For instance, different from static textbooks or lectures, AI-powered educational platforms can assess

DOI: 10.1201/9781003510635-8

students' progress in real time and provide targeted interventions when needed. Similarly, when a student struggles with a particular concept, the AI system can suggest further explanations, practice exercises, or alternative learning resources to scaffold their understanding (Chiu et al., 2023b).

In addition to enhancing the learning experience for students, AI can also reduce the burden of time-consuming administrative tasks for teachers. In fact, grading assignments, creating lesson plans, and analyzing assessments are essential but often tedious aspects of teaching (Celik et al., 2022). However, AI algorithms can automate these tasks, offering valuable time to teachers use. From the teacher's side, this valuable time can lead to more meaningful interactions with students. By leveraging AI-based technologies, teachers can focus on facilitating discussions, providing individualized feedback, and fostering critical thinking skills in their students (Nemorin et al., 2023; Seufert et al., 2021). Another persuasive reason for teachers to embrace AI-based technologies is the wealth of data-driven insights they provide (Cukurova et al., 2020). By analyzing large datasets generated from students' interactions with digital learning platforms, AI algorithms can uncover valuable insights into learning trends, misconceptions, and areas for improvement (Ley et al., 2023). This functionality enables teachers to make informed decisions about instructional strategies, curriculum design, and individualized interventions (Wang, 2021). The technological and pedagogical affordances of AI technologies could be utilized in any educational field. Literacy instruction is no exception. It is important to note that AI technologies also offer novel opportunities for literacy instruction.

AFFORDANCES OF AI-BASED TECHNOLOGIES FOR LITERACY INSTRUCTION

AI-based technologies offer a multitude of technological affordances that revolutionize literacy instruction. Personalized learning experiences are regarded as one of the prominent affordances in the ability to provide tailored to the individual needs and preferences of learners (Celik, 2023). Through sophisticated algorithms, AI systems can analyze students' reading levels, interests, and learning backgrounds to deliver customized reading materials and writing prompts. This personalized approach not only engages students but also fosters greater comprehension and fluency in literacy skills (Xiao & Hu, 2019).

Furthermore, AI enables real-time feedback on reading and writing assignments, a novelty that was previously challenging to achieve in traditional classroom settings (Huang et al., 2023). Automated feedback mechanisms powered by AI algorithms can assess students' comprehension, grammar usage, and writing structure, offering immediate insights into areas for improvement (Srinivasan & Murthy, 2021). This timely feedback not only supports students in refining their literacy skills but also promotes a growth mindset by encouraging iterative learning and improvement. Additionally, AI-based technologies facilitate access to a wealth of digital resources and tools that enrich literacy instruction. From interactive e-books and audiobooks to grammar-checking software and virtual writing assistants, AI-powered platforms offer a diverse range of resources to support reading and writing development (Huang et al., 2023). These AI tools not just enhance engagement but also provide students with opportunities for independent practice and exploration of literacy skills. In addition to their technological capabilities, AI-based technologies offer pedagogical affordances that enhance literacy instruction. One such affordance is the ability to scaffold learning through interactive and adaptive activities (Liu et al., 2023). AI-powered tutoring systems can guide students through personalized learning pathways, providing support and feedback at each step of the learning process. This scaffolded approach helps students develop critical reading comprehension strategies and writing skills while building confidence and autonomy in their learning (Rad et al., 2023).

Moreover, AI facilitates differentiated instruction by tailoring learning experiences to meet the diverse needs of students. Adaptive learning platforms can adjust the difficulty level of reading passages or writing tasks based on students' performance. For instance, if a student demonstrates strong comprehension skills in a reading passage, the adaptive learning platform might present a more complex text with advanced vocabulary and sentence structures in subsequent tasks. Conversely, if the student struggles, the platform could offer simpler texts with additional supports, such as vocabulary hints or guided questions, to help the learner improve. Thus, such platforms ensure that each learner is appropriately challenged and supported for gaining reading and writing skills (Huang et al., 2023). This individualized approach not only assists varying skill levels but also promotes equity and inclusivity in literacy instruction (Xiao & Hu, 2019). Furthermore, AI-based technologies foster collaborative learning experiences that promote peer interaction and knowledge sharing. Online platforms and tools enable students to engage in collaborative reading activities, peer editing sessions, and digital book clubs, fostering a sense of community and shared responsibility for learning (Celik et al., 2022). AI algorithms can analyze students' collaborative interactions, providing insights into group dynamics and facilitating targeted interventions to support effective collaboration in literacy practices.

AI-BASED TOOLS FOR SUPPORTING LITERACY INSTRUCTION

AI is not regarded as a single technology; rather, it is an umbrella term covering various sub-field such as machine learning and natural language processing. In essence, all these subfields serve as different analytical methods for collecting and analyzing data; ultimately, producing an outcome in an automated way (Celik et al., 2022). To benefit from technological and pedagogical affordances, AI is deployed in teaching and learning settings in different ways. In other words, AI is integrated into several instructional technologies. Previous reviews and empirical studies indicate that chatbots, intelligent tutoring, automated grading systems (AGS), and dashboards are the most common AI-based technologies (Akgun & Greenhow, 2022; Celik, 2023).

Chatbots

Chatbots can provide personalized learning experiences tailored to each learner's needs, abilities, and interests. They can assess the learner's proficiency level through interactive exercises, quizzes, and conversations, and then offer appropriate learning materials and activities to improve literacy skills such as reading, writing, grammar, and vocabulary (Liu et al., 2022). Chatbots can engage learners in interactive reading and writing activities, such as comprehension questions, grammar exercises, word games, and writing prompts. By providing immediate feedback and correction, chatbots help learners practice and reinforce literacy skills in a supportive environment. Unlike human instructors, chatbots are available 24/7, allowing learners to access literacy support whenever they need it. This flexibility enables learners to practice and reinforce their skills at their own pace and convenience, which can lead to more consistent learning outcomes (Akgun & Greenhow, 2022; Chocarro et al., 2023).

For instance, Liu et al. (2022) explored the effectiveness of using a chatbot as a book talk companion to promote students' interest in reading. The chatbot, equipped with AI, had a basic understanding of 157 books and engaged students in book talk activities. Results indicated that students perceived a strong social connection with the chatbot, which contributed to their engagement and interest in reading. Those who interacted with the chatbot maintained a higher level of interest compared to those who did not. The findings suggest that AI-powered chatbots can play a valuable role in enhancing students' reading experiences and sustaining their interest in learning.

In another empirical study, Liu et al. (2022) investigated the effectiveness of a teachable Q&A chatbot based on a learning-by-teaching approach. Participants were ninety-five fifth graders for a 9-week reading program. Teachable Q&A chatbot was trained with AI techniques in order to promote students' interest and engagement in extensive reading activities. Unlike traditional tutor chatbots, this approach proved beneficial for both highly interested active participants and low-proficiency moderate learners. However, challenges were observed among low social connection readers and low-interest active learners, suggesting a need for additional reading skill support and improved adaptability of story text to cater to diverse preferences and abilities.

Automated Grading Systems

AGS can provide instant feedback to students on their writing assignments, including essays, reports, and creative writing pieces. This immediate feedback helps students identify and correct errors in grammar, punctuation, spelling, and syntax, leading to improved writing skills over time (Celik, 2023). AGS ensure consistency in grading across multiple assignments and classrooms. This consistency is particularly beneficial in large classes or across different sections of a course, ensuring that all students receive a fair and equitable evaluation of their literacy skills (Celik et al., 2022). By automating the grading process, teachers can save significant time on manually assessing and grading written assignments. This time saving allows teachers to dedicate more time to providing targeted instruction, personalized feedback, and individualized support to students (Liu et al., 2022). These systems generate data on students' writing performance, including strengths, weaknesses, common errors, and progress over time (Mardini et al., 2024). Teachers can use these data to inform their instructional decisions, tailor their teaching strategies to address students' needs, and provide targeted interventions for struggling learners.

Mardini et al. (2024) developed an automatic short answer grading system to measure and assess higher education students' reading comprehension skills, particularly understanding, interpreting, and evaluating texts effectively. During their experimental study, they collected data from 199 undergraduate students in the Spanish language. Results showed the automatic grading system could be a novel method to deal with challenges such as time limitation, accuracy, and validity of the assessment process. It is also suggested that for using such technological and pedagogical affordances associated with AGS, teachers should have knowledge and skills. In this way, teachers might support and optimize students' learning with the help of AGS.

AI-Supported Dashboards

Dashboards can visually represent data related to students' literacy skills, such as reading comprehension levels, vocabulary acquisition, writing proficiency, and progress over time. Teachers can easily interpret this information to identify patterns, trends, and areas for improvement among individual students or groups (Celik et al., 2022). Dashboards can display these learning paths, along with recommended activities, resources, and interventions to support each student's literacy development (Srinivasan & Murthy, 2021). Dashboards provide real-time monitoring of students' literacy performance, allowing teachers to track their progress, identify struggling students, and intervene promptly when necessary. Alerts and notifications can be integrated into the dashboard to notify teachers of significant changes or concerns in students' literacy skills. AI-supported dashboards can adapt instructional strategies and materials based on students' ongoing literacy data. For example, if a student is struggling with a particular literacy concept, the dashboard can recommend targeted interventions or alternative teaching approaches to address their needs effectively.

In a study, an AI-supported dashboard entitled WiREAD was created with the primary goal of encouraging and guiding students to cultivate more meaningful conversations and interactions with peers regarding multimodal texts (Tan et al., 2017). This is intended to strengthen their connection to and appreciation of collaborative and critical reading as a valuable social activity. To accomplish this objective, the design of

WiREAD prioritized two main educational benefits: facilitating online peer discussions centered around reading and utilizing a learning analytics dashboard. Results from student feedbacks on the LA dashboard showed that there were notable advantages for learning, including the promotion of increased self-awareness and self-regulation in learning approaches.

Intelligent Tutoring Systems (ITS)

ITS can assess students' literacy skills and knowledge through diagnostic assessments, then create personalized learning paths tailored to each student's strengths, weaknesses, and learning preferences (Mohamed & Lamia, 2018). These paths may include targeted lessons, practice exercises, and enrichment activities designed to address specific literacy needs. ITS can dynamically adjust the difficulty and pace of instruction based on students' performance and progress. For example, if a student demonstrates proficiency in certain literacy skills, the system can advance them to more challenging tasks or provide additional support in areas where they struggle. ITS can provide instant feedback on students' reading, writing, grammar, and comprehension exercises (Ng et al., 2022). This feedback can include explanations of correct answers, suggestions for improvement, and targeted remediation to address common errors (Mohamed & Lamia, 2018). ITS can offer engaging, interactive activities and simulations to reinforce literacy concepts and skills. For example, students may interact with virtual reading passages, practice grammar rules through interactive exercises, or engage in collaborative writing tasks with virtual peers. ITS can provide scaffolded support to help students gradually build their literacy skills (Mohamed & Lamia, 2018). This may involve breaking down complex tasks into smaller, more manageable steps, providing hints or prompts when students encounter difficulties, and offering additional resources or examples as needed. ITS can track students' progress in real time and generate detailed reports on their literacy performance. Teachers can use these reports to monitor individual and class-wide progress, identify areas of concern, and make data-informed instructional decisions.

A meta-analysis found out ITS are more effective in improving literacy skills compared to traditional literacy instruction in terms of reading comprehension (Xu et al., 2019). According to this meta-analysis, Alphie's Alley, conText, iStart, ITSS, Project Listen, and Summary Street are the six common ITS to foster reading and writing skills in K-12 context. For instance, Alphie's Alley offers continuous feedback and support tailored to individual students' performance, tracking their progress, and addressing their diverse needs (Pai et al., 2021; Xu et al., 2019). Meanwhile, ITSS is structured to offer modeling, interactive exercises, assessments, and feedback to students, aiding them in mastering text structure strategies.

As seen from the examples, AI-based technologies offer a variety of technological and pedagogical affordances that transform literacy instruction. However, in order to utilize these affordances, the role of teachers is crucial. In other words, educational integration of AI will fail if teachers do not have the knowledge and skills to use AI technologies (Celik, 2023). Therefore, using AI technologies for literacy instruction requires teachers to have technological and pedagogical knowledge (TPK) (Cukurova et al., 2020). In addition to this knowledge, the teacher's ethical assessment of the decision of AI technologies is also essential. This is because AI technologies could make biased decisions with systematic errors (Adams et al., 2023; Sao Pedro et al., 2013), violating inclusiveness and fairness considerations in education (Castelvecchi, 2016; Shin, 2020).

A NEW APPROACH FOR AI-BASED LITERACY INSTRUCTION: INTELLIGENT-TPACK

The foundation of the technological pedagogical and content knowledge (TPACK) framework stems from pedagogical content knowledge (PCK), initially proposed by Shulman (1986, 1987). PCK encompasses an understanding of how various aspects of subject matter can be planned, adapted, and transformed to enhance student learning. Essentially, PCK combines content knowledge (CK) with pedagogical knowledge (PK), comprising the appropriate methods and strategies for teaching specific content areas. Mishra and Koehler (2006) expanded upon PCK by integrating technological knowledge (TK) to foster the understanding of teachers' knowledge for effective technology integration. This expansion resulted in technological content knowledge (TCK), TPK, and TPACK.

Given its flexibility and comprehensiveness, TPACK has been adopted by numerous researchers to explore various technological tools and pedagogical approaches. For example, Valtonen et al. (2017) applied TPACK to the teaching of twenty-first-century skills such as critical thinking and collaboration. In this regard, Celik (2023) updated TPACK based on technological (e.g., automation) and pedagogical (e.g., adaptive feedback) affordances of AI-based systems including ethical knowledge. Intelligent-TPACK focused on TK-related knowledge components, namely TK, TCK, TPK, and TPACK (see Table 5.1). The sub-domains of knowledge within the Intelligent-TPACK framework are illustrated in Figure 5.1

TABLE 5.1 The Descriptions and Indicators of Intelligent-TPACK Frameworks

Intelligent-TPACK Components	Sample Knowledge for Literacy Instruction
Intelligent-TK component addresses the knowledge required for interacting with AI-based tools and utilizing their fundamental functionalities. This aspect is closely linked to the familiarity level of teachers with the technical capabilities of AI-based tools.	• knowing how to interact with AI-based tools in daily life • knowing how to execute some tasks with AI-based technologies
Intelligent-TPK encompasses the knowledge necessary for leveraging the pedagogical affordances offered by AI-based tools, including the provision of personalized and timely feedback, as well as monitoring students' learning progress. Additionally, Intelligent-TPK emphasizes teachers' comprehension of how to interpret and respond to alerts or notifications generated by AI-based tools.	• recognizing how AI-based tools contribute pedagogically to literacy instruction • assessing the effectiveness of feedback provided by AI-based tools in literacy teaching and learning • choosing appropriate AI-based tools for students to apply their literacy skills and knowledge
Intelligent-TCK pertains to the knowledge in utilizing field-specific AI-based tools among teachers. It incorporates the extent to which teachers employ AI-based tools to enhance and update their CK. This component also addresses teachers' understanding of specific technologies that are particularly effective for facilitating subject-matter learning within their field.	• utilizing AI-based tools to search for educational material relevant to literacy instruction • knowing about different AI-based tools commonly utilized by professionals in the field of literacy education • understanding how to effectively utilize field-specific AI-based tools tailored for literacy instruction, such as intelligent tutors for reading comprehension or vocabulary development
Intelligent-TPACK serves as the foundational knowledge domain, central to focusing on teachers' professional competence in selecting and effectively utilizing appropriate AI-based tools, such as ITS. This domain encompasses the integration of TK, PK, and CK to execute teaching strategies, such as monitoring and providing timely feedback, in order to achieve instructional objectives within a specific domain.	• in literacy teaching, utilizing various AI-based tools to provide adaptive feedback tailored to individual students' needs • in literacy teaching, employing different AI-based tools to facilitate personalized learning experiences for students • in literacy teaching, utilizing a range of AI-based tools to provide real-time feedback on students' literacy skills and progress
Ethics encompasses the teacher's understanding and consideration of ethical principles and implications when assessing and making decisions regarding the use of AI-based tools. The ethical principles are regarded as transparency, fairness, accountability, and inclusiveness.	• assessing the extent to which AI-based tools in literacy instruction consider individual differences, such as race and gender, among all students • evaluating the fairness of AI-based tools' behavior toward all students in literacy teaching

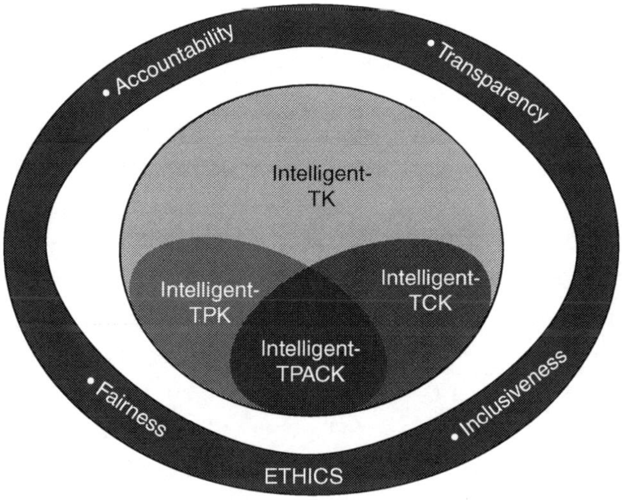

FIGURE 5.1 Intelligent-TPACK Sub-domains.

DEVELOPING INTELLIGENT-TPACK USING LEARNING ACTIVITY TYPES FOR LITERACY

AI integration into teaching and learning processes is mostly technocentric, often overlooking the dynamics and sophisticated nature of Intelligent-TPACK domains (e.g., Harris et al., 2009). It is recommended to use the Intelligent-TPACK framework as a vehicle to think about the effective use and integration of AI-based tools and AI pedagogy in literacy instruction. The Intelligent-TPACK framework is practical and may enable teachers to develop and apply interdependent knowledge domains of AI, pedagogy, content, and ethics. In this regard, we embrace using "learning activity types" suggested by Harris and her colleagues (e.g., Harris, 2008; Harris et al., 2009; Harris & Hofer, 2009). "Learning activity types function as conceptual planning tools for teachers [...] are used to prepare a plan for learning experiences" (Harris & Hofer, 2009, p. 101). These types address the content and time of an activity, such as group discussion within a particular K-6 literacy content area that matches with an AI-based tool or several AI technologies.

In our case, these are AI-enriched activity types that are for literacy teachers to build their Intelligent-TPACK in practical ways. Teachers select literacy content with learning goals for a lesson or an assessment, then decide from AI-enriched activity types for promoting students' literacy skills. As indicated by Harris et al. (2009), activity types are designed for "students' content-related learning needs and preferences" (p. 403). AI-based tools and activity types go together with the literacy content a teacher teaches. In this way, using AI-enriched activity types can represent a way of teachers' professional development for literacy instruction.

AI affordances mentioned above (e.g., personalized learning analyzing students' reading level or real-time feedback on students' writing) create opportunities to use AI-enriched activity types. However, the activity-type approach asks teachers to design learning goals and activities before selecting AI-based tools. The emphasis is always on instructional planning for optimizing student learning and the effective use of AI-based tools through which Intelligent-TPACK is developed authentically (Harris & Hofer, 2009). We expect the more teachers plan with AI-enriched activity types, the more they use time efficiently and productively.

When planning for lessons in a way AI technologies are integrated effectively, researchers, literacy educators, literacy curriculum developers, and professional development providers can benefit from the following samples of learning activity types in Table 5.2. These are attempts to simplify teaching, reading, and writing instruction into more organized, manageable experiences with the help of AI-based tools. Activity types related to literacy instruction can facilitate teachers' planning processes for more engaging lessons that challenge students to read and write. In the literacy-related AI-enriched activity types, we include more general types critical to the development of a good reader, and pre-reading, during-reading, post-reading, vocabulary, comprehension, and fluency activity types (Schmidt et al., 2011).

The activities are derived from a carefully examined collection of empirical and theoretical work around TPACK and learning activity types (e.g., Fang et al., 2023; Kandlhofer et al., 2016; Harris & Hofer, 2009; Hofer & Harris, 2011; Kim et al., 2021; Maher & Young, 2023; Mishra et al., 2023; Ng et al., 2023; Schmidt et al., 2011; Sun et al., 2023). When we describe each learning activity type, we also connect them with any compatible of the four AI-based tools defined above in this chapter. However, not all tools may be appropriate for each AI-enriched activity type. The key idea is that based on AI affordances, a specific AI-based tool should be selected intentionally to align with activity types.

AI-enriched activity types are fine-grained and granular and aim not to overwhelm students and teachers. As similar structures demonstrated, the expectations from and how to be engaged in these activity types are helpful

TABLE 5.2 AI-Enriched Activity Types for Literacy Instruction and Corresponding AI-Based Tools

Activity Type	Short Description	Chatbot	AGS	Dashboard	ITS
Reading text	AI extracts information from text, books, or an online resource	X	X	-	X
Interactive reading sessions	AI reads texts aloud and interacts with students by asking comprehension questions or highlighting vocabulary, thus enhancing reading fluency and comprehension	X	-	-	X
View images	AI examines images to generate relevant information			X	X
Summarize multimedia	AI tools help students summarize informational content from videos or audio clips, enhancing listening and comprehension skills and integrating multimodal literacy practices			X	
Think aloud	Students reflect on their thinking and AI	X			
Vocabulary analysis	AI analyzes how sentences are formed from words	X	X		X
Visual vocabulary building	AI generates visual aids or interactive games that help students learn and memorize new vocabulary through engaging and contextualized scenarios		X	X	X
Prepare presentation	AI prepares slides to demonstrate a basic understanding of a topic				X
Summarizing discussion	AI creates highlights from a synchronous or asynchronous discussion, forum, or dialogue	X	X	X	X
Debate	AI discusses opposite viewpoints in a debate	X	X	X	X
Reading strategy	Guide AI to use a five-step strategy (survey, question, read, recite, and review) to create a purpose for reading	X			X
Research	AI gathers resources on a given topic and analyzes and synthesizes what is known and unknown about the topic	X	X	X	X
Emotion recognition in texts	AI analyzes texts to identify and discuss emotional cues, helping students develop emotional intelligence and deeper comprehension of narrative texts.	X	X		X
Mock interview	AI responds to students' questions on a chosen topic	X	X		

(continued)

TABLE 5.2 (Continued)

Activity Type	Short Description	Chatbot	AGS	Dashboard	ITS
Dialogue simulation	AI simulates historical or fictional dialogues for students to engage with, allowing them to explore different perspectives and deepen their understanding of the content	X	X		X
Artifact analysis	AI examines an artifact uploaded by students		X	X	X
Customized reading challenges	AI systems adapt text complexity and provide personalized reading challenges based on individual student performance, encouraging differentiated learning	X			X
Grammar and syntax improvement	Students use AI to analyze and improve their writing samples, receiving real-time feedback on grammar, punctuation, and stylistic choices		X		X
Alphabetic knowledge	Students name and recognize the letters of the alphabet, create alphabet books using AI-generated images, listen to correct pronunciation, and take quizzes			X	X
Comparing letters and words	Students use AI to recognize patterns (phonemic awareness) and compare different letters, words, or phonemes to understand similarities and differences (decoding skills)			X	X
Develop a story	AI assists students in creating stories by suggesting plot developments, character traits, and settings based on the inputs from the students, fostering creative writing and narrative skills	X			X
Predictions	Students formulate predictions about a story or a text through questions, prompts, or polls when AI pauses reading	X		X	X
Retell	AI helps students retell what they remember about a book they read	X			X
Responding queries	Students drive AI to respond to questions, problems in a worksheet, or a prompt in a discussion board	X		X	
Create a chart or a table	AI creates students' own chart or table on a given topic			X	

Reviewing new content	Students are in conversation with AI to review literacy content			X	X
Test preparation	Students prepare for an exam/test in a practice quiz-like AI-oriented environment	X	X		
Note-taking	AI takes notes about the essential ideas about what students are reading			X	X
Write a paragraph or a short essay	AI composes a structured written document in conversation with students	X			X
Write with a creative format	AI creates a document with a stylized version with multimedia and/or text for summarizing content or a review/student note	X	X	X	X
Creating a diary of learning	AI writes a log of students' learning progress to monitor students' success			X	X
Draw a cartoon of literacy concepts	AI creates drawings, caricatures, or comics on literacy concepts	X			X
Create an advance organizer	Using teacher and/or student notes, AI organizes critical information in a written, visual, or digital format	X	X	X	X
Tracking progress	Students choose their books, and set learning goals and times through AI-driven monitoring skills			X	
After reading	AI helps students form opinions, make comments, and formulate theories and hypotheses after reading	X	X		X

Note: Based on Harris et al.'s (2009) work, activity types can be categorized into (1) knowledge-building: Helping students build their knowledge of literacy content, concepts, and processes, and (2) knowledge expression: Providing students with opportunities or encouraging them to express similar or their understanding of a set of topics. We prefer not to categorize learning activities in such a way to be more inclusive considering AI's capabilities.

for both parties (Karns, 2019; Kolodner & Gray, 2002). These activity types can leverage AI's capabilities to enhance literacy instruction by making learning experiences more interactive, personalized, and aligned with twenty-first-century skills. Such integrations not only support traditional literacy skills but also prepare students to be proficient in digital literacy and critical thinking.

The activity types listed above are described briefly here. Considering Intelligent-TPACK's flexible and practical nature, they can be customized and combined with other types that might be well-matched. It should be kept in mind that AI-enriched activity types are not merely a curriculum or unit planning on their own. Effective literacy learning requires knowledge and skills from other pedagogical and literacy content. Teachers are encouraged to think about their student's needs, expectations, backgrounds, contexts, or preferences and even access to AI-based tools when using activity types (Harris et al., 2009).

A SAMPLE OF LEARNING ACTIVITY TYPES AS A SET OF LEARNING EXPERIENCES

This sample set of activity types revolves around exploring classic literature, "Alice in Wonderland (by Lewis Carrol)," to deepen students' understanding of narrative techniques, character development, and thematic exploration through AI integration. We suggest using a chatbot, such as ChatGPT 4 or Claude, when we refer to the AI tool in this sample.

Phase 1: Pre-Reading and Exploration

Objective: Familiarize students with the context of the story, its author (Lewis Carrol), and the Victorian era to set a foundation for deeper engagement with the text.

Activity Types:

- **Reading text**: Use an AI tool to provide background articles and extracts about Lewis Carroll and the Victorian era. The AI can highlight key facts and quiz students to ensure comprehension.
- **Interactive reading sessions**: Introduce the first chapter of "Alice in Wonderland" through an AI narration tool that asks comprehension questions dynamically to engage students actively.

- **View images**: AI-driven exploration of Victorian-era artwork and culture to help students visualize the setting and social context of the story.

Phase 2: In-Depth Reading and Analysis

Objective: Analyze the text to understand character development, narrative techniques, and themes.

Activity Types:

- **Dialogue simulation**: Use AI to simulate a conversation with Alice or other characters, allowing students to ask questions and explore character motivations and feelings.
- **Emotion recognition in texts**: An AI tool analyzes the text to identify and discuss emotional cues and themes, helping students understand complex character interactions.
- **Vocabulary analysis**: AI breaks down challenging vocabulary within the text, providing definitions and usage examples in context.

Phase 3: Creative Response and Synthesis

Objective: Encourage creative engagement with the text by having students develop their own narrative pieces inspired by "Alice in Wonderland."

Activity Types:

- **Develop a story**: Students use an AI assistant to help them develop their own short stories inspired by the themes of "Alice in Wonderland." AI suggests plot twists, character traits, and settings.
- **Prepare presentation**: AI helps students prepare multimedia presentations of their stories, integrating text, images, and voice narration.
- **Summarizing discussion**: AI creates a summary of online discussion forums where students have debated themes from "Alice in Wonderland," helping to consolidate key points of agreement and contention.

Phase 4: Presentation and Reflection

Objective: Share and reflect on their creative works and understand different interpretations of the text.

Activity Types:

- **Mock interview**: Students conduct an AI-facilitated interview with "Lewis Carroll," discussing why they made certain artistic choices in their stories.
- **Create an advance organizer**: AI helps organize a class exhibition of the students' projects, summarizing their narratives and thematic explorations in a digital format.
- **After reading**: AI facilitates a reflective session where students critique each other's works and discuss how their understanding of the original text influenced their creative decisions.

Integration and Assessment

Formative Assessment: Continuous AI-powered quizzes and feedback during the reading and analysis phases to track comprehension and engagement.

Summative Assessment: Final presentations of creative projects and reflective discussions serve as summative assessments, showcasing students' depth of understanding and creative application of the text.

This AI-enriched activity set integrates the Intelligent-TPACK framework by employing technological tools to enhance pedagogical methods and deepen CK. The activities are designed to move beyond traditional reading comprehension, using AI to foster a multifaceted understanding of literature and support creative expression, aligned with modern educational objectives in literacy.

REFERENCES

Adams, C., Pente, P., Lemermeyer, G., & Rockwell, G. (2023). Ethical principles for artificial intelligence in K-12 education. *Computers and Education: Artificial Intelligence*, *4*, 100131.

Akgun, S., & Greenhow, C. (2022). Artificial intelligence in education: Addressing ethical challenges in K-12 settings. *AI and Ethics*, *2*(3), 431–440.

Castelvecchi, D. (2016). Can we open the black box of AI? *Nature News*, *538*(7623), 20.

Celik, I. (2023). Towards Intelligent-TPACK: An empirical study on teachers' professional knowledge to ethically integrate artificial intelligence (AI)-based tools into education. *Computers in Human Behavior, 138*, 107468.

Celik, I., Dindar, M., Muukkonen, H., & Järvelä, S. (2022). The promises and challenges of artificial intelligence for teachers: A systematic review of research. *TechTrends, 66*(4), 616–630..

Chiu, T. K., Moorhouse, B. L., Chai, C. S., & Ismailov, M. (2023a). Teacher support and student motivation to learn with artificial intelligence (AI) based chatbot. *Interactive Learning Environments, 32*(7), 1–17.

Chiu, T. K., Xia, Q., Zhou, X., Chai, C. S., & Cheng, M. (2023b). Systematic literature review on opportunities, challenges, and future research recommendations of artificial intelligence in education. *Computers and Education: Artificial Intelligence, 4*, 100118.

Chocarro, R., Cortinas, M., & Marcos-Matás, G. (2023). Teachers' attitudes towards chatbots in education: A technology acceptance model approach considering the effect of social language, bot proactiveness, and users' characteristics. *Educational Studies, 49*(2), 295–313.

Cukurova, M., Luckin, R., & Kent, C. (2020). Impact of an artificial intelligence research frame on the perceived credibility of educational research evidence. *International Journal of Artificial Intelligence in Education, 30*(2), 205–235.

Fang, X., Ng, D. T. K., Leung, J. K. L., & Chu, S. K. W. (2023). A systematic review of artificial intelligence technologies used for story writing. *Education and Information Technologies, 28*(11), 14361–14397.

Harris, J. (2008). *TPACK in in-service education: Assisting experienced teachers' planned improvisations*. In AACTE Committee on Innovation & Technology (Eds.), *Handbook of technological pedagogical content knowledge for educators* (pp. 251–271). Routledge.

Harris, J., & Hofer, M. (2009). *Instructional planning activity types as vehicles for curriculum based TPACK development*. In C. D. Maddux (Ed.), *Research highlights in technology and teacher education 2009* (pp. 99–108). AACE.

Harris, J., Mishra, P., & Koehler, M. (2009). Teachers' technological pedagogical content knowledge and learning activity types: Curriculum-based technology integration reframed. *Journal of Research on Technology in Education, 41*(4), 393–416.

Hofer, M., & Harris, J. (2011). *Learning activity types wiki*. College of William & Mary, School of Education. http://activitytypes.wmwikis.net

Huang, X., Zou, D., Cheng, G., Chen, X., & Xie, H. (2023). Trends, research issues and applications of artificial intelligence in language education. *Educational Technology & Society, 26*(1), 112–131.

Kandlhofer, M., Steinbauer, G., Hirschmugl-Gaisch, S., & Huber, P. (2016). Artificial intelligence and computer science in education: From kindergarten to university. In *2016 IEEE frontiers in education conference (FIE)* (pp. 1–9). IEEE.

Karns, S. J. (2019). *Pairing a learning activity types short course with collaborative curriculum design: An approach to impact teachers' technological pedagogical content knowledge (TPACK)* (Doctoral dissertation). University of Pittsburgh.

Kim, S., Jang, Y., Choi, S. et al. (2021). Analyzing Teacher competency with TPACK for K-12 AI education. *Künstl Intell, 35*, 139–151. https://doi.org/10.1007/s13218-021-00731-9

Kolodner, J. L., & Gray, J. T. (2002). *Understanding the affordances of ritualized activity for project-based classrooms.* Paper presented at the International Conference of the Learning Sciences, Seattle, WA. April 14, 2009.

Ley, T., Tammets, K., Pishtari, G., Chejara, P., Kasepalu, R., Khalil, M., ... & Wasson, B. (2023). Towards a partnership of teachers and intelligent learning technology: A systematic literature review of model-based learning analytics. *Journal of Computer Assisted Learning, 39*(5), 1397–1417.

Liu, C., Hou, J., Tu, Y. F., Wang, Y., & Hwang, G. J. (2023). Incorporating a reflective thinking promoting mechanism into artificial intelligence-supported English writing environments. *Interactive Learning Environments, 31*(9), 5614–5632.

Liu, C., Liao, M. G., Chang, C. H., & Lin, H. M. (2022). An analysis of children' interaction with an AI chatbot and its impact on their interest in reading. *Computers & Education, 189*, 104576.

Luckin, R., George, K., & Cukurova, M. (2022). *AI for schoolteachers.* CRC Press.

Maher, D. & Young, K. (2023). Artificial intelligence and literacy development in K–12 schools. In J. Keengwe (Ed.), *Creative AI tools and ethical implications in teaching and learning* (pp. 80–98). IGI Global. https://doi.org/10.4018/979-8-3693-0205-7

Mardini, G. I. D., Quintero, M. C. G., Viloria, N. C. A., Percybrooks, B. W. S., Robles, N. H. S., & Villalba, R. K. (2024). A deep-learning-based grading system (ASAG) for reading comprehension assessment by using aphorisms as open-answer-questions. *Education and Information Technologies, 29*(4), 4565–4590.

Mishra, P., & Koehler, M. J. (2006). Technological pedagogical content knowledge: A framework for teacher knowledge. *Teachers College Record, 108*(6), 1017–1054.

Mishra, P., Warr, M., & Islam, R. (2023) TPACK in the age of ChatGPT and generative AI. *Journal of Digital Learning in Teacher Education, 39*(4), 235–251.

Mohamed, H., & Lamia, M. (2018). Implementing flipped classroom that used an intelligent tutoring system into learning process. *Computers & Education, 124*, 62–76.

Nemorin, S., Vlachidis, A., Ayerakwa, H. M., & Andriotis, P. (2023). AI hyped? A horizon scan of discourse on artificial intelligence in education (AIED) and development. *Learning, Media and Technology*, *48*(1), 38–51.

Ng, D. T. K., Leung, J. K. L., Su, J., Ng, R. C. W., & Chu, S. K. W. (2023). Teachers' AI digital competencies and twenty-first century skills in the post-pandemic world. *Educational Technology Research and Development, 71*(1), 137–161.

Ng, D. T. K., Luo, W., Chan, H. M. Y., & Chu, S. K. W. (2022). Using digital story writing as a pedagogy to develop AI literacy among primary students. *Computers and Education: Artificial Intelligence*, *3*, 100054.

Pai, K. C., Kuo, B. C., Liao, C. H., & Liu, Y. M. (2021). An application of Chinese dialogue-based intelligent tutoring system in remedial instruction for mathematics learning. *Educational Psychology*, *41*(2), 137–152.

Pei-Ling Tan, J., Koh, E., Jonathan, C., & Yang, S. (2017). Learner dashboards a double-edged sword? Students' sense-making of a collaborative critical reading and learning analytics environment for fostering 21st-century literacies. *Journal of Learning Analytics*, *4*(1), 117–140.

Rad, H. S., Alipour, R., & Jafarpour, A. (2023). Using artificial intelligence to foster students' writing feedback literacy, engagement, and outcome: A case of Wordtune application. *Interactive Learning Environments*, *32*(9) 1–21.

Salas-Pilco, S. Z., Xiao, K., & Hu, X. (2022). Artificial intelligence and learning analytics in teacher education: A systematic review. *Education Sciences*, *12*(8), 569.

Sao Pedro, M. A., Baker, R. S., & Gobert, J. D. (2013). What different kinds of stratification can reveal about the generalizability of data-mined skill assessment models. In *Proceedings of the third international conference on learning analytics and knowledge* (pp. 190–194). ACM digital library. https://dl.acm.org/doi/abs/10.1145/2460296.2460334

Schmidt, D., Harris, J., & Hofer, M. (2011, February). *K-6 literacy learning activity types*. College of William and Mary, School of Education, Learning Activity Types. http://activitytypes.wm.edu/K6Literacy.html

Seufert, S., Guggemos, J., & Sailer, M. (2021). Technology-related knowledge, skills, and attitudes of pre-and in-service teachers: The current situation and emerging trends. *Computers in Human Behavior*, *115*, 106552.

Shin, D. (2020). How do users interact with algorithm recommender systems? The interaction of users, algorithms, and performance. *Computers in Human Behavior*, *109*, 106344.

Shulman, L. (1986). Those who understand: Knowledge growth in teaching. *Educational Researcher*, *15*(2), 4–14.

Shulman, L. (1987). Knowledge and teaching: Foundations of the new reform. *Harvard Educational Review*, *57*(1), 1–23.

Srinivasan, V., & Murthy, H. (2021). Improving reading and comprehension in K-12: Evidence from a large-scale AI technology intervention in India. *Computers and Education: Artificial Intelligence, 2*, 100019.

Sun, J., Ma, H., Zeng, Y., Han, D., & Jin, Y. (2023). Promoting the AI teaching competency of K-12 computer science teachers: A TPACK-based professional development approach. *Education and Information Technologies, 28*(2), 1509–1533.

Valtonen, T., Sointu, E., Kukkonen, J., Kontkanen, S., Lambert, M. C., & Mäkitalo-Siegl, K. (2017). TPACK updated to measure pre-service teachers' twenty-first century skills. *Australasian Journal of Educational Technology, 33*(3),15–31

Wang, Y. (2021). When artificial intelligence meets educational leaders' data-informed decision-making: A cautionary tale. *Studies in Educational Evaluation, 69*, 100872.

Xiao, Y., & Hu, J. (2019). Assessment of optimal pedagogical factors for Canadian ESL learners' reading literacy through artificial intelligence algorithms. *International Journal of English Linguistics, 9*(4), 1–14.

Xu, Z., Wijekumar, K., Ramirez, G., Hu, X., & Irey, R. (2019). The effectiveness of intelligent tutoring systems on K-12 students' reading comprehension: A meta-analysis. *British Journal of Educational Technology, 50*(6), 3119–3137.

CHAPTER 6

Cultivating Global Writers

The Role of AI in Creating Authentic Writing Situations for Young Learners

Arild Michel Bakken, Patrick Burke, Johannes Steinrücke, Bente R. Walgermo, Maryam Amir Haeri, Madalena Teixeira, Yolanda Álvarez Amigo, and Erik Roelofs

INTRODUCTION

Interest and engagement are crucial for literacy acquisition, as students who are engaged in reading and writing activities learn more effectively. However, stimulating interest and engagement in school contexts can be challenging. Reading and writing are by their very nature communicative activities, and a main driver behind engaging in them is a need to communicate. Out of school, children routinely write purposefully, in order to communicate, for example, within the family or with friends, on game platforms, or in different kinds of social networks. In these cases, children have real-world reasons for writing, and they are writing to an authentic audience—people who are interested in discovering what they have to communicate. In school, possibilities for such authentic writing are of course also present. The teacher is a privileged audience for the students'

DOI: 10.1201/9781003510635-9

writing, as are classmates. It is however challenging to leverage these readers to create authentic writing situations on a continuous basis. Both teacher and classmates have many other roles with regard to the students that interfere with the role as interested reader. The shared history in the classroom will, for example, often eliminate the need to communicate in writing. As a result, writing instruction is dominated by "artificial" tasks without authentic audiences. The recent entry of digital tools in schools opens up opportunities for engaging with the world beyond the classroom, for example, through blogging or exchanging texts with students in other schools or abroad. The current expansion of artificial intelligence (AI) could further enhance these opportunities for collaboration.

This chapter reports on the AILIT project (AI Literacy Network in Primary Education), a collaboration aimed at exploring how AI can be used to enhance students' motivation for writing. The project brings together universities and schools from Norway, Ireland, Portugal, Spain, and the Netherlands to build a platform leveraging AI to boost students' writing motivation. Funded by the Erasmus+ program of the European Commission, the project runs from 2022 to 2025.

The rise of generative AI in recent years has created a sense of uncertainty in the educational sector. While AI offers opportunities to engage students in creative work, it also risks seeing students withdraw from actual writing, leaving that task to machines. However, AI encompasses much more than generative AI. In this project, we examined how AI could be used to scaffold students' writing rather than doing the writing for them. The work centered around the idea of authentic writing situations. Two key AI capabilities were identified as fruitful contributors to creating such authentic situations: machine translation and recommendation. Machine translation would allow students to write for authentic peer audiences in other countries and machine recommendations of texts to read would allow them to find audiences who were interested in exactly the kind of texts they wrote.

SCAFFOLDING, INTEREST, AND ENGAGEMENT

The AILIT project aims to scaffold students' literacy work using AI. The "scaffolding" metaphor was introduced by Wood et al. (1976) in the context of an instructional situation where "an adult or 'expert' helps someone who is less adult or less expert (p. 89)". They described the scaffolding process as consisting essentially of "the adult 'controlling' those elements of the task that are initially beyond the learner's capacity, thus permitting him to concentrate upon and complete only those elements that are within his range of competence (p. 90)". Operating in the area between what is beyond and what is within the learner's capacity, the concept of scaffolding is closely related to Vygotsky's concept of the "zone of proximal development", defined as "the distance between the actual developmental level as determined by independent problem solving and the level of potential development as determined through problem solving under adult guidance or in collaboration with more competent peers" (Vygotsky, 1978, p. 86).

Wood et al. conclude their study by listing a set of "scaffolding functions" that the teacher performs when supporting the learner: (1) Recruitment (enlisting the learner's interest in the task), (2) Reduction in degrees of freedom (simplifying the task by controlling some of its elements), (3) Direction maintenance (keep the learner motivated and progressing), (4) Marking critical features, (5) Frustration control, and (6) Demonstration. The list highlights the often-overlooked fact that maintaining motivation for and interest in the task is an essential part of scaffolding. In addition to functions directly targeting the learner's competence, several of the functions target the learner's motivation, interest, and engagement. In this chapter, we understand the scaffolding of a student's writing as all steps taken to support the learner's writing at a level slightly above their current competency level, whether they target the student's competency or their interest and engagement.

Interest is a fundamental concept in education. In a recent book chapter, Hidi et al. (2023) detail the writing paradox of the 21st century: most people today are happy to engage with others in *online* written communication platforms, yet associate more *formal* writing situations with negative sentiments. Boscolo and Gelati (2019) show that this is often the case not only for students but also for their teachers. Interest can be construed as an individual's relation to specific content and their motivation to seek opportunities to engage with that content (Hidi & Renninger, 2006). In the field of writing, interest refers more specifically to how individuals engage with writing. It describes both their psychological state while they are writing and the likelihood that they will continue to seek opportunities to engage with writing over time (see Hidi & Renninger, 2006; Hidi et al., 2023).

Interest is both the gateway to and a prerequisite for meaningful engagement and learning. It is often treated as a single-phase construct, as something students either have or do not have. In opposition to this idea, Hidi and Renninger (2006) propose a four-phase model of interest development:

1. Triggered situational interest
2. Maintained situational interest
3. Emerging individual interest
4. Well-developed individual interest

Each phase has its own characteristics of students' traits and instructional requirements. Interest is a particularly valuable construct in educational contexts as humans are hardwired to develop interest (Renninger et al., 2019). This means that interest can always be strengthened for all individuals in any given domain or activity.

In the AILIT platform, we try to trigger situational interest in writing by creating authentic writing situations. Additionally, we attempt to leverage students' emerging or well-developed individual interest in specific content for reading. As students' interests are multifaceted, it is challenging to find texts that engage all students. The platform's recommender systems will be able to propose interesting texts to individual students based on the content of the texts they have written.

While interest relates to students' relationships with specific content and their willingness to engage with it, engagement pertains to the quality of the involvement itself. Lutz et al. define engagement in learning as "students' behavioral, cognitive, affective, and social involvement in instructional activities" (2006, p. 3). Engagement thus encompasses four dimensions:

1. **Emotional or affective engagement**: Positive affective reactions toward teachers, tasks, and classmates, including enthusiasm, enjoyment, pride, and happiness.
2. **Behavioral engagement**: Active participation in learning activities as demonstrated through focus, concentration, absorption, persistence, and repeated effort.
3. **Cognitive engagement**: Mental investment in learning, effortful strategy use, goal strivings, and deep thinking, evident in students' work in progress and the traces they leave behind.

4. **Social engagement**: Welcoming and active exchange of ideas and work of peers in an interdependent collaborative writing environment (Johnson & Johnson, 2009).

Engagement across all four dimensions is actively supported through the use of authentic writing and reading tasks. Authentic work characterizes "tasks that are considered meaningful, valuable, significant, and worthy of one's effort, in contrast to those considered nonsensical, useless, contrived, trivial, and therefore unworthy of effort" (Newmann et al., 1992, p. 23). By connecting to the "real world" beyond school, such tasks offer students a sense of purpose and ownership (Newmann et al., 1996; Roelofs & Terwel, 1999), thereby directly addressing the 21st-century writing paradox. In the AILIT project, the central idea is to make such authentic work possible by offering an authentic audience to the student writers, and authentic texts written by students in other countries to the student readers and editors, as explained in the following section.

THE AILIT PLATFORM

In order to scaffold motivation for reading and writing as presented in the previous chapter, we built the AILIT platform, where students can write and read what other students wrote. Some features of the platform were decided before the project proposal was submitted. After the project started, all participants gathered in a workshop to collaborate on the ideas and plan the work. The platform was built based on the results of that workshop. We consider the platform to be a pedagogical intervention exploring how AI can be used to scaffold writing.

The platform consists of different modules:

Write module (Figure 6.1): Students can write texts in a writing box, entering any text they like. The teacher can give them specific writing assignments or ask them to write freely. There are also two kinds of "AI help" in this module. When students finish writing, they click "ready to publish". They are then provided with several AI-generated images based on their writing. They can select one to become the "cover image" for their text. The text is then sent to the student's teacher for approval before publication.

Review module (Figure 6.2): Students can review machine-translated texts written by students in other countries. They receive the text in the same writing box as in the write module and can make any changes they want.

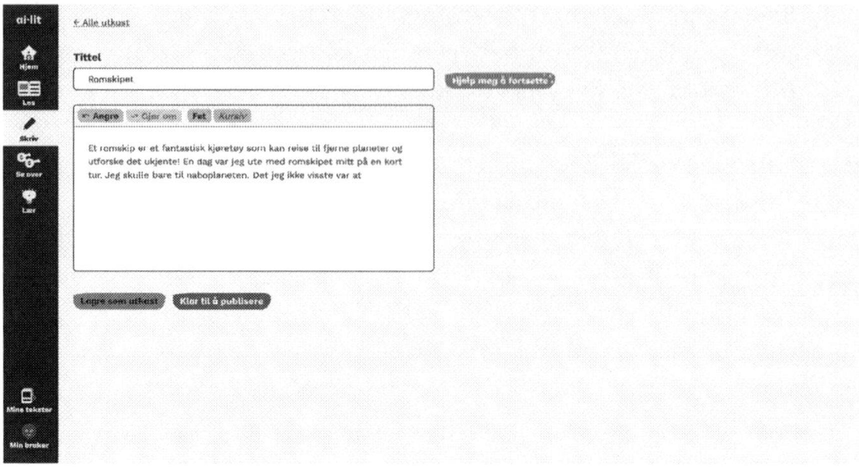

FIGURE 6.1 Write Module.

Note: The write module as seen in the Norwegian version of the AILIT platform.

FIGURE 6.2 Review Module.

Note: The review module as seen in the Catalan version of the AILIT platform. The texts and images are AI-generated for illustration purposes.

After reviewing, they click "ready to publish" and send the text to their teacher for approval. Once approved, the text is published in that language's library and will no longer be changed.

Read module (Figure 6.3): Students can read published texts in their language's library. Recommender systems will select texts for display that they are likely to be interested in.

FIGURE 6.3 Read Module.

Note: The read module as seen in the Portuguese version of the AILIT platform. The texts and images are AI-generated for illustration purposes.

THE MACHINE TRANSLATION

AI-aided machine translation lies at the core of the AILIT platform. When the student's text has been approved by the teacher, it is automatically translated into the other platform languages (Norwegian, English, Catalan, and Portuguese). The system uses Microsoft's Azure OpenAI Service and prompts GPT 4.0 to translate the text. The translated texts are then sent to the libraries of the target languages and marked as unreviewed. Students in the target country can now access this text through the review module where they can make changes to it.

Machine translation is a fairly old technology as AI applications go but one that has improved substantially in recent years. On an AI "generativity" scale, it can be seen as scoring quite low. Although it relies on large language models, just like chatbots, its output remains very close to the input given by the students—the only difference being the change of language. The cognitive work that the AI does for the student is quite removed from the core of the creative act of writing and addresses skills that the student would likely not possess (unless they know the alternate language). In this sense, the technology does not interfere with the communicative aspect of writing. The process maintains a human writer and a human reader. This AI implementation can therefore in many ways be considered a fruitful cooperation between human and machine.

At the same time, as the saying goes, "translation is treason". Any translator faces ethical dilemmas vis-à-vis the original writer, and these may be exacerbated in the case where the treacherous translator is a machine translating the work of a child. The machine translator may, for example, misrepresent the child's intentions in ways a human translator would not. It may also "flatten" the language in the translated text. Biases in the language model may result in translation choices that are not the best for making the text an authentic one in the target language. This shortcoming of the language model can however be seen as a pedagogical opportunity. The machine "needs help" from children to make the translation authentic. The fruitful cooperation between human and machine is not only between writer and translator then but also between translator and reviewer in the target language. Working on the machine translations is a high value formative literacy experience for the students, different from both writing their own texts and simply reading other students' texts. Through editing the translated text, they engage in text work that is similar to some aspects of how text work happens in life outside school. In addition, this experience promotes AI literacy by giving students a hands-on experience with the strengths and shortcomings of machine translations.

In summary, the machine translations permit the texts to travel across geographical and linguistic borders, thereby giving students an authentic audience as writers. As readers, the translations provide students with authentic texts written by peers in other countries. This "exotic" character of the texts may increase motivation for reading. Reading texts from other countries can also potentially motivate young students to learn more about the countries and people who generated the original text. The texts can also serve as building blocks for intercultural discussions and promote intercultural awareness and competence.

THE RECOMMENDER SYSTEM

The other core AI feature is a recommender system that suggests texts to the students to be read or reviewed, based on the students' personal writing interests. This is achieved through a three-step process:

1. **Identifying popular topics**: Initially, the focus is set on five topics. Only texts published in English (either original or translated) are selected. Using the BERTopic topic modeling module in Python (Grootendorst, 2022), the five most common topics are identified.

BERTopic is a topic modeling method that utilizes transformers and c-TF-IDF to build dense clusters. This method finds easily interpretable topics while keeping important terms in the topic descriptions. It fits models on a set of texts, generates topics, and returns the probabilities and topics per document. The algorithm is further restricted to identifying topics present in at least five texts. N-grams of up to three words (i.e., trigrams) are allowed when clustering the data. Each text relates to each of the resulting topics using probabilities (e.g., how likely is it that text A is about topic B).

2. **Associating topics with each student**: Knowing which topics are most likely for each text, the AILIT platform can identify favorite topics for each student. This match improves with every additional text a student contributes to the platform. Assuming a student has written three texts, the platform identifies the student's favorite topics by considering all topic probabilities per text, again resulting in five probabilities (one per topic) associated with each student.
3. Recommending texts to students: In the read and review modules, students interact with the recommender system, which displays texts that match their interests. The platform ensures that students do not see their own texts or texts they have previously interacted with. Moreover, the platform not only provides texts associated with the student's favorite topic but also introduces some variety from other texts.

The recommender system in the AILIT platform is designed to aid the goal of increasing writing interest and engagement for its users. The system draws its knowledge about a student from the student's own learning products, following a data-driven approach to learning content personalization. Students are less likely to "switch off" or leave the platform, simply because the offered learning content is tailored to their individual interests.

While this tailoring of learning content can be advantageous, there are also some challenges to consider. The main challenge when using recommender systems in educational contexts is that personalizing the learning content too much can lead to a very biased and limited scope of content that is offered to a user. Without some kind of counterbalancing, the student could be left gazing into an "AI mirror" (Vallor, 2024) where their own preferences are constantly reflected back to them. In the context of primary education, it is particularly important that students should also be urged to explore different concepts, or in this case texts on a variety of topics.

In addition, learning is more likely to take place in the zone of proximal development (Vygotsky, 1978). This means that the learning content offered to the student should be challenging, but not too challenging. In its current form, the AILIT recommender system does not yet consider the writing and reading abilities of the students. This may cause a mismatch between a student's abilities and the level of the recommended texts. Like in topic-based recommendation, this mismatch could lead to decreased motivation and engagement, which in turn affects learning. In contrast, a match in student ability and text complexity can further increase motivation and engagement.

THE "AI HELP" FEATURES

In addition to these two core AI features, other ways of using AI to scaffold writing emerged in the development workshop, labeled collectively as "AI help".

Two of these features are based on text generation with GPT 4.0. One is a button marked "help me start". If the student clicks it, they will be prompted to answer the question "What would you like to write about?" Based on their answer, the model will generate a few sentences to start the text. These phrases are then inserted into the writing box as the start of the text—where the students can modify them as they wish or delete them. The other text generation feature is a button marked "help me continue". When the student has already written a certain amount of text in the write module, they can click this button to get the model to produce a few sentences to continue their text. The output is meant as an inspiration, not to be copied directly into the text. It is shown to the right of the writing box and must be typed in manually. Both of these features are scaffolds in the sense of Wood et al. (1976), both by reducing the students' degrees of freedom, controlling frustration, and serving as demonstration. They reduce the degrees of freedom (and control frustration) by proposing a way to start the text (avoiding the "fear of the blank page") or to continue it (helping the student who is "stuck").

From the myriad possibilities available to the student at the start of their writing, or in the middle of the process, the model selects one and presents it to the student to accept, reject, or modify. Here they serve a traditional function of writing scaffolds, like writing frames (e.g., Lewis & Wray, 1996). What the AI adds to such traditional scaffolds is the dynamic interaction with the students' writing. The proposals from the generative model are responses to what the students wrote so far ("help me continue") or to the topics they proposed ("help me start"). As such, they constitute feedback on the students' initiatives.

These features also *demonstrate* how solving the problem of writing a phrase can be done by showing a product. This is more problematic for the student's learning. Contrary to how demonstration works in the account of Wood et al. (where the learner imitates what the teacher demonstrates), the student may here simply "take" the model's solution. If the student accepts the model's propositions wholesale, they will miss a learning opportunity, because it implies the model doing the cognitive work *for* the student.

This is also a problem from the perspective of literacy as communication, as it will introduce a non-human element into the text that is published. That text will then have been co-written by the student and the model, blurring the human authenticity of the text. The reader will not know the part of the human and the part of the machine in the production of the text.

The final "AI help" feature is the generation of a "cover image" for the student's text. When the student clicks "ready to publish", the system uses GPT 4.0 to generate a summary of the student's text. This summary, along with the instruction "illustrated in a children's fantasy book style, without any text", is sent to DALL-E 3. The resulting image is presented to the student, who can accept it or request a different one.

This image generation serves multiple purposes: It acts as a reward for completing the text. It provides visual feedback on the student's writing. It potentially makes the text more appealing to readers. While this feature can motivate students and enhance the visual appeal of their work, it also presents a dilemma. If the goal is to scaffold the entire process of creating multi-modal texts, having AI generate the images means students miss out on developing important visual literacy and creative skills.

ETHICAL CHALLENGES AND CONSIDERATIONS

Piloting any educational intervention with children requires careful consideration of ethical principles (Alderson & Morrow, 2020). An intervention involving novel AI tools and collaborators across multiple nations further deepens the level of ethical attention required. Aligned with the increased attention given to the use of AI in education, there is a growing awareness of the need to adequately weigh the ethical complexities of such innovations. Jobin et al.'s (2019) review of international guidelines on the general ethical use of AI identified 11 principles, including the need for transparency, justice and fairness, non-maleficence, responsibility, and privacy. Extending this review to focus specifically on the ethical use of AI in school settings, Adams et al. (2023) noted the need to focus on four additional principles: (1) pedagogical appropriateness (the extent to which it advances or diminishes educational goals), (2) children's rights (e.g., how developmentally appropriate assent is acquired), (3) AI literacy (how children's own understanding of AI is developed), and (4) teacher well-being (consideration of how the use of AI alters teacher work practices).

Extended collaboration, preparation, and review ensured that high ethical standards were maintained during the project. For instance, a joint data controller agreement was put in place to ensure transparency and protocols around the use of children's data. The project was subjected to the ethical review protocols expected of each of the partner institutions. In Dublin City University, an extensive ethical protocol was subjected to full ethics committee review. This protocol explicitly detailed how AI would be used (e.g., the prompts used when communicating with the underlying OpenAI models). The protocol incorporated plain language statements for school management, teachers, parents, and children that explicitly detailed how and why AI would be used. These statements were tailored to ensure they were age appropriate and children provided individual assent to their participation.

Procedures were put in place to ensure that children's contributions to the project would not jeopardize their privacy. This meant that children adopted "nicknames" or pseudonyms that would be known only to them and their teachers when using the AILIT platform. A failsafe was exercised to ensure that teachers approved all contributions to the platform; texts that inadvertently provided sensitive or personal information would be screened out by teachers prior to being made more widely available. The nature of the AILIT project is such that ongoing tweaks and modifications will be needed throughout its operation to ensure that educational goals (e.g., sustaining motivation) are weighed against challenges (e.g., excessive "offload" of writing to AI), ensuring that the project not only ensures non-maleficence but also provides genuine benefits for its young users.

TRYING IT OUT

The platform was tested informally in spring 2024 at the schools in Norway, Catalonia, and Portugal, to gather initial impressions on how students would respond to it. Based on these insights, the design will be adapted for the final data collection. The texts written by students during these trials will serve as a training dataset for the development of recommender algorithms to be implemented in the final version, helping to overcome the cold-start problem. The recommender systems were not implemented in the trial version.

Norway

In Norway, approximately 250 students aged 9–12 years (fourth, fifth, and sixth grades) tested the platform on a single day. We first gathered the students in a large amphitheatre to show them how the platform worked and gave them a mission: write whatever you want, and use the "AI help" if you wish. The students then went to their classrooms and performed the task, while the researchers and teachers circulated between the classrooms, gathered impressions, and offered assistance.

The students found it exciting and engaging to use the platform. Many wrote more than usual according to their teachers. A teacher showed one of the texts they had approved on the big screen and read it to the class. The student who had written the text seemed proud of his product.

It seemed like most students used the AI feature to get started, and "help me continue" was also widely used. Some "took a shortcut" by using "ctrl-c/v" to paste the output into their text, while others copied "manually" and thus processed the text, presumably learning more from the experience. Some of the students claimed they had an entire text written by AI. The teachers in many of the classes also mentioned that they thought the model wrote too much text for the students.

The image generation feature of the platform garnered significant interest from the students. However, technical limitations leading to slow generation times when many students attempted to create images simultaneously caused some frustration. This highlighted the need for robust infrastructure capable of handling high simultaneous usage.

Content-wise, some students expressed that the AI-generated images were overly benign, particularly when depicting antagonists or monsters in their stories. This feedback points to a potential mismatch between the platform's current image generation parameters and the creative expectations of young writers.

In a subsequent trial focusing on the review and read modules, students expressed enjoyment in reading texts authored by peers from other countries. However, many felt uncertain about how to effectively review these texts, indicating a need for more structured guidance in the peer review process.

Portugal

In Portugal, the platform was tested with a fifth-grade class of 18 students working in pairs. The intervention took place on four different days. On the first day, the topics for the descriptive texts were assigned randomly to the students. After the draw, the students created plans for their respective topics. The next day, they produced a text based on the plans developed in the previous session. On the third day, students entered their texts into the AILIT platform, utilizing the "help me start" feature and selecting AI-generated images to accompany their writing. The final day involved a review process where, following teacher proofreading, students made corrections to their texts before submitting them for final publication.

The students found the introductions generated by "help me start" interesting. However, significant adjustments were needed due to the linguistic norm used by the platform which is Brazilian Portuguese and not European Portuguese. Additionally, even within the Brazilian standard, some inaccuracies were identified. For example, in the expression "Fico ansiosa para mostrar o que sei, mas também fico com medo de esquecer algo" (I'm anxious to show what I know, but I'm also afraid of forgetting something)—the choice of the word "algo" (the closest translation into English is "something") is not appropriate to the discursive context; it is unclear what "algo" refers to. Moreover, the same sentence lacks the unstressed personal pronoun in the proclitic position.

Another aspect worth highlighting was the motivation generated by using the platform. On the one hand, the students felt motivated when they first used it and when they realized that it generated images for their texts. On the other hand, their motivation seemed to wane when they had to correct the suggestions provided by the platform.

At the end of the study, the students were given a post-study questionnaire to gauge the impact of using the platform. The results showed that students felt motivated by the use of a novel resource in their writing activities. They also believed that AILIT helped them to develop their writing, because it gave them many ideas to start writing. They would like to do more writing tasks using this type of platform. Only one student found AILIT challenging to use.

Catalonia

In Catalonia, the AILIT platform was tested with a group of 60 students aged between 9 and 11 years. The results from this trial were particularly encouraging, with several positive aspects observed throughout the process.

One of the most notable features of the platform, as observed in the Catalan trial, was its ability to adapt to the individual writing pace of each student. This adaptive quality fostered an inclusive and equitable classroom environment, allowing students of varying abilities to engage meaningfully with the writing process at their own speed.

The AI features played a crucial role in stimulating students' creativity. By offering topic suggestions and assistance with narrative structuring, the platform encouraged students to explore their imaginations more freely. This resulted in a diverse range of interesting and original pieces of writing, demonstrating how AI can be leveraged to encourage creative thinking and personal expression.

Engagement levels during the writing activity were notably high. Elements such as the "cover image" generation made students more committed and motivated to actively participate in the task. The increase in motivation was reflected in greater involvement and effort by the students throughout the writing process.

One of the most enriching aspects of the platform was the opportunity for sharing and reading texts from students of other countries. This feature allowed students to encounter different perspectives and writing styles, broadening their worldview. The texts were translated into Catalan, which facilitated understanding while still allowing students to appreciate cultural and linguistic diversity. This exchange fostered a sense of global connection and respect for other cultures, adding an invaluable dimension to the educational experience.

The AI-generated images proved to be a point of particular interest and learning for the students.

In summary, the trials of the AILIT platform across these three diverse settings provided valuable insights into its potential as an educational tool.

Students showed improvements in their writing and were motivated. The platform demonstrated its capacity to engage students, stimulate creativity, and foster cross-cultural understanding. However, it also highlighted areas for improvement, such as the need for better localization of AI-generated content and more structured support for peer review processes. These findings will be instrumental in refining the platform for its full implementation, ensuring it can effectively meet the diverse needs of students and educators across different linguistic and cultural contexts.

CONCLUSION

The development and testing of the AILIT platform across schools in Norway, Catalonia, and Portugal has yielded valuable insights into the potential of AI-assisted writing in multicultural educational contexts. Students predominantly found the platform highly engaging, with this engagement stemming from multiple factors. The prospect of an international audience reading their texts served as a significant motivator, while the ability to generate images based on their writing added an exciting visual dimension to the process. Many students also appreciated the AI-assisted writing support, which provided helpful scaffolding, particularly at the start of their writing process. Moreover, the novelty of engaging with a different kind of writing assignment was inherently motivating for many participants. However, the use of generative AI, particularly for text generation, presented both opportunities and challenges. In some instances, these features became quite dominant, potentially overshadowing the main purpose of the platform: the sharing of texts across borders. Many teachers observed that AI sometimes performed too much of the work for the students, potentially limiting learning opportunities. This highlights the need for careful calibration of AI assistance to ensure it enhances rather than replaces student effort and learning. Despite these challenges, the platform successfully facilitated the sharing of texts across different countries and languages, promoting intercultural awareness and competence.

This cross-cultural exchange emerged as one of the most promising aspects of the AILIT project, offering students a unique opportunity to engage with peers from diverse linguistic and cultural backgrounds.

The trials also revealed important technical and cultural considerations. While popular, the image generation feature highlighted the need for robust technical infrastructure to support simultaneous use by many students.

Slow response times due to high demand sometimes led to frustration, underscoring the importance of scalability in educational technology. Additionally, the importance of considering linguistic variations and cultural contexts in AI-generated content became evident. For instance, the differences between Brazilian and European Portuguese in AI-generated text highlighted the need for localization and cultural sensitivity in educational AI applications.

LOOKING AHEAD

Looking ahead, several key areas for refinement have been identified. In the final version of the platform, the text generation features will be either removed or adapted to better align with the concept of scaffolding. We are considering proposing writing frames instead of finished texts, or asking questions to prompt student reflection about their texts instead of providing ready-made answers. These approaches aim to maintain the supportive aspect of AI while ensuring that students remain actively engaged in the writing process.

There is also a need to develop clearer guidelines and support for students when reviewing texts from other countries, enhancing the peer review process. This will not only improve the quality of feedback but also deepen students' engagement with texts from different cultural contexts. Technical improvements will focus on addressing both the limitations and content concerns of the image generation feature to make it more effective and engaging. We aim to strike a balance between child-friendly content and the creative expressions desired by students.

The implementation of recommender systems, which were not included in the test version, will be informed by the texts generated during these trials. This feature has the potential to enhance the platform's ability to suggest relevant reading material to students, further personalizing the learning experience and potentially increasing engagement with diverse texts.

Throughout this process of refinement, ongoing attention to ethical issues, including privacy, data protection, and the appropriate use of AI in educational contexts, will remain a priority. The AILIT project will continue to navigate the complex ethical landscape of AI in education, ensuring that the platform's development aligns with best practices and regulatory requirements. This includes maintaining strict protocols for data handling and continuously assessing the impact of AI features on student learning and well-being.

As the project moves forward, we plan to conduct a more systematic investigation to disentangle the relative contributions of different factors to student engagement. This will help in fine-tuning the platform to maximize its educational benefits while mitigating potential drawbacks. Our goal is to create a more robust and educationally sound platform that harnesses the power of AI to create authentic writing situations while preserving the essential role of student creativity and effort in the writing process.

Ultimately, the AILIT platform shows promise in creating a novel, engaging environment for literacy development that spans linguistic and cultural boundaries. By carefully balancing AI assistance with student autonomy and by fostering genuine cross-cultural communication, the platform has the potential to make a significant contribution to literacy education in an increasingly interconnected and technologically advanced world. As we continue to refine and develop this tool, we remain committed to the core goal of enhancing student engagement in writing while ensuring meaningful and equitable learning experiences for all participants.

The journey of the AILIT project thus far has demonstrated both the exciting possibilities and the complex challenges of integrating AI into literacy education. As we move forward, we are guided by the belief that technology, when thoughtfully implemented, can open new avenues for learning, creativity, and global understanding. The continued development of the AILIT platform represents not just an advancement in educational technology but a step toward a more connected, literate, and empathetic global community of young learners.

ACKNOWLEDGMENT

This work was co-funded by the Erasmus+ Programme of the European Union.

REFERENCES

Adams, C., Pente, P., Lemermeyer, G., & Rockwell, G. (2023). Ethical principles for artificial intelligence in K-12 education. *Computers and Education: Artificial Intelligence*, *4*, 100131. https://doi.org/10.1016/j.caeai.2023.100131

Alderson, P., & Morrow, V. (2020). *The ethics of research with children and young people: A practical handbook* (2nd ed.). SAGE. https://doi.org/10.4135/9781529682694

Boscolo, P., & Gelati, C. (2019). Motivating writers. *Best practices in writing instruction* (3rd ed.; pp. 51–78). Guilford Press.

Grootendorst, M. (2022). BERTopic: Neural topic modeling with a class-based TF-IDF procedure. *arXiv preprint arXiv:2203.05794*. https://doi.org/10.48550/arXiv.2203.05794

Hidi, S., Magnifico, A. M., & Renninger, K. A. (2023). Students developing as writers: How and why interest makes a difference. In *The Routledge international handbook of research on writing* (pp. 477–492). Routledge. https://doi.org/10.4324/9780429437991

Hidi, S., & Renninger, K. A. (2006). The four-phase model of interest development. *Educational Psychologist, 41*(2), 111–127. https://doi.org/10.1207/s15326985ep4102_4

Jobin, A., Ienca, M., & Vayena, E. (2019). The global landscape of AI ethics guidelines. *Nature Machine Intelligence, 1*(9), 389–399. https://doi.org/10.1038/s42256-019-0088-2

Johnson, D. W., & Johnson, R. T. (2009). An educational psychology success story: Social interdependence theory and cooperative learning. *Educational Researcher, 38*, 365–379. https://doi.org/10.3102/0013189X09339057

Lewis, M., & Wray, D. (1996). *Writing frames: Scaffolding children's non-fiction writing in a range of genres*. Reading and Language Information.

Lutz, S. L., Guthrie, J. T., & Davis, M. H. (2006). Scaffolding for engagement in elementary school reading instruction. *Journal of Educational Research, 100*(1), 3–20. https://doi.org/10.3200/JOER.100.1.3-20

Newmann, F., Marks, H. M., & Gamoran, A. (1996). Authentic pedagogy and student performance. *American Journal of Education, 104*(4), 280–312. www.jstor.org/stable/1085433

Newmann, F., Wehlage, G., & Lamborn, S. (1992). The significance and sources of student engagement. In F. Newmann (Ed.), *Student engagement and achievement in American secondary schools* (pp. 11–39). Teachers College Press.

Renninger, K. A., Bachrach, J. E., & Hidi, S. E. (2019). Triggering and maintaining interest in early phases of interest development. *Learning, Culture and Social Interaction, 23*, 100260. https://doi.org/10.1016/j.lcsi.2018.11.007

Roelofs, E., & Terwel, J. (1999). Constructivism and authentic pedagogy: State of the art and recent development in Dutch National Curriculum in secondary education. *Journal of Curriculum Studies, 31*(2), 201–227. https://doi.org/10.1080/002202799183232

Vallor, S. (2024). *The AI mirror: How to reclaim our humanity in an age of machine thinking*. Oxford University Press.

Vygotsky, L. S. (1978). *Mind in society. The development of higher psychological processes*. Harvard University Press.

Wood, D., Bruner, J. S., & Ross, G. (1976). The role of tutoring in problem solving. *Journal of Child Psychology, Psychiatry, & Applied Disciplines, 17*, 89–100.

III

Theoretical Grounding and Future Applications

CHAPTER 7

The Song Need Not Remain the Same

AI Literacies in the Lives of Youth

Christopher Proctor and Ryan M. Rish

With greater and greater frequency, we find ourselves in conversations, meetings, and even invitations for writing where the term artificial intelligence (AI) literacy or AI literacies (often used interchangeably) is named as if it had a commonly shared and stable definition. In the contexts of education policy, teacher education, and research on learning, we are experiencing an urgency driven by funders and popular media to solve the "AI Problem" for (not with) youth. This urgency is predicated on the assumption that AI is transforming everything and poses a potential existential threat. AI literacy is seen as a form of power and control; providing AI literacy (to those assumed not to have it) will allow people to regain control over their lives, protect themselves from AI, earn a living, and participate fully in society.

The current wave of urgency around AI education in the United States results from the confluence of US science policy and popular excitement following the widespread availability of generative AI tools. Two of the National Science Foundation's Ten Big Ideas (n.d.) guiding research investment were the "Future of Work at the Human-Technology Frontier" and "Harnessing the Data Revolution," both of which have come to fruition in the recent progress of AI technologies (U.S. National Science Foundation,

DOI: 10.1201/9781003510635-11

n.d.). The President's Council of Advisors on Science and Technology, which guides national science priorities, released a report on AI in 2024. The National Science Foundation issued two "Dear Colleague" letters in 2023, each introducing grant funding in AI education. Meanwhile, popular awareness of AI has exploded in the last several years. Although machine learning technologies have been invisibly incorporated into our lives for decades, the broader public became aware of the power of generative AI in the last several years through the release of generative applications such as Midjourney and ChatGPT.

Education has been a major emphasis of AI-related scientific policy and popular media coverage. The rapidly growing body of research on AI education has largely embraced "literacy" as a framing for what needs to be learned about AI. An "AI literacy framework for families" (Druga et al., 2023) has been proposed; theoretical articles have conceptualized AI literacy (e.g., Ng et al., 2021); a workshop at the leading conference on human–computer interaction asked "What is AI literacy?" (Long et al., 2023); and a literature review was published on AI literacy in K12 education (Casal-Otero et al., 2023). In some of this research, the term "literacy" does little work beyond grouping learning objectives together, e.g., "We refer to this set of competencies as AI literacy" (Long & Magerko, 2020, p. 598); in other cases, AI literacy is either defined or identified as a construct needing definition, often with reference to prior discourses of computational literacy or digital literacy. But despite the prominence of *literacy* as a way of thinking about AI education, it is curious that the emerging field of AI education appears almost wholly unaware of the decades of research in literacy studies which questioned and refined the concept, as well as many preceding cycles in which *literacy* has been proposed for new media, relying on the same assumptions and repeating the same conceptual and practical missteps.

Discourse around AI education emphasizes its newness, but these arguments are a familiar refrain echoing past arguments for how everyone needs to learn a set of skills and practices, packaged as literacy, regardless of individual, social, or historical context. This all too familiar *song* was first named *The Literacy Myth* by Harvey Graff (1979), and though times have changed and we benefit from over 40 years of literacy studies research, we all too easily fall back into the pattern of presuming that literacy by itself has unique and innate power to transform lives and improve society (Graff, 2022).

Evidence of the persistence of this myth is the inherent value that the term "literacy" is perceived to have when ascribed to any set of skills, competencies, or areas of knowledge. We have yet to come across an exhaustive list of areas of study, policy, and commerce that have co-opted the term literacy in a move to elevate its status and potential effectiveness (e.g., financial literacy, mental health literacy, recreational literacy, culinary literacy). As Graff (1979) documented historically, literacy has been synonymous with progress, while the lack of literacy (or illiteracy) represents stagnation and decay. Everything is better with literacy and inferior without. Literacy is framed as a necessary precursor to individual and social progress, so it comes as no surprise that AI literacy is considered essential for progress, lest we become defenseless victims to the infrastructure of computing technologies that shapes our daily lives.

Fortunately, we have worked our way out of the conceptual trappings of the literacy myth many times before, most recently in the shift from computational thinking to computational literacies (Kafai & Proctor, 2021). The goal of this chapter is to retrace the past and remind ourselves of what we have learned and accomplished with over 40 years of literacy studies research. We do so in the hope of establishing some heuristics for our thinking around AI in the lives of youth lest we fall back into the rut of the literacy myth and its seductive promises. We also point to some ways forward for when we find ourselves in interdisciplinary collaboration with colleagues who may be using the terms AI literacy or AI literacies without considering the ideologies and practices that accompany those terms which have ramifications for the lives of youth. In the rest of this chapter, we summarize six lessons from literacy studies and suggest how they could help reframe AI literacies' research and practice.

LITERACIES ARE SITUATED WITHIN AND ACROSS SOCIAL CONTEXTS

Though not in direct response to the historical analysis of the literacy myth provided by Graff (1979), concurrent ethnographic research of literacy by psychologists Scribner and Cole (1981), anthropologists Heath (1983) and Street (1984), and compositionist Brandt (2001), among others, revealed that literacy varied across the social domains of people's lives. Their collective work which came to be known as the New Literacy Studies (NLS) provided a reframing of our understanding of literacy and a set of conceptual tools (i.e., literacy practice, literacy event) to be used in ethnographic investigations of literacy. We emphasize that this research was ethnographic to highlight the significance of people defining the meaning and value of different forms of literacy in their lives, rather than researchers or policymakers. We will return to this significance later in the chapter.

Parallel to Graff identifying the literacy myth historically, Street (2000) working anthropologically referred to that set of assumptions about literacy as the autonomous model. The autonomous model assumes that literacy, or the ability to read and write, has effects on other social and cognitive processes independent of "the social conditions and cultural interpretations of literacy associated with programmes and educational sites for its dissemination" (Street, 2005, p. 417). The problem with the autonomous model of literacy is that it assumes that literacy is a set of reading and writing skills which are powerful regardless of identity and social position—that anyone can acquire, use, and benefit from. The autonomous model of literacy is the basis for arguments that everyone needs a particular form of literacy (e.g., "computer science literacy for all"), and that it is a matter of equity to identify those who need to be provided this form of literacy to transform their lives.

The literacy myth of the autonomous model also has implications in reverse to justify blaming the marginalized when literacy does not come through for them. If everyone can succeed once they have literacy, and literacy is provided to everyone, then everyone can succeed. When someone does not succeed, it follows that they themselves or the social group or category to which they belong are to blame. This backfiring of the autonomous model of literacy can be used as an explicit tool of oppression (e.g., the use of literacy tests to disenfranchise Black voters in the south of the United States), but it can also occur more subtly. For example, one effect of widespread computing education is the production of computationally governable citizens (Williamson, 2015).

In contrast, Street (2000) argued that the ideological model of literacy subsumes the autonomous model by foregrounding the ideologies of particular forms of literacy situated in social arrangements, such as families, schools, faith communities, commerce, and workplaces. (By *ideology*, we mean a system of ideas and beliefs based on lived experience but not a distinct political commitment.) Rather than consider literacy as a universal, neutral set of skills, NLS ethnographic research considered literacy to be multiple situated social practices. NLS ethnographic research revealed the particular significance of forms of literacy in different domains of people lives based on what they were accomplishing, with whom, within what social arrangements, and for what social consequences, as well as the meaning and value they ascribed to those practices. To acknowledge how greatly literacy can vary in use and meaning within and across these differences, NLS scholars began using the plural form of literacies to name multiple and distinct social practices (i.e., literacy practices) defined by the people who enact them.

If we are to build on the NLS foundation with AI literacies (plural), we need to retain a few key characteristics of this framework. First, AI literacies are not an autonomous, neutral set of skills, but rather are varied ideological social practices that have different meaning and value across people, social domains, and institutions. The ninth-grade student using AI to write an essay for their teacher is not enacting the same literacy practice as the religious official using AI to write their sermon or homily for their congregation. They are engaged in different social practices, for different purposes, in relationship to different intuitions and social arrangements, and for different social outcomes. Second, the people enacting the literacy practices are the ones who define the meaning, value, affect, and ideology. We understand what role AI plays within these literacy practices by making inductions from observations and interviews with the people enacting those social practices. Therefore, any conversation about AI literacies needs to begin with specific ethnographic examples. Though, we must also avoid the temptation to hastily extract characteristics from those examples and render them as a neutral and universal set of skills and habits of mind. A few current framings of AI literacy adopt this ethnographic stance (e.g., Druga et al, 2023), but most put forward their own prescriptive framing of what skills and practices should be adopted.

LITERACIES VARY WITHIN AND ACROSS POWER RELATIONS

Beyond recognizing the existence of multiple literacies, we should recognize that they operate in the context of power relations which enable and constrain participants' ability to enact them, inform the willingness of others and institutions to validate and sanction them, and shape the value which is attributed to their enactment in any given social context. NLS research foregrounds how ideology shapes literacy practices within and across social domains in people's lives. For example, schools, and in particular English Language Arts classrooms in the United States, often operate within an assimilationist ideology that sanction particular literacy practices (e.g., standard English, essayist prose) and marginalize others as deficient, constituting linguistic injustice (e.g., Baker-Bell, 2020). Street and Street (1991) characterize this marginalization of literacy practices and the people who enact them as "pedagogization," or the rendering of unsanctioned literacy practices as noncomplementary with school-sanctioned literacy practices (e.g., Heath, 1983) with a deficit perspective (McCarthey, 2000) and/or considering unsanctioned literacy practices as "inferior attempts at the real thing, to be compensated for by enhanced schooling" (Street & Street, 1991, p. 143). Youth are then caught up in institutions, wherein literacy practices and the people who enact them are valued and treated differently based on how commensurate their literacies are with those sanctioned by the institution (e.g., school). Since U.S. schools tend to reflect white, middle-class values and social practices, those students whose literacy practices are situated in white, middle-class social domains are valued and regarded differently from their peers whose literacy practices may be situated in more diverse social domains.

When enacting literacy practices, people negotiate among the ideologies that frame the literacy practices they *bring along* with them and the ones that others are attempting to *bring about* in the situation (Goff & Rish, 2020). Sometimes, the relationships between the ideologies people are negotiating among are not compatible. For example, two people on a sales call may be negotiating between *zero sum* and *mutual benefit* ideologies; the ELA teacher and their students may be negotiating among *assimilationist* and *pluralist* ideologies, and the religious official writing their sermon or homily may be negotiating among *intolerance* and *acceptance* ideologies within their congregation. Bloome and his colleagues (2000) named possible relationships among literacy practices, including but not limited to: *oppositional*, the out-right rejection of literacy practices as resistance to a dominant cultural group (e.g., Ogbu, 1991); *assimilative*, the adoption of literacy practices to become part of the dominant cultural group (e.g., Guthrie, 1985); and *adaptive*, the recasting of literacy practices so that they are consistent with one's own culture (e.g., Kulick & Stroud, 1991). Youth are engaged daily in these negotiations among literacy practices and the ideologies that frame them within and across the social domains of their lives.

The questions for our consideration of AI literacies are What ideologies are youth negotiating when enacting literacy practices that involve AI? What is the relationship between the AI literacies they *bring along* with them to a social arrangement such as an ELA classroom and the literacy practices the ELA teacher is attempting to support and *bring about* among the students? We may find that there are any number of relationships among the literacy practices involving AI that youth are negotiating, including but not limited to: *adopting, adapting, resisting*, and *refusing*. We fear that AI could become yet another means for supporting assimilationist ideologies in ELA classrooms depending on how the ELA teacher positions and frames the use of AI among youth (e.g., authoritative source, mentor text, genre model, text to be interrogated).

At the same time, generative AI has disrupted some of the mechanisms by which sanctioned literacies are recognized and rewarded. For example, it has become near impossible to catch students passing off AI texts as their own writing. Anyone can now effortlessly produce a properly formatted essay, lab report, or working computer code. This fact fundamentally destabilizes schools' processes of evaluating and sorting students according to their performance of sanctioned literacies and will perhaps also disrupt the role education plays in sorting youth into their later social class positions. The disruption of dominant literacies could create an opening for schools to embrace syncretic ideologies (Gutiérrez, 2014), but there is already an evidence of a reactionary response: increasingly invasive efforts to maintain the status quo through an arms race of monitoring tools to catch students using AI tools.

LITERACIES VARY IN SCALE AND DURABILITY

Social practices mediated by reading, writing, and related semiotic systems (i.e., literacy practices) are defined in part by the extent to which they are shared and mutually recognized by people within and across social domains, as well as the extent to which they are concretized within institutions and related social arrangements. Two people engaged in the same activity may or may not be enacting the same literacy practice. For example, two students in an ELA classroom who are writing a personal essay may attribute different meaning, affect, and value to the literacy practice. One student may report writing the personal essay to earn a grade, in which case the literacy practice may be framed around compliance with the teacher's expectations. Another student may be writing the same personal essay with a relative or a loved one as the primary audience, in which case the literacy practice may be framed around a relationship with the intended audience. In both cases, the students may be expected to comply with particular genre constraints or formulas (e.g., five paragraphs, standard English, first person), in which case they may be using language in ways that are particular to the institution of school. Further, this may not be their first personal essay for them, indicating that the literacy practices they are enacting have a history. However, there is no promise that this literacy practice will continue to be relevant and useful to them once they are no longer writing for a classroom assignment. Last, some characteristics of their literacy practices are deeply concretized as an enduring genre within the institution of schooling (with no indication of widespread change on the horizon) and recognized across a macro scale (i.e., five paragraph personal essay).

For AI literacies among youth, we cannot assume they do or do not have a history of enacting literacy practices with AI. We cannot assume that the way we ask them to consider using AI will be commensurate with their past experiences, if any. Further, any AI literacies that we hope our youth to take up will have to be reconciled with the literacy practices that students *bring along* with them based on their history and the literacy practices that are presently sanctioned and valued by the school. Simply adding AI literacies, however they are defined ideologically and supported by teachers, to a set of school-sanctioned literacy practices provides no guarantee students will adopt them with fidelity and enact them in ways that have durability beyond the social domain of schooling.

Likewise, we cannot assume that any literacy practice has a patterned predictability and durability, both in terms of its history and its future. Some literacy practices are emergent, ephemeral, and fleeting as social arrangements and relationships shift and change. Every day literacy practices are shaped by feeling, affect, embodiment (Pahl & Rowsell, 2020), and take on different characteristics with movement across space and places (Stornaiuolo et al., 2017). A literacy practice that has value in one moment may not in the next, and a literacy practice may be encountered in one context and become more durable over time in a completely different context. We see this often in the lives of youth as they use language and related semiotic systems creatively and not always for reasons that school may consider purposeful or rational (Leander & Boldt, 2012).

NOT ALL PRACTICES ARE DEFINED BY THE TOOL

The identification and naming of literacy practices is significant because in most cases the modifier is considered to be the most essential characteristic of the literacy practice. Some examples include the type of place, urban literacies (Kinloch, 2015); the identity of the people involved, Black immigrant literacies (Smith, 2023); the purpose of the social practices, agitation literacies (Muhammad, 2019); restorative literacies (Wolter, 2021); the ideology of the social practices, social justice literacies (Boyd, 2017), critical literacies (Pandya et al., 2022); and the semiotic systems, multimodal literacies (Albers & Sanders, 2010). Additionally, literacy practices are often named for the tool or mediational means that is used to enact the social practices (e.g., digital literacies). In many cases when the tool is the modifier, literacy is being used within an autonomous model and the term is primarily being co-opted to elevate the status of what we would otherwise call competencies, set of skills, or knowledge. However, if literacies (plural) is being used with a type of mediational means/tool as the modifier, we would expect that it is being framed within an ideological model of literacy (though this is not always the case). The question is: to what extent is the tool the most essential characteristic of the literacy practice?

Using standardized testing as an example, students are often expected to answer multiple choice questions and produce specific genres of writing on an abbreviated timescale (e.g., short answer, extended response). The literacy practices required to be successful on these standardized tests are rehearsed in preparation for the exam, enacted on the day of the exam, and then never used again (unless taking a similar standardized test in the future). The literacy practices of producing the specific genres of writing and filling out the multiple-choice answer sheet only have value within domains where such exams are consequential to the person taking the exam (and the institution that may be rated on the test takers' scores). We might refer to this literacy practice as *test taking literacies* to point to the essential characteristic of the literacy practice (in this case the purpose). However, it would be odd if we named this literacy practice after the tool used, #2 pencil literacies. While it is true that the specific tool is required for enacting this literacy practice, we could argue that it is not the defining characteristic.

Therefore, when considering any literacy practice that involves AI, we should consider the extent to which AI is the defining characteristic. Returning to two earlier examples, using AI may or may not be a defining characteristic for the ninth-grade student writing an essay for their teacher or for the religious leader writing their sermon or homily for their congregation. We need to consider what is revealed and concealed, as well as what is valued and devalued, when we foreground the tool or mediational means as the defining characteristic of the literacy practice under consideration. Framing either of these examples as AI literacies implies that using AI is what matters most in each scenario. If using AI is seen as the essential characteristic of the practice, then the teacher, tool designer, or policymaker (each of whom controls what counts as "using AI") also become the arbiter of which literacy practices are sanctioned and supported.

AVOIDING *A PRIORI* DEFINITIONS OF LITERACIES

In our view, research activity under the banner of New Literacies represents a cautionary tale for AI literacies. Though not their intention, Lankshear and Knobel (2006) provided a definition of New Literacies that was taken up in ways that runs contrary to the ethnographic and anthropologic NLS foundation on which it based. They noticed that new technologies created the potential for literacy practices that differed from those we were accustomed to considering among youth and adults. They defined New Literacies as social practices that involved new technologies but also liberatory new ways of using them, resulting in collective and distributed authority and expertise. Wikis were new ways of writing; the distributed authorship of Wikipedia redefined what counts as evidence and who gets to be an authority. However, the transformative potential of new technologies can easily blunted when they are co-opted into existing scripts (Cuban, 2003), so New Literacies scholars (e.g. Kist, 2005) sought out examples of the practices they imagined, and advocated for the potential of new digital and networked tools.

Because this project was committed to the potential of specific technologies, literacy practices were only relevant to the research when they used certain technologies in certain ways. Such operationalization of an *a priori* definition of a particular literacy practice puts the researcher and the practitioner in a deductive mode where they are seeking out evidence to support their idealized literacy practice. Unanswered is the question whether those same participants in those studies would have named the ontology of their literacy practices as the most significant element to them. In other words, rather than working inductively from an ethnographic perspective that leaves open the question of what are the most essential characteristics of literacy practices to the participants, much New Literacies research went hunting for examples to support their idealized model. The result was often a valuation of the literacy practices being considered based on the extent to which they represented the idealized model: non-example, peripheral case, or paradigmatic case (Lankshear & Knobel, 2006).

Research and practice on AI literacies runs the risk of falling into a comparable pattern of asserting what AI practice should look like rather than learning what works alongside users. This risk is magnified by the recent urgency to teach and research AI. When school systems demand AI literacy but also insist on predefined learning objectives to teach and measure, they implicitly demand the autonomous model of literacy. Meanwhile, a research proposal may feel more focused, with greater potential impact (and thus more likely to be funded), when it specifically defines the kinds of AI use it is looking for and the outcomes which are hypothesized to result.

AGENCY IS SLIPPERY

With traditional print literacies, there was no difficulty in distinguishing the reader or writer from the text. Agency—the capacity to form intentions and the power to act on them—was a property of the reader/writer, whose semiotic action was mediated by text. New media technologies play a more active role in organizing, contextualizing, and interpreting meanings, and therefore complicate the locus of agency. NLS has been particularly interested in how individual and collective agency is mediated by semiotic systems, and how those systems reciprocally shape the possibilities and meanings of literacy practices. Readers and writers have some agency to determine how they will use tools, but tool designers and increasingly the tools themselves are also agentic, shaping tools' use and co-author the resulting meanings.

Post-humanist perspectives on literacy as a social practice have broadened considerations of how agency is distributed in any given social arrangement (Burriss & Leander, 2024). Informed by actor-network theory (Latour, 2005), agency is extended to non-human actors within the social context. Rather than only considering how the design of an object makes some actions easier (affordances) and some actions more difficult (constraints), actor-network theory goes a step further to suggest that objects not only mediate but also "authorize, allow, afford, encourage, permit, suggest, influence, block, render possible, and so on" (Latour, 2005, p. 72). Agency is distributed across people and objects and actions are taken within assemblages of people and objects. Actor-network theory is a particularly helpful theoretical lens for thinking about generative AI, where it is much more difficult to distinguish the reader or writer from the text, and where literacy practices are not only enacted by people but also in part by objects such as AI.

Even though agency may be distributed, we should not consider all actors equal in today's AI-powered assemblages and networks of literacy. People are not passive dupes whose actions are wholly determined by semiotic structures; they are adaptive within situations and prone to take actions based on thoughtful reflection or unpredictable whimsy. Youth, and particularly those growing up in a world that was not built for them, are often particularly adept at repurposing tools in unanticipated ways (Vogel et al., in press). At the same time, however, the agency of AI tools will likely continue to grow as they "read" us (e.g., automatic essay graders, automatic resume evaluators, meeting summary tools) and "write" on our behalf (e.g., chatbots, auto-generated email, AI writers, and programmers) in more and more social situations.

Current framings of AI literacy seldom embrace this complexity, defaulting instead to either an optimistic assumption that AI are tools like any other with agency resting in users, or to a pessimism which sees today's AI as a step toward superintelligence, which threatens human agency or even human existence. Instead, we propose that the ethnographic stance developed by NLS be extended to exploration of how, in each specific situation, humans, computers, and other symbolic systems all participate in meaning-making via flexible and shifting roles. Should humans be granted a special ontological status, with intrinsic rights and dignity? Today it is easy to answer in the affirmative, but it is also easy to imagine a near future where the answer is much murkier.

Finally, we suggest that theories that were developed to account for semiotic agency within human culture (e.g. linguistic anthropology and sociology of language) may be particularly helpful for making sense of the agency of large language models which model and reproduce human discourse. For example, language ideologies (Irvine & Gal, 2000) are cultural ideas that shape how listeners interpret language and perceive speakers. Large language models enact language ideologies they learned from training data when they participate in discourse as listeners and speakers. Social constructs such as race and gender, which we also use to make sense of speakers and their speech, are also reproduced and reenacted by large language models. Further, race and gender are coded into and associated with other variables in algorithms that replicate and intensify hierarchical outputs and discriminatory allocation of access and resources, as well as undue attention, surveillance, and scrutiny (Buolamwini, 2023). Benjamin (2019) named the racial discriminatory aspects of algorithmic bias The New Jim Code. Following, while we acknowledge that people should be granted a larger consideration of agency within assemblages and networks, we are also aware that algorithms and related AI are shaping those social, material, and digital contexts in ways that exacerbate persistent societal inequities and injustices, including discriminatory practices and policies.

LOOKING AHEAD

Each technological revolution of the last 50 years has been met with similar hopes and fears and has been followed by similar proposals for the kind of literacy we need now. We view these as verses with the same refrain of the literacy myth. Our purpose in this chapter has been to trace the origin of the song to which these verse belong, as well as present six lessons learned in response. However, it is easy to imagine how the tired song may repeat itself:

An aspirational model of AI literacy is developed, along with curricula which rely on best practices to ensure consistent outcomes. The model is then incorporated into institutions and policy with the promise that AI literacy will improve people's lives, and with the premise that it is needed because most people are AI illiterate. In schools, AI literacies are taught and assessed from an assimilationist ideology that does not take into consideration the literacy practices and identities youth *bring along* with them. Research then shows an AI literacy gap falling along existing inequities, creating yet another divisive statistic that is used against the most vulnerable and marginalized.

We argue that if the song is *not* to remain the same with AI literacies, then we must begin with considering what people, particularly youth, are doing with AI currently, in classrooms as well as in their daily lives. Without knowing how people are actively and passively using AI to enact social and literacy practices, we are setting ourselves up to repeat past patterns and harms. We imagine a different possible future, within which researchers and practitioners take time to understand how AI is currently being used within the literacy practices of youth, as well as the value, meaning, and affect youth attribute to those practices. Researchers and practitioners work from the understanding that any AI practices they would like to introduce come with ideologies that need to be reconciled with the ideologies of youths' existing everyday literacies. Researchers and practitioners do not expect wholesale adoption and fidelity of the AI literacies they are introducing but rather learn alongside people what is useful and valuable. Researchers and practitioners resist the urgency to standardize and assess AI literacies and avoid the temptation to scale and commercialize related processes and procedures. They allow for the possibility that the AI literacies being introduced may or may not have significance to people's lives outside of the context in which they are being introduced. For example, if AI literacies are solely situated in school-based social contexts and school-sanctioned literacy practices, it should come as no surprise if people do not bring them along to other domains of their lives outside of school.

We recognize that our observations about the history of literacy studies, our arguments about current iterations of AI literacy, and our hopes for how we might avoid perpetuating the literacy myth and its related harms are in tension with dominant practices of education (which insists on specifying what is to be learned a priori, and measuring it accordingly) and positivist research (which expects *a priori* operationalization of constructs and their hypothesized effects). Nonetheless, when we find ourselves in conversations, meetings, and invitations for writing about AI, we will be working steadfastly to change the tune.

REFERENCES

Albers, P., & Sanders, J. (Eds.). (2010). *Literacies, the arts, & multimodality*. National Council of Teachers of English

Baker-Bell, A. (2020). *Linguistic justice: Black language, literacy, identity, and pedagogy*. Routledge.

Benjamin, R. (2019). *Race after technology: Abolitionist tools for the New Jim Code*. Polity.

Bloome, D., Katz, L., Solsken, J., Willett, J., & Wilson-Keenan, J.-A. (2000). Interpellations of family/community and classroom literacy practices. *The Journal of Educational Research*, *93*(3), 155–163. https://doi.org/10.1080/00220670009598704

Boyd, A. S. (2017). *Social justice literacies in the English classroom: Teaching practice in action*. Teachers College Press.

Brandt, D. (2001). *Literacy in American lives*. Cambridge University Press.

Buolamwini, J. (2023). *Unmasking AI: My mission to protect what is human in a world of machines*. Random House.

Burriss, S. K., & Leander, K. (2024). Critical posthumanist literacy: Building theory for reading, writing, and living ethically with everyday artificial intelligence. *Reading Research Quarterly*, 59(4), 560–569. https://doi.org/10.1002/rrq.565

Casal-Otero, L., Catala, A., Fernández-Morante, C., Taboada, M., Cebreiro, B., & Barro, S. (2023). AI literacy in K-12: A systematic literature review. *International Journal of STEM Education, 10*(1), 29. https://doi.org/10.1186/s40594-023-00418-7

Cuban, L. (2003). *Oversold and underused: Computers in the classroom.* Harvard University Press.

Druga, S., Yip, J., Preston, M., & Dillon, D. (2023). The 4 As: Ask, adapt, author, analyze: AI literacy framework for families. In M. Ito, R. Cross, K. Dinakar, & C. Odgers (Eds.), *Algorithmic rights and protections for children* (pp. 193–232). The MIT Press. https://doi.org/10.7551/mitpress/13654.003.0014

Goff, B., & Rish, R. (2020). What's brought along and brought about: Negotiating writing practices in two high school classrooms. *Learning, Culture and Social Interaction, 24,* 100291. https://doi.org/10.1016/j.lcsi.2019.02.016

Graff, H. (1979). *The literacy myth: Literacy and social structure in the nineteenth-century city.* Academic Press.

Graff, H. J. (2022). The new literacy studies and the resurgent literacy myth. *Literacy in Composition Studies, 9*(1), 47–53.

Guthrie, G. P. (1985). *A school divided: An ethnography of bilingual education in a Chinese community.* Erlbaum.

Gutiérrez, K. (2014). Syncretic approaches to literacy learning: Leveraging horizontal knowledge and expertise: Integrative research review. *Literacy Research Association Yearbook, 63, 48–61.*

Heath, S. B. (1983). *Ways with words: Language, life and work in communities and classrooms.* Cambridge University Press.

Irvine, J. T., & Gal, S. (2000). Language ideology and linguistic differentiation. In P. V. Kroskrity (Ed.), *Regimes of language: Ideologies, polities and identities* (pp. 35–84). School of American Research Press.

Kafai, Y. B., & Proctor, C. (2021). A revaluation of computational thinking in K-12 education: Moving towards computational literacies. *Educational Researcher, 51*(2), 146–151.

Kinloch, V. (2015). *Harlem on our minds: Place, race, and the literacies of urban youth.* Teachers College Press.

Kist, W. (2005). *New literacies in action: Teaching and learning in multiple media* (Vol. 75). Teachers College Press.

Kulick, D., & Stroud, C. (1991). Conceptions and uses of literacy in Papua New Guinea village. In B. Street (Ed.), *Cross-cultural approaches to literacy* (pp. 30–61). Cambridge University Press.

Lankshear, C., & Knobel, M. (2006). Sampling "the New" in new literacies. In *The new literacies sampler.* (pp. 2–17). Peter Lang.

Latour, B. (2005). *Reassembling the social: An introduction to actor-network-theory.* Oxford University Press.

Leander, K., & Boldt, G. (2012). Rereading "A Pedagogy of Multiliteracies": Bodies, texts, and emergence. *Journal of Literacy Research*, *45*(1), 22–46. https://doi.org/10.1177/1086296X12468587

Long, D., & Magerko, B. (2020). What is AI literacy? Competencies and design considerations. In *Proceedings of the 2020 CHI conference on human factors in computing systems*. Association for Computing Machinery, (pp. 1–16). https://doi.org/10.1145/3313831.3376727

Long, D., Roberts, J., Magerko, B., Holstein, K., DiPaola, D., & Martin, F. (2023). AI literacy: Finding common threads between education, design, policy, and explainability. In *Extended abstracts of the 2023 CHI conference on human factors in computing systems* (pp. 1–6). https://doi.org/10.1145/3544549.3573808

McCarthey, S. J. (2000). Home–school connections: A review of the literature. *Journal of Educational Research*, *93*(3), 145–153. https://doi.org/10.1080/00220670009598703

Muhammad, G. E. (2019). Protest, power, and possibilities: The need for agitation literacies. *Journal of Adolescent & Adult Literacy*, *63*(3), 351–355.

Ng, D. T. K., Leung, J. K. L., Chu, S. K. W., & Qiao, M. S. (2021). Conceptualizing AI literacy: An exploratory review. *Computers and Education: Artificial Intelligence*, *2*, 100041. https://doi.org/10.1016/j.caeai.2021.100041

Ogbu, J. (1991). Cultural diversity and school experience. In C. Walsh (Ed.), *Literacy as praxis* (pp. 25–51). Ablex.

Pahl, K., & Rowsell, J. (2020). *Living literacies: Literacy for social change*. MIT Press.

Pandya, J. Z., Mora, R. A., Alford, J. H., Golden, N. A., & De Roock, R. S. (2022). *The handbook of critical literacies*. Routledge.

Scribner, S., & Cole, M. (1981). *The psychology of literacy*. Harvard University Press.

Smith, P. (2023). *Black immigrant literacies: Intersections of race, language, and culture in the classroom*. Teachers College Press.

Stornaiuolo, A., Smith, A., & Phillips, N. (2017). Developing a transliteracies framework for a connected world. *Journal of Literacy Research*, *49*(1), 68–91.

Street, B. (1984). *Literacy in theory and practice*. Cambridge University Press.

Street, B. (2000). Literacy events and literacy practices. In M. Martin-Jones & M. Jones (Eds.), *Multilingual literacies: Comparative perspectives on research and practice* (pp. 17–29). John Benjamin.

Street, B. V. (2005). AT LAST: Recent applications of new literacy studies in educational contexts. *Research in the Teaching of English*, *39*(4), 417–423. https://doi.org/10.58680/rte20054482

Street, J. C., & Street, B. V. (1991). The schooling of literacy. In D. Barton & R. Ivanič (Eds.), *Writing in the community* (pp. 106–131). Sage.

United States National Science Foundation. (n.d.). *NSF's 10 Big Ideas*. U.S. National Science Foundation. www.nsf.gov/news/special_reports/big_ideas/human_tech.jsp; www.nsf.gov/news/special_reports/big_ideas/

Vogel, S., Suárez, E., Semel, B., & Proctor, C. (Eds.) (in press). *Learning machines, humans learning: Critical perspectives on languaging in digitally-mediated environments*. de Gruyter Mouton.

Williamson, B. (2015). Educating the smart city: Schooling smart citizens through computational urbanism. *Big Data & Society, July-December*, 1–13. https://doi.org/10.1177/20539517156177

Wolter, D. L. (2021). *Restorative literacies: Creating a community of care in schools*. Teachers College Press.

CHAPTER 8

Building a Future with AI

Entry Points for Reimagining Literacy in Higher Education

Jens Lloyd, Kristen Hawley Turner, Alex Rudniy, and Sandra Jamieson

The future is an ambivalent presence on college campuses. It can be a positive force, the point toward which the efforts of students, faculty, and staff are directed, the destination toward which we are all striving. But it can also be a looming threat, the point at which enrollments drop, funds dry up, and programs decline. The future, then, for better or worse, is ever-present for those of us in higher education, with many of us eager to assert our perspectives about the futures we do (and do not) want to work to support.

The arrival of generative AI into this future-saturated environment has elicited conflicting reactions from faculty. Vee et al. (2023) recently cataloged these responses as (1) "prohibition," (2) "leaning in," (3) "critical exploration," and (4) "a chaotic blending of all the options" (Potential Paths). The first two are stark contrasts, with the former entailing an outright rejection and the latter entailing an eager embrace, while the third encourages students "[to] probe the limits of the technology while learning how to use it." The fourth, though, is what best describes "the current scenario, and the most likely path of the near future" for literacy instruction in higher education. This is a risky response and one that signals tremendous

 DOI: 10.1201/9781003510635-12

uncertainty about literacy in a world where GenAI technologies are increasingly prevalent.

For our purpose in this chapter, we attempt to avert the chaos and promote exploration by reflecting on what we've been experiencing as a cross-disciplinary team of teachers and scholars since the popular advent of GenAI in late 2022. The chaos inevitably stems in part from treating GenAI as an inscrutable force that is exerting a hard-to-define, all-encompassing power over the shape of literacy in our world. In the face of this, we must create entry points that allow us and our students to begin to make sense of this seemingly inscrutable force. These entry points are not domains of knowledge to master but rather lines of inquiry that can lead to better understanding how and why GenAI impacts literacy practices. To that end, we want to consider how a college education can contribute to reimagining literacy in the age of AI by identifying and delineating four entry points: the long history of AI, public discourse surrounding GenAI, expectations for incorporating GenAI into one's own practices, and the impact of new technologies on literacy development. While these do not exhaust all that a college education can contribute to literacy at this important moment, they do indicate the topics that have been among the most persistent and influential for us during this initial period of widespread GenAI use. The entry points span disciplinary boundaries and, thus, invite us to think capaciously about how to help our students navigate their lives with GenAI now and into the future.

We recognize that reimagining literacy must be a broad-based effort encompassing more than just formal educational spaces. Literacy is a field of study characterized by the desire to consider "how literacy is lived" (Rowsell & Pahl, 2015, p. 2) in a range of environments rather than just how it is acquired in school. Still, we feel a distinctive kind of AI-infused literacy can flourish in higher education because, ideally, college curricula permit structured pedagogical encounters that help students develop the relevant skills while also questioning and contextualizing the uses of these skills. If the future is to be increasingly populated by AI technologies, then the issue is not bringing our students into contact with AI but bringing our curricula into alignment with the world our students already inhabit.

But it's about more than embracing the curricular opportunities presented by GenAI; it's about appreciating and amplifying how literacy exists in the lives of college students. This is a key insight of a recent working paper published by a joint task force of the Modern Language Association (MLA) and the Conference on College Composition and Communication (CCCC), which argued that "AI cannot simply be used in colleges and universities as it might be in other organizations for efficiency or other purposes" (2023, p. 4). Why? Because literacy in college—the reading and writing that students do for courses and, also, for co-curricular and extracurricular purposes—is not primarily a productivity-oriented endeavor. Writing in college composition courses, for instance, is often about more than completing assignments in the most efficient fashion. Instead, literacy for college students helps "to support [their] intellectual and social development and to foster exploration and creativity" (p. 4). Accordingly, we think it would be a mistake if higher education attempted to mimic the approaches to AI that exist in other settings, especially work or professional settings. Attempts to reimagine literacy in higher education should aim to enable students to live in the world they inhabit and, also, to play an active role in constructing the kind of futures they want for themselves.

The emphasis on actively constructing the future is critical to what we hope to accomplish in this chapter. At the core of much of the discussion surrounding AI are concerns about our ability to influence the future. Do we imagine the future as something rushing toward us and, thus, something largely beyond our control? Or is the future something we're approaching and, thus, something we can play a role in actively constructing?

Facer (2011) offered opposing terms—future-proofing and future-building—for grasping what's at stake in how we choose to conceptualize the future. Facer challenged the troubling notion that education is best when it serves prevailing economic and technological imperatives and insisted, instead, that we think of technology and society as tied together in a "process of co-production" (p. 7). In other words, we have more power than we might think with regards to adopting and adapting to new technologies such as GenAI. The future is not dictated by technological developments and "our concern as educators when we inquire into the future … should not simply be one of preparing ourselves for an inevitable future and attempting to 'future-proof' our systems" (Facer, 2011, p. 10). Rather, based on the affordances of new technologies, we can make choices about what we want the future to look and feel like—and take a stance of future-building.

Surely, there's comfort to be found in predicting a particular future and planning for that future to come to fruition. But

> *we need to remember that the future is not set in stone, that technology is not some magical force driving us down one inevitable path, and that education is also a force to be reckoned with when it comes to shaping progressive futures.*
>
> *(Facer, 2011, p. 10)*

Facer's words, written over a decade ago, well before the popular advent of GenAI, remind us that, in this moment, we can avoid a form of instrumentality that views GenAI as just a new tool and formal education as merely a means to equip students to use that tool. Instead, drawing upon Facer's future-building approach, as well as the social epistemic orientation of literacy studies, we can recognize GenAI as an emerging part of our reality and formal education as one prominent means of helping our students and, for that matter, ourselves in negotiating the uses and applications of this technology.

Reimagining literacy in the age of AI through the lens of future-building places the present within a narrative of change that links it to the past. So, rightfully, the past is where our reimagining begins. Contrary to perceiving GenAI as an entirely novel phenomenon of our digital age, Entry Point #1 delves into humanity's long history with AI to help students and faculty contextualize their engagement with GenAI. Turning from the past to the present for Entry Point #2, we open a line of inquiry into how popular discourse about GenAI reveals a persistent set of harmful assumptions that limit the potential of literacy instruction. Just as there is much to be gleaned from scrutinizing expectations embedded in popular discourse, Entry Point #3 encourages students to think critically about their own expectations and to recognize that GenAI will not always be the ideal partner for their literacy practices. Finally, with Entry Point #4, we reiterate the intricate connections between literacy and technology—connections that are especially important to reiterate *now* if we hope to implement pedagogies that can meet the moment, which can ensure that higher education plays a vital role in shaping the age of AI.

ENTRY POINT #1: HUMANITY'S LONG HISTORY WITH AI

A future-building approach encourages us to see the future as open and flexible, but also rooted in decisions made in the past. As we seek entry points to the seemingly inscrutable force that is GenAI, the history of human attempts to create and control artificial intelligence presents opportunities for discussing with students the ways in which our contemporary efforts are inspired, influenced, and even constrained by what has come before. Indeed, students will probably be fascinated to learn from science historians that humanity's path to AI stretches back at least to ancient times with examples like the mechanical "tripods" in the *Iliad* of Homer, the ivory statue Galatea brought to life by the goddess Venus, and the Talmud's artificial creatures called golems, and extends through the Renaissance to the artificial life described in *Leviathan* by Thomas Hobbes (Buchanan, 2005; Nilsson, 2009). Exploring history, whether ancient or more contemporary, is a way for students to learn how humans have already imagined, theorized, developed, and implemented AI and to contemplate how their own engagement with GenAI fits into this longer-than-expected continuum.

While older historical examples might surprise students, the mid-20th century is a contemporary focal point that offers many significant paths for students to explore. The roots of modern AI may be traced to a 1941 science fiction story by Isaac Asimov that outlined the Three Laws of Robotics (Pez, n.d.). Asimov's imaginative work motivated numerous scholars across the fields of AI, robotics, and computer science. Wiener (1949), whose cybernetic theory posited that principles of feedback loops and control mechanisms could explain the behavior of both living organisms and machines, hypothesized that one day computers might exceed the abilities of chess grandmasters and would learn from experiences. Turing (1950) explored the feasibility of computer intelligence comparable to human cognition, introducing "the Turing test" to assess whether a machine can process information, interpret language, and communicate with humans in a way that is indistinguishable from human behavior (Haenlein & Kaplan, 2019). The term "Artificial Intelligence" was first introduced in 1956 by John McCarthy at the Dartmouth Summer Research Project on Artificial Intelligence that brought together experts from diverse fields and marked the beginning of AI as a distinct field (Stone et al., 2016), and, in the following years, AI experienced a significant expansion primarily fueled by grants provided by DARPA, the Defense Advanced Research Projects Agency (Brachman et al., 2020).

The 1960s witnessed a series of notable AI developments that can help students better contextualize and evaluate today's advances. One significant work from this period was the Symbolic Automatic INTegrator, a computer program for solving elementary symbolic integration problems commonly encountered in freshman calculus courses (Slagle, 1963). Following that, the ANALOGY program demonstrated the ability to solve geometric analogy questions similar to those on IQ tests (Evans, 1968), while the Mac Hack Six program competed against humans in chess tournaments and earned itself a chess rating (Greenblatt, et al., 1967). A major milestone was the creation of ELIZA in 1966. Often regarded as the first chatbot, ELIZA used scripts to imitate various conversation styles, with a Rogerian psychotherapist being the most famous (Bassett, 2019). Versions of ELIZA are available online and, thus, provide a hands-on opportunity for students to delve into the past of AI.

However, as a warning for contemporary students that technological progress is not always linear, this wave of innovation was soon met with significant challenges. The first AI winter, spanning approximately from 1974 until 1981, was caused by technological limitations and economic downturn, resulting in a reduction in government funding in the United States and United Kingdom and stagnation in AI research. Despite these obstacles, advancements in AI continued to emerge (Shin, 2019). The 1970s witnessed several significant theoretical developments, including case grammars, a linguistic theory focusing on the syntactic and semantic roles of nouns in sentences (Fillmore, 1975). The 1980s saw the widespread adoption of ontologies, which were used to represent entities, ideas, and events, along with their properties and the relationships between them (Gruber, 1995). During the same period, expert systems that employed rule-based approaches and decision trees to simulate the decision-making processes of human experts emerged as the most commercially successful AI applications (Quinlan, 1987).

Recent decades have been transformative in AI history and provide students with recognizable and relatable instances of how AI impacts daily life, including literacy practices. The 1990s was marked by significant advancements in Recurrent Neural Networks and the introduction of Long Short-Term Memory networks, which have become foundational to modern AI, particularly in the domains of natural language processing, speech recognition, and sequence prediction (Chauvin & Rumelhart, 1995; Hochreiter & Schmidhuber, 1997). In the 2000s, significant progress was made in developing statistical language models, machine translation, and word embeddings—dense vector representations of words capturing their semantic meanings (Bengio et al., 2003; Koehn, 2010). The 2010s witnessed an explosive growth in AI technologies. These included Word2Vec and GLoVe for word representation where word similarities could be computed by applying mathematical operations to numerical vectors (Mikolov et al., 2013; Pennington et al., 2014). Advances in computer vision included YOLO models for object detection (Redmon et al., 2016), and GenAI technologies such as Generative Adversarial Networks and Variational Autoencoders that allowed the creation of visual content from text descriptions or other types of input (Goodfellow et al., 2014; Kingma & Welling, 2014).

This brings us to the present decade, one defined by the state-of-the-art development of large language models (LLMs), including OpenAI's GPT series of increasing size and capability, which concluded with GPT-3 in 2020 and GPT-4 in 2023. LLMs applications extend from text generation and advanced dialogue systems to translation, summarization, writing computer code, and beyond (Brown et al., 2020; Gallifant et al., 2024). Advances in computer vision include DALL-E and Stable Diffusion, models based on different approaches for generating detailed images from text (Ramesh et al., 2021; Rombach et al., 2022). While these developments will be familiar to students, recognizing them as part of the most recent phase of humanity's long history with AI encourages students to appreciate that their use of AI emerges from this foundation. The future can remain open and flexible, but it cannot be severed from what has come before. Whether creative spark or necessary context, the historical examples documented in this section might very well help students decide what comes next in this long history with AI. It's a history we are all inheriting, and there are plenty of resources from the past to study as we go about the work of integrating GenAI into our present and future.

ENTRY POINT #2: POPULAR DISCOURSE ABOUT GENAI

Without a grounding in history, it is easy to forget that GenAI did not spring forth fully formed at the end of 2022 when ChatGPT burst into the public consciousness via numerous clickbait headlines. This unfortunate introduction led to divergent responses that require unpacking if we are to build the futures we want with AI. There is a need to interrogate the language faculty use to think and talk about GenAI and the ways this language shapes how we approach student work. Currently, students use GenAI for everything from brainstorming and editing to summarizing and explaining concepts. But, as with Wikipedia over the years, many have learned not to admit this dependence because of the swirl of conflicting messages about the resources we use as we write. Understanding this disparity allows us to navigate the second point of entry: popular discourse.

Headlines in late 2022 were not the first that questioned the use of GenAI in writing. A 2020 opinion piece announced "A robot wrote this entire article. Are you scared yet, human?" (GPT-3, 2020). But, it turns out, we were not yet that scared. Then came December 2022, term papers, and ChatGPT. By the end of the month, the media had convinced faculty, administrators, and parents that we should be very, very scared. Headlines like "'Flood of cheating': Expert warns new tool will be a game changer for cheaters" (*CNN*, 2022), or the *Washington Post*'s "Teachers are on the alert for inevitable cheating after release of ChatGPT" (Meckler & Verma, 2022) asserted that the mere existence of a tool that could be used to cheat would inevitably produce a nation of morally bankrupt college graduates if we didn't act fast. The *New York Post* reported that it may be too late: "Professor catches student cheating with ChatGPT: 'I feel abject terror'" (Mitchell, 2022). While Meckler and Verma report "near panic" by all "across the education system" (2022), the language was not simple panic but moral panic. The "abject terror" felt by the professor who caught someone cheating with ChatGPT arose within a "higher education [environment] already plagued by rampant cheating" (Mitchell, 2022). As with the moral panic created by the media around the mythical "Super Predators" of the 1990s, the response incited by these headlines was policing, which came in the form of policies, penalties, and investment in detection software.

Had the media turned its attention to GPT earlier, we might have seen a more nuanced approach, exploring, for instance, the ways chatbots can complicate the notion of authorship and originality rather than facilitate cheating. In August 2021, Vauhini Vara published a set of nine short "AI-Assisted" stories, "Ghosts," in the *The Believer Magazine*. Trying to discover how to tell a difficult story, she began each piece and asked GPT-3 to finish it. Each version included more of Vara's story, prompting GPT-3 to create a new ending, then she selected among options and added her next section. The collection was published with each voice—Vara's and the bot's—clearly identified. Other writers had also been drawing on the creativity of AI to introduce details they would not typically use, adding freshness to characters and plots.

The questions these experiments raise are much more interesting than those tied to policing the use of GenAI: What does it mean to write? Who owns texts and ideas? How might we rethink the creative act itself? What do we mean by collaboration? A focus on the generation of words rather than on ownership and exchange paves the way for the future-building stance that GenAI requires. If the media had presented GenAI authorship as a generative act rather than a moral act, educators might have moved more quickly to the kinds of pedagogies we propose in this chapter. Sadly, though, this is part of a pattern. Every few decades the media drums up a new literacy crisis. *Time*'s 1955 concern that Johnny couldn't read was followed by *Newsweek*'s 1975 alarm that, even with his college degree, Johnny couldn't write either, and then, a few decades later, by *Time*'s assertion that students had been seduced by the "sophisticated distribution of term papers through so-called paper mills" provided by the internet (Jamieson, 2022). GenAI perfectly fits the ongoing crisis narrative in which inadequately prepared and morally bankrupt students cheat their way through college.

By encouraging distrust of students, such media reports also provoke extreme responses to technology. Before faculty tried to ban GenAI, they banned cell phones, the internet, Wikipedia, and even laptops. Exploring the popular discourse surrounding these earlier efforts could provide contemporary students with a renewed appreciation for tools they take for granted in their literacy practices. Consider the case of embedded grammar tools. Initially, when Microsoft Word became ubiquitous on student computers, many faculty—including authors of this chapter—banned the built-in spell- and grammar-checking functions. It must be remembered that, up until these tools first appeared in the 1980s, the presence or absence of error had been a significant part of the grade for written work. With technologies that helped student writers in this area, those who graded by circling errors would need to change both their rubrics and their pedagogy. And they did. Today, it's almost impossible to imagine an instructor *not* expecting students to use these embedded editing tools.

These tools emerged from the AI-based "Writer's Workbench," which was developed by Lorinda Cherry and Nina Macdonald in the mid-1970s. Cherry offered a response to those who would police the software:

> *My feeling about a lot of those tools is their value in education is as much pointing out to people who are learning to write that they have choices and make choices when they do it. They don't think of a writing task as making choices per se. Once they get it on paper they think it's cast in stone. So [this software] makes them edit.*
>
> *Qtd. in Silverman, n.d.*

As she notes, this software transformed the way we talk about the teaching of writing as a series of student-initiated choices, but it did not replace grammar instruction. The argument for incorporating GenAI into the college classroom picks up where this earlier argument left off and invites a second transformation in the teaching of writing specifically and in the ways we approach literacy instruction in college more broadly. Refocusing our attention from policing to pedagogy requires that teachers consider the ways the narrative of moral panic shapes not only how we think about technology but also how we think about our students—and how our pedagogies invite them to think about and test out their expectations for new technologies like GenAI, which is the focus of the next section.

ENTRY POINT #3: EXPECTATIONS FOR USING GENAI

As college students incorporate GenAI into their literacy practices, they will need to grapple with the often-lofty expectations associated with these technologies. Running parallel to the moral panic described in the previous section, there is plenty of boosterism surrounding AI-laden futures. Yet, in fact, it can be argued that "no research field has promised so much and delivered so little as AI" (Vee et al., 2023). An anecdote from one of Jens' classes illuminates the bind students face when using GenAI as a writing partner. In Spring 2023, Jens taught an intermediate writing-intensive course. With ChatGPT dominating news headlines, Jens facilitated a discussion about GenAI early in the semester and then made space for students to experiment with these technologies. One student, though especially eager, faced considerable challenges when ChatGPT failed to supplement their writing process. On the day a rough draft was due for a personal narrative assignment, the student reported to Jens that they spent five hours trying unsuccessfully to prompt ChatGPT for initial ideas and an outline. Dejected, the student decided to not complete the rough draft.

This anecdote indicates the way in which expectations for using GenAI as a writing partner can influence the writing process. The student at the center of this anecdote expected to generate writing with ChatGPT and, when that failed after a lengthy session of prompting, they decided not only to stop using GenAI but also to stop work on the assignment entirely. Perhaps the student would benefit from improved AI prompting skills or a better understanding of the assignment, especially the personal or subjective nature of it. These, though, are technical hurdles that do not explain why the student stopped working on the assignment entirely. What seems to have stymied this student as much as anything was the emotional letdown arising from not being able to do what they expected to do as a writer with GenAI.

Importantly, then, this anecdote suggests that, when considering students' expectations for using GenAI as writing partners, we also need to consider their expectations for writing more generally. It's not uncommon for some students entering college to view writing, especially writing in academic contexts, as a formulaic, uninspired activity. If students who already approach writing with some degree of prescribed rigidity expect GenAI to effortlessly supplement their writing process, then we're likely to end up with many anecdotes like the one related above. At times, because GenAI technologies can function as "genre-singling machines" (Graham, 2023, p. 164), they may be ideal partners for helping students pick out and learn the conventions for writing in specific academic contexts. But, at other times, the ease with which GenAI can produce content that replicates certain genres may do more harm than good by limiting a student's ability to adapt that content to respond to the demands of certain assignments.

An obstacle to helping all students view GenAI as a complex participant in their writing process is the extent to which, currently, this technology is received with a mix of "awe, wonder, fear, and other forms of 'magical' thinking" (Morrison, 2023, p. 157). Though bound to happen with new technologies that disrupt our sense of what is normal, the response is particularly pernicious in the case of GenAI because the excitement for these technologies that simulate human-generated text is so contradictory to the humdrum view of writing affected by some college students. If we recognize that the enchanting facade of AI is belied by its reliance on "brute force processing power … and some clever procedures" (Morrison, 2023, p. 157), then we can redirect our focus:

> *What's really magic, actually, is writing… . Writing is an act of communication, of persuasion, of instruction, of exploration. What an amazing, unlikely, hopeful thing writing is:* to think beyond the present moment, to develop a system of inscription and abstraction to catch and save and share ideas, to imagine an audience, to desire to reach them.
>
> *p. 158*

Writing can be—and should be—all of these things for college students. Frankly, from our perspective, what makes GenAI an exciting development is the promise that it may ignite in some students a novel expectation for writing to be an activity that is as beguiling and strange as it is clarifying and familiar.

To close this section, we return to the anecdote: When the student showed up to class without a rough draft of the narrative assignment and explained the unsuccessful encounter with ChatGPT, Jens engaged the student and their peers sitting nearby in a short conversation about the assignment. At the end of the conversation, the student, after hearing about the ideas of their peers and putting them in dialogue with their own ideas, articulated a firm plan for how to start their narrative. The point of this anecdote is not to emphasize the triumph of human interaction over failed attempts to prompt an AI. Instead, the point is to emphasize that, like any other participant involved in the at times beguiling and strange activity of writing, GenAI will not always be the ideal partner. This section focused mostly on students using GenAI as writing partners because that has been a conspicuous component of our experience as teachers since the popular advent of these technologies. As the next section indicates, though, students will be partnering with GenAI for all sorts of multimodal literacy practices, so helping students manage expectations across these different modalities will be essential.

ENTRY POINT #4: TECHNOLOGY'S IMPACT ON LITERACY DEVELOPMENT

College students find themselves at a complex point in their literacy development. Not only are they in a time of deep identity formation, something inextricably linked to their literacy practices, but they are also navigating curricula that ask them to think broadly about writing at the same time they need to develop specific disciplinary literacies. They inhabit a context that can both be "schoolish" (Whitney, 2011, p. 55) and authentic. Additionally, students in college have come of age in a digital generation that is distinct from the experiences of the professors and other mentors who guide them as they develop their future selves. While most college students have never known a world without email, Web 2.0, social media, and mobile devices, many of their professors learned to write papers longhand and have had to adapt to a barrage of new technologies over the course of their lives.

It is no wonder, then, that students might take to future-proofing, rather than future-building, in this moment of seismic shift. Not only is the introduction of GenAI into their lives the first time many of them have been confronted with technology that fundamentally impacts what they know about reading, writing, and communicating writ large, but their faculty are also facing yet another technology that has the potential to upend systems and practices. It is a time of wobble, and as Fecho (2011) explained, "When the wobble in our lives becomes too great to be withstood, it needs to be understood" (p. 101).

With regard to GenAI, it's important for everyone to understand the moment for what it is—a point of evolution—and to reflect on their own agency in how technology will impact their practices. Even in the shift from complex oral language to early writing, questions were raised about the impact on humanity. According to Plato's *Phaedrus*, Socrates thought that the introduction of writing into an oral culture would ruin the brain (Ong, 2002). Writing was as much an alien technology to early philosophers as GenAI is to English professors today. Bruce (2003) laid out a timeline that shows how technology has impacted literacy over time. Moving from orality to print literacy, Bruce then captured new literacies (Leu et al., 2004) that developed near the turn of the 21st century: video, digital, multimedia, hypertext, and virtual reality. At each point, Bruce (2003) contended, "We change along with the world around us, and who we become is determined by how we react to change. When a change occurs, it is often disruptive" (p. 30). Since Bruce published, at least two more phases could be added to the timeline: social media and GenAI. The technologies that have been introduced in the last two decades have dramatically impacted the way that humans communicate.

Even so, as authentic, real-world practices continue to evolve at a rapid pace, classroom pedagogy typically privileges earlier forms of literacy. Perhaps this is because K-12 schools and institutions of higher education have been slow to adopt wide-scale practices that fully embrace inquiry-based curricula that promote multimodal composition and instead rely on very traditional modes of assessment. College instructors have not focused enough on how new technologies like GenAI can help students expand their worldview and share their perspectives broadly and ethically. In short, a focus on what it means to be literate in a digital age that now includes widely accessible AI technologies is sorely missing from college curricula.

According to the National Council of Teachers of English (2019), literacy in a digital age is "interconnected, dynamic, and malleable" and involves "communicative and sociocultural practices shared among communities."

Literacy in this context includes print-based, linear texts, as well as digital, multimodal, networked compositions. Many of these aspects are again at a turning point with the explosion in GenAI technologies, and, as this chapter argues, it is essential that teachers and students see this moment with "historical consciousness" (Bruce, 2003, p. 13). Turner and Pankiewicz (2023) suggested that to achieve this view, writers and teachers of writing must ask a fundamental question in this age of AI: What is writing? To answer this question in a context where multimodal, networked texts dominate communication, students—and we, as their instructors and mentors—must acknowledge that the brain works differently to consume and create digital texts than it does for analog. Accepting that literacy practices are different because of the technologies with which humans engage over time and valuing all literacies in the classroom will lead to a future-building stance as professors expand the kinds of tasks they ask of students, and students see the literacy practices of the real world enacted in their academic sphere.

Technologies have the power to shift practice in a few ways. They can help us be more efficient, and they can also help us redefine what we do. As college instructors craft assignments, we should consider how GenAI provides opportunities for students to be more efficient and to redefine their literacy practices. For example, a professor who simply asks students to write a response to a question related to content is inviting students to use GenAI strictly for efficiency. The tool can respond to such questions with relatively little effort on the part of the student. However, if the professor asked students, first, to have GenAI create a response to the question and, second, to analyze the GenAI response, build on it, and weave it into their reflective thinking on a broader topic, noting where GenAI got it right and where they needed to think more deeply about what they know and believe, not only has the instructor prompted deeper thinking on the part of the students, but they have also encouraged students to consider how to redefine their own practices moving forward.

Creating assignments that require the use of GenAI by accepting that some literacy practices might be more efficiently done by a bot and considering how the technology can reshape the kinds of literacies students develop will help to push college students into a future-building mindset. Without this kind of instruction, students may not realize that GenAI can be both a tool of efficiency *and* a tool of redefinition. It is this juxtaposition where they can lean into future-building as new technologies continue to change what it means to be literate and participatory in the world.

CONCLUSION

The entry points we offer in this chapter are intended to start conversations in higher education that break through the inscrutability of GenAI and its effects. On our campus and elsewhere, we have witnessed conversations across disciplines that have given GenAI too much power over the fate of literacy practices. Ultimately, though, as each entry point in this chapter suggests, we have agency to develop, use, and refine GenAI. Rather than allowing our futures to be built *by* GenAI, we can choose to build them *with* GenAI. It is the process of recognizing and claiming this agency that will help us all—students and faculty alike—to future-build in the age of AI.

REFERENCES

Bassett, C. (2019). The computational therapeutic: Exploring Weizenbaum's ELIZA as a history of the present. *AI & Society*, *34*(4), 803–812. https://doi.org/10.1007/s00146-018-0825-9

Bengio, Y., Ducharme, R., Vincent, P., & Jauvin, C. (2003). A neural probabilistic language model. *Journal of Machine Learning Research*, *3*(6), 1137–1155. https://doi.org/10.1162/153244303322533223

Brachman, R., Gunning, D., & Burke, M. (2020). Integrated AI systems. *The AI Magazine*, *41*, 66–82. https://doi.org/10.1609/aimag.v41i2.5300

Brown, T., Mann, B., Ryder, N., Subbiah, M., Kaplan, J. D., Dhariwal, P., Neelakantan, A., Shyam, P., Sastry, G., Askell, A., Agarwal, S., Herbert-Voss, A., Krueger, G., Henighan, T., Child, R., Ramesh, A., Ziegler, D., Wu, J., Winter, C., Hesse, C., Chen, M., Sigler, E., Litwin, M., Gray, S., Chess, B., Clark, J., Berner, C., McCandlish, S., Radford, A., Sutskever, I., Amodei, D. (2020). Language models are few-shot learners. *Advances in neural information processing systems. 33*, 1877–1901. proceedings.neurips.cc/paper/2020/hash/1457c0d6bfcb4967418bfb8ac142f64a-Abstract.html

Bruce, B. C. (Ed.). (2003). *Literacy in the information age: Inquiries into meaning making with new technologies*. International Reading Association.

Buchanan, B. G. (2005). A (very) brief history of artificial intelligence. *The AI Magazine*, *26*(4), 53–60. https://doi.org/10.1609/aimag.v26i4.1848

Chauvin, Y., & Rumelhart, D. E. (Eds.) (1995). *Backpropagation: Theories, architectures, and applications.* Psychology Press.

CNN. (2022). 'Flood of cheating': Expert warns new tool will be a game changer for cheaters. Retrieved December 5, 2024, from www.cnn.com/videos/business/2022/12/26/cheat-app-chatgpt-chatbot-nr-vpx.cnn

Evans, T. (1968). A program for the solution of geometric-analogy intelligence test questions. In M. Minsky (Ed.), *Semantic information processing* (pp. 271–353). MIT Press.

Facer, K. (2011). *Learning futures: Education, technology and social change.* Routledge.

Fecho, B. (2011). *Teaching for the students: Habits of heart, mind, and practice in the engaged classroom.* TC Press.

Fillmore, C. J. (1975). Some problems for case grammar. *Languages (Paris), 9*(38), 65–80.

Gallifant, J., Fiske, A., Levites Strekalova, Y. A., Osorio-Valencia, J. S., Parke, R., Mwavu, R., Martinez, N., Gichoya, J. W., Ghassemi, M., Demner-Fushman, D., McCoy, L. G., Leo, A. C., Pierce, R. (2024). Peer review of GPT-4 technical report and systems card. *PLOS Digital Health, 3*(1), Article e0000417. https://doi.org/10.1371/journal.pdig.0000417.

Goodfellow, I., Pouget-Abadie, J., Mirza, M., Xu, B., Warde-Farley, D., Ozair, S., Courville, A., & Bengio, Y. (2014). Generative adversarial nets. *Advances in neural information processing systems*,27,2672–2680. arxiv.org/abs/1406.2661

GPT-3. (2020). A robot wrote this entire article. Are you scared yet, human?. *The Guardian.* www.theguardian.com/commentisfree/2020/sep/08/robot-wrote-this-article-gpt-3

Graham, S. S. (2023). Post-process but not post-writing: Large language models and a future for composition pedagogy. *Composition Studies, 51*(1), 162–168.

Greenblatt, R. D., Eastlake, D. E., & Crocker, S. D. (1967). *The Greenblatt chess program.* AFIPS '67 (Fall).

Gruber, T. R. (1995). Toward principles for the design of ontologies used for knowledge sharing? *International Journal of Human-Computer Studies, 43*(5–6), 907–928. https://doi.org/10.1006/ijhc.1995.1081

Haenlein, M., & Kaplan, A. (2019). A brief history of artificial intelligence: On the past, present, and future of artificial intelligence. *California Management Review, 61*(4), 5–14. https://doi.org/10.1177/0008125619864925.

Hochreiter, S., & Schmidhuber, J. (1997). Long short-term memory. *Neural Computation, 9*(8), 1735–1780. https://doi.org/10.1162/neco.1997.9.8.1735

Jamieson, S. (2022). The AI "Crisis" and a (re)turn to pedagogy. *Composition Studies, 50*(3), 153–158.

Kingma, D. P. & Welling, M. (2014). *Auto-encoding variational Bayes.* 2nd International Conference on Learning Representations, ICLR 2014, Banff, AB, Canada, April 14–16, 2014, Conference Track Proceedings.

Koehn, P. (2010). *Statistical machine translation.* Cambridge University Press.

Leu, D. J., Jr, Kinzer, C. K., Coiro, J., & Cammack, D. W. (2004). Toward a theory of new literacies emerging from the Internet and other information and communication technologies. In R. B. Ruddell, & N. Unrau (Eds.). *Theoretical models and processes of reading* (5th edition, pp. 1570–1613). International Reading Association.

Meckler, L., & Verma, P. (2022). ChatbotGPT worries teachers who seek to detect cheating by AI. *The Washington Post*. www.washingtonpost.com/education/2022/12/28/chatbot-cheating-ai-chatbotgpt-teachers/

Mikolov, T., Chen, K., Corrado, G., & Dean, J. (2013). Efficient estimation of word representations in vector space. *arXiv.Org*. https://doi.org/10.48550/arxiv.1301.3781

Mitchell, Alex. (2022) "Professor catches student cheating with ChatGPT: 'I feel abject terror.'" *The New York Post*. nypost.com/2022/12/26/students-using-chatgpt-to-cheat-professor-warns/

MLA–CCCC Joint Task Force on Writing and AI. (2023). *MLA–CCCC Joint Task Force on writing and AI working paper: Overview of the issues, statement of principles, and recommendations*. Modern Language Association of America/Conference on College Composition and Communication.

Morrison, A. (2023). Meta-writing: AI and writing. *Composition Studies*, *51*(1), 155–219.

National Council of Teachers of English. (2019) "Definition of literacy in a digital age." ncte.org/statement/nctes-definition-literacy-digital-age/

Nilsson, N. J. (2009). Dreams and dreamers. In *The quest for artificial intelligence* (pp. 3–9). Cambridge University Press.

Ong, W. J. (2002). *Orality and literacy: The technologizing of the word*. Routledge.

Pennington, J., Socher, R., & Manning, C. D. (2014). GloVe: Global vectors for word representation. In Moschitti, A., Pang, B., Daelmans, W. (Eds). *Proceedings of the 2014 conference on empirical methods in natural language processing (EMNLP)* (pp. 1532–1543). Association for Computational Linguistics

Pez, J. (n.d.). *The history of the positronic robot and foundation stories. Part 1: 1940-1941*. www.asimovonline.com/oldsite/Robot_Foundation_history_1.html.

Quinlan, J. R. (Ed.). (1987). *Applications of expert systems: Based on the proceedings of the second Australian conference on applications of expert systems, Sydney, NSW*. Addison-Wesley Longman Publishing.

Ramesh, A., Pavlov, M., Goh, G., Gray, S., Voss, C., Radford, A., Chen, M., & Sutskever, I. (2021). *Zero-shot text-to-image generation*. Proceedings of the 38th International Conference on Machine Learning (ICML 2021).

Redmon, J., Divvala, S., Girshick, R., & Farhadi, A. (2016). You only look once: unified, real-time object detection. *2016 IEEE conference on computer vision and pattern recognition (CVPR)*, 779–788). https://doi.org/10.1109/CVPR.2016.91

Rombach, R., Blattmann, A., Lorenz, D., Esser, P., & Ommer, B. (2022). High-resolution image synthesis with latent diffusion models. *2022 IEEE/CVF conference on computer vision and pattern recognition (CVPR)*, 10674–10685. https://doi.org/10.1109/CVPR52688.2022.01042

Rowsell, J., & Pahl, K. (Eds.). (2015). *The Routledge handbook of literacy studies*. Routledge.

Shin, Y. (2019). The spring of artificial intelligence in its global winter. *IEEE Annals of the History of Computing, 41*, 71–82.

Silverman, D. (n.d.) Text processing and writer's workbench. *A history of unix*. Github. https://dspinellis.github.io/oral-history-of-unix/frs122/unixhist/text.htm

Slagle, J. R. (1963). A heuristic program that solves symbolic integration problems in freshman calculus. *Journal of the ACM, 10*, 507–520.

Stone, P., Brooks, R., Brynjolfsson, E., Calo, R., Etzioni, O., Hager, G., Hirschberg, J., Kalyanakrishnan, S., Kamar, E., Kraus, S., Leyton-Brown, K., Parkes, D., Press, W., Saxenian, A., Shah, J., Tambe, M., & Teller, A. (2016). Artificial intelligence and life in 2030: The one hundred year study on artificial intelligence. *arXiv* (Cornell University). https://doi.org/10.48550/arxiv.2211.06318

Turing, A. M. (1950). Computing machinery and intelligence. *Mind, 59*(236), 433–460. www.abelard.org/turpap/turpap.htm.

Turner, K. H., & Pankiewicz, G. (2023). Developing writers in a new digital age: Ethical stances for writers and teachers. In J. D. Dehart (Ed). *Critical roles of digital citizenship and digital ethics* (pp. 99–115). IGI Global. DOI: 10.4018/978-1-6684-8934-5.ch007

Vee, A., Laquintano, T., & Schnitzler, C. (Eds.) (2023). *TextGenEd: Teaching with text generation technologies*. The WAC Clearinghouse. https://doi.org/10.37514/TWR-J.2023.1.1.02

Whitney, A. E. (2011). In search of the authentic English classroom: Facing the schoolishness of school. *English Education, 44*(1), 51–62.

Wiener, N. (1949). *Cybernetics; or, control and communication in the animal and the machine*. Technology Press.

CHAPTER 9

Framing a Critical, Historical, Proactive View of AI Literacies in "Zero-Gravity" Spaces

Raúl Alberto Mora and Manuela Yepes-Mora

INTRODUCTION: PROBLEMATIZING EXISTING ARTIFICIAL INTELLIGENCE (AI) IMAGINARIES IN LITERACY

We would like to start looking at AI's present landscape by foreshadowing the three elements of the framework we proposed in the title.

The Historical

If we start thinking about how AI (Fetzer, 1990; McCarthy, 2004; PK, 1984), or the "branch of science and technology that creates intelligent machines and computer programs to perform various tasks which requires human intelligence" (PK, 1984, p. 65), has been portrayed in the media *historically*, the first thing one finds is an overarching dystopian view about it (Cave & Dihal, 2019). For example, look at movies depicting AI. One famous reference is Hal 9000 from *2001 Space Odyssey* (Kubrick, 1968). In the 1980s, the movie *War Games* (Badham, 1983) created mass hysteria about a computer leading us to thermonuclear war through a video game. The 1990s also gave us plenty of dystopian fodder through *The Matrix* Saga (Wachowski & Wachowski, 1999). We cannot forget the reference to Issac Asimov through the movie adaptation of *I, Robot* (Proyas, 2004). And

DOI: 10.1201/9781003510635-13

finally, how can we talk about AI and dystopia without referencing *The Terminator* (Cameron, 1984)?

The Proactive

After briefly introducing the historical element, let us discuss the *proactive.* One major problem we have witnessed as we problematize the views about AI literacies is the visceral reactions against technology and AI (Chamorro-Premuzic, 2023). The proposed solutions only seem to focus on the immediateness of solving our problems today. We're not thinking about five years from now; we're not thinking about ten years from now. Such shortsightedness risks missing out on the possibilities that these technologies may afford us to revise and reinvent our educational policies, curricula, and instructional and pedagogical practices (Grájeda et al., 2024; Köchling et al., 2024).

The Critical

Finally, let us discuss the *critical* element in this introduction. Before we move on, we wish to point out that challenging media visions and some apparent shortsightedness do not equate to dismissing the ramifications and consequences of AI's increasingly ubiquitous presence. There are serious questions that we must analyze. After all, serious questions are worth considering about the risks of intellectual theft that have plagued image generators (Farrant, 2023) and the perils of AI misuse in the workplace (Hinds, 2023). We must keep an eye on the so-called Digital Wildfires (O'Byrne et al., 2022), as we have dis/misinformation, fake news, and extreme biases that we need to control while remaining vigilant and thinking about better futures. The critical element of this framework entails raising serious questions about what AI can do and who leads the debates and conversations. Following Wolodelsky's (2023) invitation, it is worth interrogating whether we want to let the people at Silicon Valley and the CEOs of the technological companies be the only ones indicating what we should do with AI. We, as a society, must be the ones who dictate the tempo and make the decisions regarding AI.

Ch(e)atGPT, a Game Changer?

At this point, we would be remiss if we did not bring up the ongoing debates regarding ChatGPT (Ciampa et al., 2023; Opara et al., 2023)... with that little "(e)" we added in the heading. That slight shade concerns the tone of the recent conversations in media and educational circles about ChatGPT, the inevitable cheating this generative AI tool will generate, and how that will disrupt our instructional practices (Fütterer et al., 2023; Yu, 2023). To be clear, we cannot rule out the chance that *some* students will use ChatGPT for that. However, that is a different view from assuming that cheating is students' default setting. In this sense, it is worth noting this provocation by Smith (2023) from an article in *The Chronicle* at Duke University, "We shouldn't be asking if students are cheating via ChatGPT, but rather why they feel the need to." We will return to this question later in the chapter.

An Even Narrower View of AI?

Equating AI with just ChatGPT is part of the problem surrounding current conversations. The other issue we have found is this reductionist view of the purposes of generative AI. If just equating AI with one app is wrong, just seeing AI tools as gizmos for mere entertainment is equally problematic. Let me share two (among many) examples found on social media: One depicts AI examples of what The Avengers cast would look like if made in the 1970s, 1980s, or 1990s (www.instagram.com/reel/C-aB97yPi4q/?utm_source=ig_web_copy_link&igsh=MzRlODBiNWFlZA==). Another depicts different movie franchises as if directed in the style of Wes Anderson movies, including *Star Wars* or *The Lord of the Rings* (https://youtu.be/KrjL_TSOFrI?si=b4Etwp8LLpJZePod). Make no mistake: The videos are very creative and fun. But we must also question if there could be something else we could do with generative AI tools besides sheer entertainment.

RESISTANCE, THE BIGGER PICTURE, AND THIS CHAPTER

This chapter provides a moment to move away from prohibition and resistance and embrace symbiosis, co-creation, and coexistence possibilities. This chapter proposes one roadmap to examine AI literacies (Ng et al., 2021), as well as a working definition of AI literacies, as the basis for our proposed critical, historical, and proactive framework,

> *AI literacies broadly cover three main areas:* First, they explore the *use* of AI tools for textual creation and interpretation, as AI can bring together multiple linguistic and semiotic resources as part of this textual design process. Second, they describe how to *assess* the use of AI tools, thinking about which and how to use them. This assessment considers AI tool use not just for the sake of using them but as a form of awareness of the technical and design affordances

> that AI provides for meaning-making. Finally, they refer to the ability to *critically question* if, when, and why to incorporate AI tools into the textual creation endeavor as we attempt to balance the advances in AI technology with the ongoing ethical debates regarding such technologies.
>
> *Mora, 2024, Defining the Term, pa. 2*

The Bigger (Historical) Picture

To move forward into better framing AI tools, we need to come to terms with two ideas. First, we must accept that, even if conversations around AI have become a more significant part of today's zeitgeist, their presence as part of digital spaces is not novel (Newell, 1982; Brooks, 1999). Digital spaces have been here for a very long time (Burriss & Leander, 2024). If we think about the emergence of video games, with games such as Pong in the 1970s or the Atari consoles in the 1980s, video games (a realm where AI is highly present) are not novel. They have evolved and grown with the rest of us. Now, think about the Internet and the World Wide Web. We have been plotting these spaces at least since the 1960s and navigating (surfing?) them for over 30 years already. We have been using image creators since we had the first portable computers at home, those with floppy disks. Even today's suggestions for writing specific kinds of e-mails or letters found in Grammarly of Gemini are, at their core, not so dissimilar to Clippy, the infamous virtual assistant that plagued Microsoft Office at the end of last century (Rossen, 2023). So, digital spaces are not something that just happened because ChatGPT or AI tools showed up. They have been here for a while (Toosi et al., 2021).

Along these historical lines, yes, we must also embrace the present resistance and fears to AI, but as part of the very essence of human nature. This tension is something that Mora and Semingson (2023) also recalled in their conversations about AI literacies, "If we went all the way back to the Stone Age, there must have been backlash when someone proposed turning stones into specialized tools. But, as there was backlash, there was also creation, progress, and change" (p. 56). Embracing this tension as something that is human nature will also go a long way toward creating better frameworks for AI literacies.

Finally, we must also come to terms with the fact that, barring a total collapse of our entire civilization, it is doubtful that AI tools and digital technologies, by extension, are going anywhere. In that sense, this chapter will also revisit the idea of *symbiosis*. That idea is another that we can find in the media, sometimes hiding amid the dystopia. Recall, for example, that scene in *Matrix: Reloaded* (Wachowski & Wachowski, 2003), where one of the members of the Council of Zion talks to Neo and, looking at the city, says, "I like to be reminded the city survives because of these machines. These machines keep us alive while other machines are coming to kill us. Interesting, isn't it? The power to give life and the power to end?" All dystopian undertones aside, this chapter's proposed framework and examples explore the idea that we can harness ubiquity and make it part of our lives and educational settings as possibilities for resistance (Agnew et al., 2023).

TOWARD A CRITICAL, HISTORICALLY PROACTIVE APPROACH TO AI, PART 1: FOUNDATIONAL NOTES

Here, we propose three vantage points for discussing AI literacies: a *critical* view, a *historical* view, and a *proactive* view. This section will outline some of the foundational elements of each view.

Zero-Gravity Spaces

Mora et al. (2019) proposed the "zero-gravity spaces" metaphor to describe online, digital, and virtual spaces, realms where AI literacies seem to thrive (Burden, 2008; Matsuba, 1999). When thinking about zero-gravity spaces, Mora et al. introduced the example of zero-gravity airplanes that train astronauts before they fly into space. The idea of these places is simple: once you remove gravity from the equation, you can do things with your body that you cannot do otherwise: you can fly, you can jump, you can leap, you can go in circles. Digital and virtual spaces, then, are spaces where the traditional limitations of geographical and physical spaces disappear, and new possibilities for meaning-making and text creation emerge.

In the case of AI literacies in these zero-gravity spaces, we can see the possibilities for interplay and connectivity that these generative tools may provide (Chamola et al., 2024). In these instances, it is vital to remember the ethics of care needed in these spaces (think about the plane example: just because you may float doesn't mean you can't get hurt, as there may be objects and other people floating). We argue that AI in these spaces affords new ways to creatively connect information and design resources (Gong, 2021).

Critical Views of Literacy and Multimodality

Critical literacy (Mora, 2014) and its intersections with digital literacies (Ávila & Pandya, 2013; Ávila, 2021), multimodality (Mora, 2017; Mora et al., 2022), and most recently, AI (Burriss & Leander, 2024; Leander & Burriss, 2020) provide a powerful blueprint for our proposed model. At its core, critical literacy reminds us that there are multiple forms of power dynamics surrounding textual creation and interpretation, particularly when we look at digital spaces and AI (Leander & Burriss, 2020). They also remind us that there are issues of access and accessibility related to these digital technologies (Aleman & Martinez, 2024), which we must also counter as a matter of social responsibility (Pandya et al., 2021). The intersections with multimodality, or what Mora describes as Multimodal Critical Consciousness (Mora, 2017), have become a possibility to engage with textual creation through AI, where we can remix creativity and ethics as driving forces behind AI use.

Cultural Historical Activity Theory

Another critical element in this framework comes from Cultural Historical Activity Theory (e.g., Sannino & Engeström, 2018). One essential theme in discussions of Activity Theory, particularly in the works of Leont'ev and Engeström (Cong-Lem, 2022), is the presence of conceptual and practical tools (Mora & Lopera Gómez, 2001; Grossman et al., 1999), as essential features of societal evolution and operation. From this view, the notion of appropriation as gradual mastery (Grossman et al., 1999) becomes an integral part of this conversation surrounding AI (El Maouch & Jin, 2024; Karanasios et al., 2021). So long as we consider these tools as foreign to our development, resistance will ensue. Once we begin to see these tools as extensions of ourselves and our possibilities for growth, resistance may make room for more creativity (Lim et al., 2024).

Playful Literacies

Finally, playful literacies (Ehret et al., 2023; Lammers et al., 2022; Wohlwend et al., 2017) bookend the conceptual foundations behind this framework. At their core, playful literacies involve "creat[ing]and re-creat[ing] narratives, shar[ing] meanings, propos[ing] new ones, transform[ing] and remediat[ing] objects, compos[ing] with real and imagined technologies, and collaborat[ing]" (Lammers et al., 2022, p. 81). Ehret et al. (2023) argued that play and playful literacies can no longer be conceived as something only children do. Instead, they claim that play is vital for human development, regardless of age, and therefore essential to societal growth.

If we relate this to AI literacies, the idea of play becomes paramount. Although some fears around AI stem from ethical quandaries (as we pointed out earlier in the chapter), other fears come from a lack of experimentation and concerns about these tools' actual learning curves (Mora, 2019). A playful approach to AI would enable students, teachers, and even their families (Druga et al., 2022) to have time to experiment with these tools (Cannon et al., 2018) and to make choices about their use and how to weave them into our educational settings (Cortez et al., 2024).

TOWARD A CRITICAL, HISTORICALLY PROACTIVE APPROACH TO AI, PART 2: DISRUPTING FATALISM

The first part of our discussion of our framework situated the conceptual underpinnings to our work. This next section will elaborate on how to counter some of the existing views of AI literacies, which are still grounded in fatalistic and dystopian views. While we acknowledge the existing concerns, one of the goals of our proposal to frame AI literacies is to move past these fatalistic views surrounding AI, as we said at the beginning. We cannot stay fatalistic; we cannot stay in dystopia if we want to move to utopia. It is worth recalling some of Freire's (1979) ideas and how he reminded us about the importance of Utopia as a way to think about the future. We will highlight three major issues our framework wishes to disrupt.

Disrupting Deficit Thinking

Earlier in the chapter, we pointed out that the risk of looking at AI literacies stems from the deficit views of students and teachers. Ofelia García et al. (2021) described these views as *abyssal thinking*, which applied to AI, surface in these expectations that AI equals cheating. So, the only way forward is prohibition or absolute control of these tools (Abd-Eliall et al., 2019). Although we are not contesting the need for ethical safeguards and believe these conversations should happen in our educational settings (Fyfe, 2023), we are questioning why this seems to be the *default setting* in some academic discussions. If we just conceive AI literacies from a prohibitive lens that only views students under this lens and forces teachers to operate only under these deficit settings, it ultimately curtails their creativity.

Disrupting Unnecessary (and Non-existent) Divides in Zero-Gravity

One troublesome conversation we continue to hear regarding digital literacy practices has to do with the ill-conceived notion of digital natives and digital immigrants, a divide that Raúl has long questioned in previous work (see Mora, 2011 for an illustration) due to its links to geography and physical spaces, analog concepts that neither represent what happens in digital spaces nor need any further compartmentalization (Raúl still recalls a webinar during the pandemic in Colombia where the presenter decided to add a third category named digital *tourists*). The zero-gravity metaphor (Mora et al., 2019) predicates on the idea that once we remove those physical limitations ingrained in the native/immigrant divide, we realize that people can play, in this case, with AI tools in different ways (Shaw et al., 2024). Granted, there are levels of expertise in these spaces, but they are the effect of the various experiences navigating these spaces and not just issues of age or mother language (two issues that seem to ground any discussions about natives and immigrants in physical spaces).

Preventing Marginalization in AI Literacies

One final concern about these views surrounding AI literacies (some stemming from existing views about digital literacies) is how these deficit and fatalistic views may add layers to the existing digital divides. If we continue to perpetuate these divides, we risk now only marginalizing, disenfranchising, and even infantilizing our youth (Higgs & Stornaiuolo, 2024). We see this often when adults (and teachers) may dismiss social media content by default just because it's on Instagram or TikTok. There is a dismissive attitude that equates Instagram Reels of TikTok videos as low-brow (Bourdieu, 1984) and lacking any intellectual value. Granted, content on these sites may qualify as such, but that cannot be the default setting or expectation. However, Raúl has used these sites for students to create content for his assignments, and one can see the amount of work it takes to make a good quality video that may be between 30 and 60 seconds.

This marginalization of these tools, which we sometimes see in dismissive positions regarding ChatGPT or digital image creators, also returns to the renewed vision of play and playfulness that this framework supports. If we want to create more engaging possibilities with AI (Bradley et al. 2024), we must stop thinking that play is a waste of time. We must stop treating these tools as luxuries for a precious few and find ways to make them more accessible to different groups. We must also move past issues of ableism (Williams, 2024) and ageism (Stypinska, 2021) that plague some practices. Perpetuating these practices is doing a severe disservice to all participating in these spaces and these communities.

TOWARD A CRITICAL, HISTORICALLY PROACTIVE APPROACH TO AI, PART 3: BUILDING A SYMBIOTIC RELATIONSHIP

Beyond the issues we highlighted in the previous section regarding some views of AI literacies, there is another issue we wish to highlight to open this section: Sometimes, the conversations around AI tools and literacy practices place them as isolated, distant, and even disconnected from ourselves. One key element we introduced in our discussion of Cultural Historical Activity Theory was the relationship we develop with tools as extensions of our bodies and minds and ways to overcome some of our shortcomings. Why do we have binoculars, for example? Because our sight is minimal compared to that of other animals. We have built cameras to help us move beyond our limited peripheral vision. Our arms are only so long, so we need extensions. We have invented all kinds of boards and skis so we can move as fast as other animals on different surfaces. The list goes on, but the main issue is how we have developed these links to the tools we use. This is what we like to think about when we talk about this symbiotic relationship with tools.

Now, transfer these initial tools to the different digital tools we use. Think, for example, about what we pack in our backpacks: We make sure to pack our laptops, smartphones, and tablets if we use those also. We ensure that we have our power cords, adapters, and even a power bank in case your phone runs out of battery. Some others also carry a smartwatch with them in addition to their smartphones. Traveling seems increasingly paperless, as we can access our boarding passes and bus and train tickets through different apps.

The Everyday Cyborg: A New Symbiosis with AI?

One element that characterizes our proactive approach is how we rethink our relationships with digital tools (Loh et al., 2023), particularly the idea that we do not depend on just one tool for anything. Instead, we integrate multiple tools for different purposes. As we rethink our relationships with AI, we have found Lizárraga's (2023) notion of the *everyday cyborg* insightful. Lizárraga argues that

> *Today, we live in the age of the everyday cyborg where cutting-edge digital technologies, specifically, allow us to instantly connect and to share knowledge in order to take action in the world but also to author narratives of our present and future.*
>
> *pp. 22*

We do not envision AI literacies as foreign to our everyday lives and experiences. Instead, we advocate envisioning them in ways similar to the tools of the old. We see them as integrated tools (Bender, 2024), extensions of our minds, ways to enhance our imaginations, and ways to display our creative playfulness in ways that might be more difficult otherwise.

TOWARD A CRITICAL, HISTORICALLY PROACTIVE APPROACH TO AI, PART 3: CONSIDERATIONS

Now that we have laid out some of the conceptual elements that profile our framework, let us discuss what a critical, historically proactive approach to AI looks like. Mora and Semingson (2023) outlined a first thought that serves as the basis for this section,

> *We suggest the conversation about AI and ChatGPT move past the reactions that mostly aim at limiting, outlawing, and curtailing AI's presence in classrooms [...] What we need is [...] a more critical, proactive approach to how to maximize this existing hybrid of humans and machines we are witnessing in our classrooms.*
>
> *p. 56*

Our critical, historically proactive view starts from this realization that we are "everyday cyborgs" in many ways and have symbiotic relationships with digital and virtual tools. AI, in this case, would be just an extension of these symbioses, and outlawing these tools only has a short-term effect (we already tried with calculators, and that was not a success story for math teachers, for instance). This section will outline some considerations for this approach and two recent experiences involving AI in the creative process.

A(I) Matter of Trust, Challenge, and Possibility

To talk about a critical and proactive view means starting from a place of trust. We must trust that our students can exercise judgment with these tools (Higgs & Stornaiuolo, 2024). The ethics of care was talking about that idea of caring. Caring for our students means also trusting their judgment. A greater breadth of approach also goes into a cultural challenge. Challenge your students to be creative and not simply let the tools think of them (Fyfe, 2023; Gong, 2021). So, we must create challenging opportunities for creativity and ingenuity and understand the possibilities for the coalescence of humans and the more-than-human (Leander & Burriss, 2020). In other words, we want our students to maintain their agency regarding decision-making, design, and meaning-making instead of simply outsourcing their brainpower to AI. This would entail inviting AI tools to work with us and help us co-construct those messages, those texts, and that language (Cortez et al., 2024).

Acknowledge What's Going On in Zero-Gravity

So, what's going on in these zero-gravity spaces? Think about social media, popular culture, and how AI keeps emerging in these scenarios. These stories are threaded; they move across different media and they move across different forms of communication. A lot of collaborative textual creation is happening in these spaces. And there is also a lot of rule-breaking and rule-bending. That happens as you start making up words, and you can propose new expressions (think urbandictionary.com, for instance). Zero-gravity spaces, where AI resides, will afford us the possibility to create and recreate language. And then that gives us ownership of playful ownership of language and text in the sense that we feel the language is something we can use and matters to us.

Another consideration comes from Raúl's work on gamifying educational spaces. One big lesson we can extrapolate to AI literacies is the importance of the *ethos* of using the tools, where we break traditional uses of tools for their sake or novelty. Instead, this AI ethos looks at the purpose and learning potential of incorporating AI, for example, in our educational settings. We want to think of a good reason for using them beyond entertainment (as we questioned at the beginning of the chapter). Nothing is wrong with the fun element, but we're missing our educational opportunities if that is the only purpose.

TOWARD A CRITICAL, HISTORICALLY PROACTIVE APPROACH TO AI, PART 3: EXAMPLES

Mora and Semingson (2023) proposed two avenues for AI literacies: the idea of a "digital muse" and multimodal text creation mediated by AI. We will now illustrate these two avenues with two recent examples: an exercise that Raúl did in his class and how Raúl and Manuela wrote this chapter.

The "Writing Muse" Value of AI for Composing

Mora and Semingson (2023) explained the idea of the "digital muse" as the possibility "to generate starter ideas, outlines, and questions [...] but with the caveat that you do not want to rely on it verbatim, only as a starting point or a spark" (p. 57). They also proposed infusing different AI tools into the writing process, understanding that one tool will never be fully encompassing, and we must carefully consider their inclusion in our writing process (Beck & Levine, 2024). So, let us document how AI tools became that digital muse for this chapter.

As we will disclose at the end of this chapter, the basis for this text comes from three lectures in November 2023 and April 2024. Raúl recorded all the lectures using his smartphone and then transcribed them using Otter.ai. When Manuela joined the project, they had synchronous conversations using WhatsApp to discuss the chapter and introduce Manuela to AI. She accessed different introductory texts in a shared Google Drive folder. To create the outline for this chapter, they made a prompt from the abstract from one lecture on ChatGPT, which they later contrasted with the outlines that Otter.ai created from the transcripts. Manuela read through all the outlines and proposed a mixed version, the basis for the outline that guided writing this chapter. Once the outline was in place, Raúl took excerpts from the three lectures and placed them along the outline to see how the draft was shaping up. The process of writing the draft mixed fleshing out the transcripts, writing new texts, and using Grammarly to correct some sentences along the way.

The Digital Muse in Our Classrooms. Writing, particularly when facing academic texts, is never easy. Students may often encounter writer's block and concerns about articulating their ideas. Think, for example, how we can start writing by mixing transcribed voice memos, where students can flesh out an idea by using generative AI tools such as ChatGPT, Gemini, and Copilot to suggest outlines. We can then work collaboratively in class using those outlines to help students start writing their drafts. While doing this, we can also have conversations with our students regarding where we should draw the line (Fyfe, 2023) about using these tools and how much control we want to give the tools over our writing.

Multimodal Text Cre(AI)tion

This example stems from a course on bilingualism that Raúl taught at his university in the second semester of 2023. This activity aimed to help students reflect on the benefits and pitfalls of AI in education while taking a stand on these current debates. The assignment required students to create a storyboard outlining their overall vision for the multimodal essay and an initial list of tools. Regarding the multimodal essay, let us share the description as shown in the course syllabus (Mora, 2023),

> *You will develop your project as a multimodal essay to upload to YouTube. One key meta-element of this essay is that you will have to create the different multimodal resources that make the video (images, music, narration, etc.) using AI tools. You can visit Futuredia (https://*futurepedia.io) for a detailed list of available apps. You should choose FREE apps to use (I want to make it very clear that you must not pay any fees to access the apps for this assignment!) Yes, you can use ChatGPT to help you create outlines or storyboards, but you must disclose in the end credits to the video all the apps that you used for this assignment.
>
> *See Mora & Semingson, 2023, for an illustration*

During the last session of the course, Raúl met with the students to watch the multimodal essays and discuss the lessons learned. Students shared the usefulness of this exercise to understand the possibilities of AI use in their classes, expand their AI resource toolkit beyond the "usual suspects" (i.e., ChatGPT or DALL-E), and reflect on the ethical matters behind AI, including issues related to data and human involvement (see Figure 9.1 to watch the student videos).

Multimodal Text Cre(AI)tion in Our Classrooms. Creating multimodal texts in our classes always adds a layer of playfulness to our activities. The classroom should always be a place for exploration and inquiry. In the case of AI literacies, this means opening spaces to explore these tools and the possibilities to create other textual forms that involve more active learning. And, just as in the previous example, the use of multimodal AI

FIGURE 9.1 QR-Code for Multimodal Text Cre(AI)tion Videos YouTube Playlist.

tools may also foster teachable moments about when and how to use these tools so that our students' creations are genuinely theirs, even if these tools assist their creativity.

TOWARD A CRITICAL, HISTORICALLY PROACTIVE APPROACH TO AI, PART 4: LESSONS LEARNED ABOUT AI IN ZERO-GRAVITY

As we developed this framework and revisited the experiences using AI, it is fitting to reflect on the lessons we learned from the perspective of someone who has talked about AI in education (Raúl) and someone who has explored it in her life and is interested in inquiring about it as a professional subject (Manuela). We now share with our readers three lessons we learned while looking at AI tools and writing this chapter. While brief, these lessons should help teachers' decision-making when infusing AI tools into their practice.

Lesson 1: Avoid Single-Tool Overreliance

The first lesson is quite simple: if you want to be creative in these zero-gravity spaces, the best thing you can do is not to over-rely on one tool. Don't overuse ChatGPT, thinking it is a Swiss Army knife. Like any other AI tool or software, there are limitations as to what it can do. It is also essential to recognize that these tools cannot compensate for a lack of knowledge or skills. Some generative AI tools only go as far as your capacity to create good prompts, for example.

Lesson 2: Human Agency over Tools

In this sense, the second big lesson is to remember that even in the middle of this AI landscape, we still have the agency to broker these tools and find common ground as we create different textual forms. No meta-tool can replace human ingenuity. But, when one brings all these tools together, they can provide possibilities to enhance creativity. Also, make sure there is a sense of a level playing field when you propose it. Returning to this idea of ethos, we fear that folks sometimes worry too much about looking for the most advanced and sophisticated tools. Sometimes, that means the most expensive tool, where you have to pay fees, something not many people (especially think of children and youth at school or college) can afford to pay regularly. It is better to always seek freely available tools without paying a subscription.

Lesson 3: Minimalism Is a Powerful Approach

When playing with, in this case, AI tools, we suggest taking a minimalist approach (Mora & Golovátina-Mora, 2020), where you go with tools whose learning curve is much friendlier. Regarding educational projects, we also stress that students use free tools. The last we want in our classes is to create an arms race around the most expensive tools, which will further those digital divides we cautioned against earlier in the chapter. The last thing we want in our classes is for students to stop thinking about being creative as they play with tools and create texts because they are more concerned about who brings the shiniest tool to our classes. We want them to focus on developing and the context, not necessarily on the shiny objects.

CODA

As we finished this chapter, we reflected on the possibilities and the idea that AI literacies can help us build better futures. Along the way, we returned to that initial reference to Terminator at the beginning of the chapter and the narratives that this movie saga has driven regarding AI and machines. Raúl has never taken a pessimistic tone as a scholar in his work. As Manuela's uncle, he wants her to remain optimistic about the future, especially as she embarks on her college experience. In addition, as Raúl tells his students when teaching critical theory, one comes to critical work because one is unhappy with how things are going. However, one continues to be engaged with criticality because one hopes things can and will improve. In that sense, it was worth recalling Sarah Connor's words at the end of *Terminator*

2: Judgment Day (Cameron, 1991), "'The unknown future rolls toward us. I face it for the first time with a sense of hope, because if a machine, a Terminator, can learn the value of human life, maybe we can too."

So, we end this chapter by considering whether we can have a better future. And saying, Yes, we can. Once we submit this chapter and the edited book it is part of, both Manu and Raúl will pack our laptops in our backpacks, she will go to school, Raúl will go back to his work, and, together, we will start working on how to build those better futures for education and society from our different fronts.

ACKNOWLEDGMENTS

This chapter summarizes ideas from the keynote address *Language, literacy, and educational policy in "zero gravity" spaces: Moving past ChatGPT, inviting symbiotic futures for our educational systems* (IV Seminário Multiletramentos, Hipermídia e Ensino "Language Policies, Identities and Technologies," Universidade Estadual de Campinas (Unicamp), Brazil in November 2023), and the invited lectures *Artificial intelligence as a "digital muse": Exploring AI's true possibilities for textual creation* and *A historical proactive framework to look at AI in language education: An evolving proposal* (delivered at the University of Białystok, Poland, in April 2024). This chapter also includes ideas from the extended conversations between Raúl and Manuela to refine and clarify the ideas in this chapter.

REFERENCES

Abd-Elaal, E. S., Gamage, S. H., & Mills, J. E. (2019, December). Artificial intelligence is a tool for cheating academic integrity. In *30th annual conference for the Australasian Association for Engineering Education (AAEE 2019): Educators becoming agents of change: Innovate, integrate, motivate* (pp. 397–403). Engineers Australia.

Agnew, W., McKee, K. R., & Kay, J. (2023). Technologies of resistance to AI. In *Proceedings of 2023 ACM Conference on Equity and Access in Algorithms, Mechanisms, and Optimization (EAAMO '23)* (pp. 1–13). https://conference2023.eaamo.org/papers/EAAMO23_paper_154.pdf

Aleman, E., & Martinez, R. (2024). "It's Like They Are Using Our Data Against Us." Counter-cartographies of AI literacy. *Reading Research Quarterly, 59*(4), 665–667. https://doi.org/10.1002/rrq.574

Ávila, J. (2021). *Critical digital literacies: Boundary-crossing practices*. Brill.

Ávila, J., & Pandya, J. Z. (Eds.). (2013). *Critical digital literacies as social praxis: Intersections and challenges*. P. Lang.

Badham, J. (1983). *War games* [Film]. United International Pictures.

Beck, S. W., & Levine, S. (2024). The next word: A framework for imagining the benefits and harms of generative AI as a resource for learning to write. *Reading Research Quarterly, 59*(4), 706–715. https://doi.org/10.1002/rrq.567

Bender, S. M. (2024). Awareness of artificial intelligence as an essential digital literacy: ChatGPT and Gen-AI in the classroom. *Changing English, 31*(2), 161–174. https://doi.org/10.1080/1358684X.2024.2309995

Bourdieu, P. (1984). *Distinction: A social critique of the judgement of taste.* Harvard University Press.

Bradley, L., Perry, M., Fassetta, G., Ryan, S. D., & Nelson, E. L. (2024). Denaturalizing "intelligence" in higher education: AI as a rupture to imagining and manifesting sustainable and anti-colonial literacies. *Reading Research Quarterly, 59*(4), 579–589. https://doi.org/10.1002/rrq.540

Brooks, R. A. (1999). *Cambrian intelligence: The early history of the new AI.* MIT press.

Burden, D. J. (2008). Deploying embodied AI into virtual worlds. In T. Allen, R. Ellis, & M. Petridis (Eds.), *Applications and Innovations in Intelligent Systems XVI. SGAI 2008* (pp. 103–115). Springer.

Burriss, S. K., & Leander, K. (2024). Critical posthumanist literacy: Building theory for reading, writing, and living ethically with everyday artificial intelligence. *Reading Research Quarterly, 59*(4), 560–569. https://doi.org/10.1002/rrq.565

Cameron, J. (1984). *The terminator* [Film]. Orion Pictures.

Cameron, J. (1991). *Terminator 2: Judgment day* [Film]. Orion Pictures.

Cannon, M., Potter, J., & Burn, A. (2018). Dynamic, playful and productive literacies. *Changing English, 25*(2), 180–197. https://doi.org/10.1080/1358684X.2018.1452146

Cave, S., & Dihal, K. (2019). Hopes and fears for intelligent machines in fiction and reality. *Nature Machine Intelligence, 1*(2), 74–78. https://doi.org/10.1038/s42256-019-0020-9

Chamola, V., Bansal. G., Das, T. K., Hassija, V., Reddy, N. S. S., Wang, J. Zeadally, S., Hussain, A., Yu, R., Guizani, M., & Niyato, D. (2024). Beyond reality: The pivotal role of generative AI in the metaverse. *IEEE Internet of Things Magazine, 7*(4), 126–135. https://doi.org/10.1109/IOTM.001.2300174

Chamorro-Premuzic, T. (2023, Feb. 27). Why are humans biased against AI? *Forbes.* www.forbes.com/sites/tomaspremuzic/2023/02/27/why-are-humans-biased-against-ai/

Ciampa, K., Wolfe, Z. M., & Bronstein, B. (2023). ChatGPT in education: Transforming digital literacy practices. *Journal of Adolescent & Adult Literacy, 67*(3), 186–195. https://doi.org/10.1002/jaal.1310

Cong-Lem, N. (2022). Vygotsky's, Leontiev's and Engeström's cultural-historical (activity) theories: Overview, clarifications and implications. *Integrative*

Psychological and Behavioral Science, 56(4), 1091–1112. https://doi.org/10.1007/s12124-022-09703-6

Cortez, A., Lizárraga, J. R., & Rivero, E. (2024). AlgoRitmo literacies in gaming: Leveraging Chicanx Praxis to reimagine AI systems. *Reading Research Quarterly, 59*(4), 609–623. https://doi.org/10.1002/rrq.539

Druga, S., Christoph, F. L., & Ko, A. J. (2022, April). Family as a third space for AI literacies: How do children and parents learn about AI together?. In S. Barbosa, C. Lampe, C. Appert, D. A. Shamma, S. Drucker, J. Williamson, & K. Yatani (Eds.), *Proceedings of the 2022 CHI conference on human factors in computing systems* (pp. 1–17). https://doi.org/10.1145/3491102.3502031

Ehret, C., Flint, T. K., Lammers, J. C., Magnifico, A. M., & Mora, R. A. (2023). Playful literacies across ages and contexts: New horizons for pleasure, affect, & living texts. *English Teaching: Practice & Critique, 22*(2), 133–136. https://doi.org/10.1108/ETPC-06-2023-199

El Maouch, M., & Jin, Z. (2024). Between meanings and senses-making spaces: Agency and ownership emergence formalization from cultural-historical activity theory position, for an AI-friendly model. *Integrative Psychological and Behavioral Science, 58*(1), 99–137. https://doi.org/10.1007/s12124-023-09770-3

Farrant, T. (2023, Mar 27). From lawsuits to tech hacks: Here's how artists are fighting back against AI image generation. *Euronews.* www.euronews.com/culture/2023/03/27/from-lawsuits-to-tech-hacks-heres-how-artists-are-fighting-back-against-ai-image-generatio

Fetzer, J. H. (1990). What is artificial intelligence?. In *Artificial intelligence: Its scope and limits.* Studies in Cognitive Systems, vol 4. Springer. https://doi.org/10.1007/978-94-009-1900-6_1

Freire, P. (1979). *Conscientização: Teoria e prática da libertação – Uma introdução ao pensamento de Paulo Freire.* Cortez e Moráes.

Fütterer, T., Fischer, C., Alekseeva, A., Chen, X., Tate, T., Warschauer, M., & Gerjets, P. (2023). ChatGPT in education: Global reactions to AI innovations. *Scientific Reports, 13*(1), 15310. https://doi.org/10.1038/s41598-023-42227-6

Fyfe, P. (2023). How to cheat on your final paper: Assigning AI for student writing. *AI & Society, 38*(4), 1395–1405. https://doi.org/10.1007/s00146-022-01397-z

García, O., Flores, N., Seltzer, K., Wei, L., Otheguy, R., & Rosa, J. (2021). Rejecting abyssal thinking in the language and education of racialized bilinguals: A manifesto. *Critical Inquiry in Language Studies, 18*(3), 203–228. https://doi.org/10.1080/15427587.2021.1935957

Gong, Y. (2021). Application of virtual reality teaching method and artificial intelligence technology in digital media art creation. *Ecological Informatics, 63*, 101304. https://doi.org/10.1016/j.ecoinf.2021.101304

Grájeda, A., Córdova, P., Córdova, J. P., Laguna-Tapia, A., Burgos, J., Rodríguez, L., Arandía, M, & Sanjinés, A. (2024). Embracing artificial intelligence in the arts classroom: Understanding student perceptions and emotional reactions to AI tools. *Cogent Education, 11*(1), 2378271. https://doi.org/10.1080/2331186X.2024.2378271

Grossman, P. L., Smagorinsky, P., & Valencia, S. (1999). Appropriating conceptual and pedagogical tools for teaching English: A conceptual framework for studying professional development (ED 431198). ERIC. https://files.eric.ed.gov/fulltext/ED431198.pdf

Higgs, J. M., & Stornaiuolo, A. (2024). Being human in the age of generative AI: young people's ethical concerns about writing and living with machines. *Reading Research Quarterly, 59*(4), 632–650. https://doi.org/10.1002/rrq.552

Hinds. R. (2023, Nov 27). How to decode the very mixed reactions to AI in the workplace. *Reworked.* www.reworked.co/digital-workplace/how-to-decode-the-very-mixed-reactions-to-ai-in-the-workplace/

Karanasios, S., Nardi, B., Spinuzzi, C., & Malaurent, J. (2021). Moving forward with activity theory in a digital world. *Mind, Culture, and Activity, 28*(3), 234–253. https://doi.org/10.1080/10749039.2021.1914662

Köchling, A., Wehner, M. C., & Ruhle, S. A. (2024). This (AI) n't fair? Employee reactions to artificial intelligence (AI) in career development systems [Advance online publication]. *Review of Managerial Science.* https://doi.org/10.1007/s11846-024-00789-3

Kubrick, S. (1968). *2001: A space Oddisey* [Film]. Metro-Goldwyn-Mayer.

Lammers, J. C., Magnifico, A. M., & Wang, A. (2022). Playful multiliteracies: Fan-based literacies' role in English Language Arts pedagogy. *Journal of Adolescent & Adult Literacy, 66*(2), 80–90. https://doi.org/10.1002/jaal.1253

Leander, K. M., & Burriss, S. K. (2020). Critical literacy for a posthuman world: When people read, and become, with machines. *British Journal of Educational Technology, 51*(4), 1262–1276. https://doi.org/10.1111/bjet.12924

Lim, J., Leinonen, T., & Lipponen, L. (2024, July). How can artificial intelligence be used in creative learning?: Cultural-historical activity theory analysis in Finnish kindergarten. In *International conference on artificial intelligence in education* (pp. 149–156). Springer Nature Switzerland. https://doi.org/10.1007/978-3-031-64312-5_18

Lizárraga, J. R. (2023). Cyborg sociopolitical reconfigurations: Designing for speculative fabulation in learning. *Journal of the Learning Sciences, 32*(1), 21–44. https://doi.org/10.1080/10508406.2022.2154159

Loh, C. E., Sun, B., & Weninger, C. (2023). "Because I have my phone with me all the time": The role of device access in developing Singapore adolescents' critical news literacy. *Journal of Adolescent & Adult Literacy, 66*(5), 319–329. https://doi.org/10.1002/jaal.1281

Matsuba, S. N. (1999). Speaking spaces: virtual reality, artificial intelligence and the construction of meaning. In A. Nijholt, O. Donk, & B van Dijk (eds.) *TWLT 15 Interactions in Virtual Worlds: Proceedings of the Fifteenth Twente Workshop on Language Technology* 131–140. Universiteit Twente

McCarthy, J. (2004). *What is artificial intelligence?* https://cse.unl.edu/~choueiry/S09-476-876/Documents/whatisai.pdf

Mora, R. A. (2011, September). Understanding what literacy is and where it comes from: Lessons and implications from a study of teachers and teacher educators. In *Keynote presentation at the 14th National ELT Conference, Bogotá, D.C., Colombia (ED547649)*. ERIC. https://files.eric.ed.gov/fulltext/ED547649.pdf

Mora, R. A. (2014). Critical literacy as policy and advocacy: Lessons from Colombia. *Journal of Adolescent & Adult Literacy, 58*(1), 16–18. https://doi.org/10.1002/jaal.329

Mora, R. A. (2017). Multimodal critical consciousness. LSLP Micro-Papers, 51. www.lslp.org/uploads/3/8/9/7/38976989/lslp-micro-paper-51-multimodal-critical-consciousness.pdf

Mora, R. A. (2019). Multimodal texts and tools in preservice methods courses: From consumption to design. In A. Palalas (Ed.), *Blended language learning: International perspectives on innovative practice* (pp. 359–388). China Central Radio & TV University Press. www.academia.edu/38545822/Multimodal_texts_and_tools_in_preservice_methods_courses_From_consumption_to_design

Mora, R. A. (2023). *Bilingualism integrative roundtable* [Syllabus]. Universidad Pontificia Bolivariana, Sede Central Medellín (Colombia).

Mora. R. A. (2024). AI literacies. *LSLP Micro-Papers, 96.* www.lslp.org/uploads/3/8/9/7/38976989/lslp-micro-paper-96-ai-literacies.pdf

Mora, R. A., & Golovátina-Mora, P. (2020). Video composition as multimodal writing: Rethinking the essay as post-literacy. *KnE Social Sciences, 4*(13), 4–12. www.neliti.com/publications/513704/video-composition-as-multimodal-writing-rethinking-the-essay-as-post-literacy

Mora, R. A., Lee, K., & Gaviria, C. A. (2019, April). *The role of second/additional languages to rethink CDL in the 21st century.* Annual Meeting of the American Educational Research Association, Toronto.

Mora, R. A. & Lopera Gómez, M.C. (2001). Games in the classroom: more than just having fun. *HOW Journal, 8*(1), 75–82. www.howjournalcolombia.org/index.php/how/article/view/220/269

Mora, R. A., & Semingson, P. (2023). AI and literacy education: Consider the challenges, embrace the possibilities, make your classroom even more human. *Literacy Today, 41*(1), 54–58. https://publuu.com AI and literacy education: Consider the challenges, embrace the possibilities, make your classroom even more human /flip-book/24429/445819/page/56

Mora, R. A., Tobón-Gallego, A. E., Mejía-Vélez, M. C., & Agudelo, E. (2022). Bridging multimodality and criticality to language education with a twist from the Global South: Multimodal critical consciousness as multimodal conscientização. In S. R. Barros & L. C. de Oliveira (Eds.), *Paulo Freire and Multilingual education: Theoretical approaches, methodologies and empirical analyses in language and literacy* (pp. 261–279). Routledge. https://doi.org/10.4324/9781003175728-18

Newell, A. (1982). Intellectual issues in the history of artificial intelligence. In R. Crisley (Ed), *Artificial intelligence: Critical concepts* (pp. 25–70). Routledge.

Ng, D. T. K., Leung, J. K. L., Chu, S. K. W., & Qiao, M. S. (2021). Conceptualizing AI literacy: An exploratory review. *Computers and Education: Artificial Intelligence, 2,* 100041. https://doi.org/10.1016/j.caeai.2021.100041

O'Byrne, W. I., Crandall, B. R., Dail, J. S., Goering, C. Z., Mora, R. A., Price-Dennis, D., & Witte, S. (2022). Digital wildfires: Tending to social media in the ELA classroom. In M. T. Christel & W. Kist (Eds.), *Bringing critical media literacy into ELA classrooms (NCTE Special Issues,* Vol. 2; pp. 19–26). NCTE. https://wiobyrne.com/wp-content/uploads/2023/01/Digital-Wildfires.pdf

Opara, E., Mfon-Ette Theresa, A., & Aduke, T. C. (2023). ChatGPT for teaching, learning and research: Prospects and challenges. *Global Academic Journal of Humanities and Social Sciences, 5*(2), 33–40. https://ssrn.com/abstract=4375470

Pandya, J. Z., Mora, R. A., Alford, J. H., Golden, N. A., & de Roock, R. S. (2021). Introduction to the handbook of critical literacies: The current state of critical literacy around the world. In J. Z. Pandya, R. A. Mora, J. H. Alford, N. A. Golden, & R. S. de Roock (Eds.), *The handbook of critical literacies* (pp. 3–9). Routledge. https://doi.org/10.4324/9781003023425-2

PK, F. A. (1984). What is artificial intelligence? In J. Karthikeyan, T. S. Hie. & N. Y. Jin (Eds.), *Learning outcomes of classroom research* (pp. 65–73). L Ordine Nuovo Publication.

Proyas, A. (2004). *I, robot* [Film]. 20th Century Fox.

Rossen, J. (2023, Jul. 31). The tragic life of Clippy, the world's most hated virtual assistant. *Mental Floss.* www.mentalfloss.com/article/504767/tragic-life-clippy-worlds-most-hated-virtual-assistant

Sannino, A., & Engeström, Y. (2018). Cultural-historical activity theory: Founding insights and new challenges. *Cultural-Historical Psychology, 14*(3), 43–56. https://doi.org/10.17759/chp.2018140304

Shaw, M. S., Toliver, S. R., & Tanksley, T. (2024). The internet doesn't exist in the sky: Literacy, AI, and the digital middle passage. *Reading Research Quarterly, 59*(4), 690–705. https://doi.org/10.1002/rrq.537

Smith, H. (2023, Feb. 27). ChatGPT and the role of the university. *The Chronicle*. www.dukechronicle.com/article/2023/02/02272023-smith-chatgpt

Stypinska, J. (2021, December). Ageism in AI: new forms of age discrimination in the era of algorithms and artificial intelligence. In *CAIP 2021: Proceedings of the 1st international conference on AI for people: Towards sustainable AI* (p. 39). European Union Digital Library.

Toosi, A., Bottino, A. G., Saboury, B., Siegel, E., & Rahmim, A. (2021). A brief history of AI: how to prevent another winter (a critical review). *PET Clinics, 16*(4), 449–469. https://doi.org/10.1016/j.cpet.2021.07.001

Wachowski, La., & Wachowski, Li. (1999). *The matrix* [Film]. Warner Brothers.

Wachowski, La., & Wachowski, Li. (2003). *The matrix reloaded* [Film]. Warner Brothers.

Williams, D. P. (2024). Disabling AI: Biases and values embedded in artificial intelligence. In D. J. Gunkel (Ed.), *Handbook on the ethics of artificial intelligence* (pp. 246–261). Edward Elgar Publishing.

Wohlwend, K. E., Buchholz, B. A., & Medina, C. L. (2017). Playful literacies and practices of making in children's imaginaries. In K. A. Mills, A. Stornaiuolo, A. Smith, & J. Z. Pandya (Eds.) *Handbook of writing, literacies, and education in digital cultures* (pp. 136–147). Routledge.

Wolodelsky, E. (2023, date). *Ilusiones y riesgos de la inteligencia artificial*. Critical Media Literacy Conference of the Americas, Tierra del Fuego, Argentina.

Yu, H. (2023). Reflection on whether Chat GPT should be banned by academia from the perspective of education and teaching. *Frontiers in Psychology, 14*, 1181712. https://doi.org/10.3389/fpsyg.2023.1181712

Index

Note: Figures are indicated by *italics*; Tables are indicated by **bold**; Endnotes are indicated by the page number followed by 'n' and the endnote number e.g., 20n1 refers to endnote 1 on page 20.

Made in the USA
Columbia, SC
21 May 2026

0e427564-ad7d-4b76-901d-9c35d01f414aR01